SPOTLIGHT

LOS ANGELES & ORANGE COUNTY BEACHES

ALAN BISBORT & PARKE PUTERBAUGH

Contents

How to Use This Book

Beaches are identified with numbers, which correspond to the numbers on the map.

Write-ups of each community or locale open with a general essay describing its physical look and layout, attractions and activities, history and sociology, and anything else that might enhance a useful overview. We've also supplied contact information for local chambers of commerce, convention and visitors bureaus, and tourist development councils.

Additional information follows under the following headings: Beaches, Recreation and Attractions, Accommodations, Coastal Cuisine, and Nightlife.

BEACHES

We offer the lowdown on what you can expect to see and do at every publicly accessible beach. This includes a description of a beach's natural features and any other relevant observations. Each beach also has its own "beach profile": a listing of practical information, including directions, activities, parking and day-use fees, hours, facilities, and contact number. A **BEST (** symbol also accompanies the profiles of best beaches.

Each beach profile also includes symbols for certain activities beyond the beach basics of swimming and sunbathing. Since one can go fishing on virtually any beach, we haven't included a special fishing symbol. However, our jetty and pier symbols indicate when those particular angling opportunities are available. The activity symbols are as follows:

Biking/jogging

Camping (developed campground or campgrounds)

Diving/snorkeling (popular spot for diving and/or snorkeling)

Hiking (trail or trails for nature observation and/or exercise)

Jetty (rock structure extending seaward from the mouth of an inlet or harbor, making for good fishing, snorkeling, and surfing)

Pier (wooden or concrete structure from which people fish or stroll)

Surfing (sufficiently sizable and well-formed waves that draw more than the occasional surfer)

Volleyball (volleyball nets and standards on the beach or park grounds)

Nude beach (clothing optional)

We've also included information on facilities available at each beach:

- Concession (food and drink available at or near beach)
- Lifeguards (year-round, unless identified as "seasonal")
- Picnic area
- Restrooms
- Showers
- Visitors center (staffed facility with information and exhibits)

RECREATION AND ATTRACTIONS

This selective listing is a kind of quick-and-dirty Yellow Pages that we've compiled for selected communities.

- Bike/Skate Rentals (bicycles, in-line skates, and other fun stuff)
- Boat Cruise (sightseeing trips on the water)
- Dive Shop (diving equipment and/or dive trips)
- Ecotourism (canoe/kayak outfitter or site for ecotourist outing)
- Fishing Charters (guided fishing trips)
- Horseback Riding
- Lighthouse
- Marina (boat dockage)
- Pier
- Rainy Day Attraction (something to do indoors when the weather is inclement)
- Shopping/Browsing (shopping district, center, or mall of note)
- Sportfishing
- Surf Report (surf forecast)
- Surf Shop (surfboards and surf gear)
- Vacation Rentals (beach houses and/or condos for short-term rental)

ACCOMMODATIONS

We offer a general overview of lodging options, as well as brief descriptions of selected hotels, motels, and resorts we'd recommend when planning a beach vacation. Our write-ups are based on actual stays and site visits. Because room rates fluctuate, we provide general guidelines of price range. Our $–$$$$ symbols are offered as general indicators of the nightly charge in season for a standard room with two beds.

$ = inexpensive (under $80 per night)

$$ = moderate ($80–129)

$$$ = moderately expensive ($130–179)

$$$$ = expensive ($180 and up)

COASTAL CUISINE

We offer a general overview of the dining scene, as well as descriptive write-ups of restaurants specializing in seafood and/or regional cuisine that are located on or near the beach. We cast a favorable eye upon places that have been around a while and have maintained a reputation for consistency and quality. Our $–$$$$ symbols are general indicators that reflect the median cost of an à la carte dinner entrée.

$ = inexpensive ($10 and under)

$$ = moderate ($11–17)

$$$ = moderately expensive ($18–24)

$$$$ = expensive ($25 and up)

NIGHTLIFE

Our concept of nightlife is people gathering to relax or blow off steam after the sun sets. Our listings run the gamut from tiki bars and coffeehouses to clubs with live music or deejays—in other words, anywhere you can kick back and have fun during and after sunset. We've made the rounds, looking for the liveliest good times. And we let you know when you're better off not wasting your time.

MAP SYMBOLS

Expressway		Interstate Freeway		Airfield	
Primary Road		U.S. Highway		Airport	
Secondary Road		State Highway		City/Town	
Unpaved Road		County Highway		Mountain	
Ferry		Lake		Park	
National Border		Dry Lake		Pass	
State Border		Seasonal Lake		State Capital	

LOS ANGELES COAST

We could have written a separate book about Los Angeles County's coastline, home to everything from the *Queen Mary* ocean liner in Long Beach to chainsaw jugglers in Venice Beach to the rich and famous who live in the secluded Malibu Colony. Just the familiar ring of the names of its beaches is enough to evoke images of endless summers, surfers, swimmers, and sun-worshippers. Who can resist the lure of Santa Catalina Island; Redondo, Hermosa, and Manhattan Beaches, down along the South Bay; Venice, Santa Monica, and Marina del Rey, all part of the pulse of daily life in Los Angeles? Even Malibu's 27-mile stretch is like a preview of the wilds one finds farther up the coast at Big Sur.

As beleaguered as this county can get during periods of fire, heat, storms, and mudslides, Los Angeles deserves an "A" for making its beaches safe and accessible to millions of residents and tourists each year. It is the nation's second largest metropolitan area, behind only New York City, so its beaches have got to serve about as many bodies as McDonald's serves hamburgers. We love the beaches of Los Angeles County, whose parks department could serve as a model of how to provide public access, service, and upkeep. In Los Angeles County, all the so-called state beaches are actually managed by the county under a lease arrangement. The only exception is Leo Carrillo State Park, up north along the Ventura County line.

It's just the rest of the so-called City of Angeles that drives us batty—from the gridlocked freeways and compulsive car culture to the loony celebrity culture to the fact that seemingly every single L.A. denizen has a cell phone glued to his or her ear or is pecking maniacally at a Blackberry, iPhone, or some other high-tech gadget, completely abstracted from the physical world they do their best to ignore. (End of sermon.)

© SONDRA STOCKER/COURTESY OF THE SANTA MONICA CVB

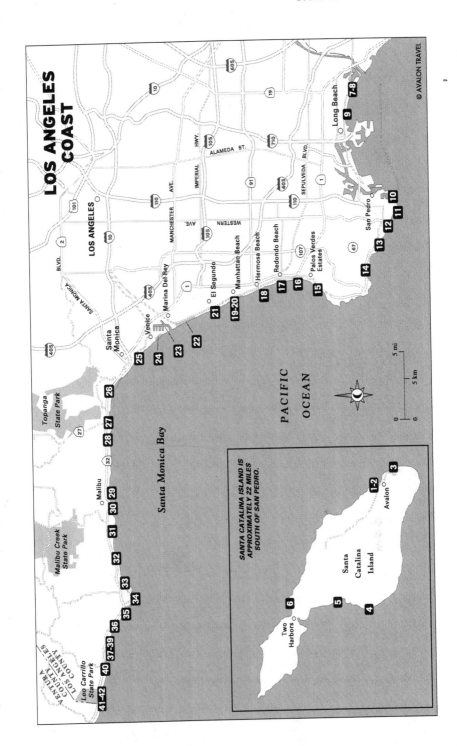

BEST BEACHES

◖ **Hermosa City Beach,**
page 34

◖ **Zuma County Beach,**
page 70

◖ **Leo Carrillo State Park,**
page 73

Los Angeles County has 74 miles of publicly accessible coastline, with many of the beaches more expansive than you might imagine and less crowded than you might think. So select a sandy oasis and let the maddening world that lies east of the ocean breezes go about its stressful scurrying while you fine-tune your tan and find out what California dreaming is really all about.

Santa Catalina Island

To visit Santa Catalina Island is to step back into the past. The prehistoric past, that is. Most of the island—86 percent of its 76 square miles, to be exact—is owned and protected by the Santa Catalina Island Conservancy, a nonprofit outfit that has maintained it as a wilderness preserve since 1972. Consequently, Catalina looks the way it did when sun-worshipping Native Americans inhabited it 4,000 years ago. Even the Spaniards, who arrived with Juan Rodríguez Cabrillo in 1542 and again with Sebastian Vizcaino in 1602, didn't leave any scuff marks behind. Today, only 3,500 or so live on the island—and most of them, by far, are concentrated in the town of Avalon.

Catalina is a rugged, rocky island 21 miles long and eight miles wide. Its jagged green hills rise out of the Pacific Ocean. Mount Oriaba, at 2,069 feet, is the highest peak. On days when the Santa Ana winds blow Southern California's smog away, Los Angelenos can clearly see the island.

Because the natural order has been allowed to prevail, Catalina Island is a different world from mainland California. The ecosystem is unique, with several species of plants and animals endemic to the island. The most celebrated flora is the Catalina ironwood, a tree that teeters on the brink of extinction; only two wild groves are left. A total of 395 species of plant life are native to Catalina, and a fascinating variety of animals make their home here. The island has its own subspecies of ground squirrel and fox, the latter a beautiful but elusive creature. Buffalo freely roam the island's interior. An herd of 14 buffalo was brought here in 1924 for the filming of *The Vanishing American;* now it numbers 400. Attempts to remove introduced herds of goats, sheep, and cattle have helped to restore indigenous vegetation. Wild pigs, goats, and deer also have the run of the place, though attempts to wipe out these feral intruders have met with less success. Some of the world's finest purebred Arabian horses are raised at El Rancho Escondido, a private ranch that is separate from the conservancy.

Unfortunately for humans (but fortunately for plants and wildlife), visitors can't easily reach many of the island's natural wonders, because exploration is fairly restricted. A permit is needed to travel anywhere more than a mile beyond the city limits of Avalon. Hiking and biking permits can be obtained by dropping by the **Santa Catalina Island Conservancy**'s headquarters in Avalon (125 Claressa Avenue, 310/510-1421), where you'll find trail maps, rules and regulations, and other information about the island. These permits can also be ob-

GETTING TO AND FROM CATALINA ISLAND

Although passenger ferries to Santa Catalina Island leave from several mainland points – including Long Beach, San Pedro, Dana Point, and Newport Beach – the logistics are about the same. The cost of parking on the mainland is not included in the fare, and generally costs $10-12 a day at the terminal. The extremely relaxing passage over to Catalina takes anywhere from an hour to two hours, one-way, depending on whether you take old-school ferries or express service. It costs an additional $5 to bring a bike or a surfboard.

- **Catalina Express:** Boats run year-round from San Pedro, Long Beach (from downtown and the *Queen Mary*), and Dana Point terminals to Avalon and Two Harbors. Round-trip fare is $66.50-68.50 for adults and $53 for kids 2-11. For more information, contact Catalina Express, Berth 95, San Pedro, CA 90731, 213/519-1212 or 800/481-3470, www.catalinaexpress.com.

- **Catalina Ferries:** Convenient for suburban Los Angelinos, this boat leaves from Marina del Rey (Fisherman's Village) and takes 90 minutes to Avalon and two hours to Two Harbors. Cost is $85 round-trip for adults and $66 for kids. (This includes a $10 fuel surcharge, added July 2008.) For more information, contact Catalina Ferries, 13737 Fiji Way, Marina del Rey, CA 90292, 310/305-7250, www.catalinaferries.com.

- **Catalina Flyer:** This triple-decker catamaran departs daily from Balboa Pavilion in Newport Beach. Round-trip fare is $68 for adults, $51 for kids 3-12. For more information, contact Catalina Flyer, Balboa Pavilion, 400 Main Street, Newport Beach, CA 92661, 949/673-5245 or 800/830-7744, www.catalinainfo.com.

- **Island Express:** This company flies helicopters from heliports at the San Pedro and Long Beach boat terminals to its pad near Avalon. Space is limited (only six passengers). Round-trip fare is $164, and the trip takes only 15 minutes. Hourly flights depart 8 A.M.-sunset. For more information, contact Island Express, 310/510-2525 or 800/228-2566, www.islandexpress.com.

tained at Two Harbors Visitor Services and Airport in the Sky. Hiking permits are free. Biking permits cost $50 per person and $75 per family and are good for a year (from May 1 through April 30). Hikers and bikers must return by dusk—unless, of course, they're camping and have the necessary permits for that.

Camping is a whole other matter. There are five campgrounds on the island: Two Harbors, Hermit Gulch, Little Harbor, Black Jack, and Parson's Landing. Camping reservations can be made at any of them by calling 310/510-8368. Alternatively, camping reservations can be made through the Santa Catalina Island Company by mail, fax, or online at www.catalina.com/camping. You can call the Santa Catalina Island Company at 310/510-2800

and ask that a camping brochure and request form be mailed to you. Finally, if you're on the island, you can book a campsite at three places in Avalon (Hotel Atwater, 125 Sumner Street, 310/510-1788; Pavilion Lodge, 150 Metropole Avenue, 310/510-2500; Discovery Tours, Crescent Avenue, across from Green Pleasure Pier, 310/510-2000), or at one place in Two Harbors (Two Harbors Visitor Services, at the foot of the main pier). Camping fees are $12 per adult and $6 per child ages 2–11. The season runs late March through the end of October; fees drop somewhat the rest of the year.

Here's a quick lowdown on the campgrounds. **Hermit Gulch Campground** is only 1.5 miles from Avalon, nestled in Avalon Canyon near the Wrigley Memorial and Botanical

PARADISE FOUND: CATALINA ISLAND'S LITTLE HARBOR BEACH

Though most of Santa Catalina Island's visitors confine their explorations to Avalon, there is an up-island sanctuary worth checking out. Little Harbor Beach is a crescent-shaped semitropical paradise midway down the windward, southwest-facing side of the island. Mountains rising to heights of more than 2,000 feet form a stunning backdrop to the wide, sandy cove. There are actually three beaches in one: There's Little Harbor proper, which has a beachside campground; a small, unnamed cove that's a Gauguin-in-Tahiti paradise; and Shark's Cove. These adjacent coves, separated by rocky protrusions, amount to about one-third of a mile of wild, gorgeous beach out of range of civilization.

Getting to this end of the island is half the fun, particularly if you enjoy a long hike. The cross-island hike to Little Harbor can be undertaken from Avalon or Two Harbors, the island's two population centers. The trek from Avalon is longer and more arduous, following a calf-bruising 17-mile trail that ascends spiny ridges and drops into canyons. The 6.8-mile walk from Two Harbors can be made either along the main road, which passes by Little Harbor en route to Avalon, or via the Banning House Road Trail. The latter is more interesting and invigorating, hugging the coastline and making significant elevation changes.

The 42-site campground at Little Harbor has outdoor showers, chemical toilets, and running water. Camping fees are $12 for adults and $6 for children, per person per day. Some visitors arrive via private boat, anchoring offshore. Anglers catch halibut and sun worshippers catch rays on the beach. Little Harbor is protected from the ocean by a small peninsula and offshore reef, making it excellent for snorkeling and scuba diving. Shark Harbor, which adjoins Little Harbor, gets wave action and is good for bodysurfing and boogie boarding. Have no fear of the name, however. Shark Harbor is named for a rock that looks like the dorsal fin of a great white.

Kayaks, diving gear, backpacking equipment, and more can be rented at Two Harbors. The Santa Catalina Island Company runs buses out to Little Harbor, arranges inter-island and cross-channel transportation, assists in travel planning, and issues camping and hiking permits.

For more information, contact the Santa Catalina Island Company, P.O. Box 737, Avalon, CA 90704, 310/510-2800, ext. 1412, www.visitcatalinaisland.com.

Garden. It's stocked with restrooms, showers, picnic tables, vending machines, grills, microwave, ice, and on-site ranger. **Two Harbors** is at a narrow isthmus about 20 miles up-island from Avalon, and there are primitive tent sites, less primitive tent cabins, and downright comfy "Catalina Cabins" with beds, refrigerator, heater, closet, and outdoor community kitchen. **Black Jack** is in the island's interior at the highest elevation. **Little Harbor** faces west onto two sandy beaches and is seven miles from Two Harbors; sites have picnic tables, fire rings, and barbecue grills, and the campground has chemical toilets, cold showers, and

potable water. **Parson's Landing** is the most remote campground, lying up at the north end of the island. You'll find chemical toilets but no fresh water and no showers. You're on your own, but you're on the beach. It's a shadeless beach, however.

All of these permits and prohibitions are sensible and laudable. They keep the island free of Jeep-driving bozos waving shotguns at the wild buffalo. The flip side to this, though, is that most visitors are off-loaded into the harborfront encampment of Avalon and see little more of the island. Avalon lies on the eastern side of Catalina, facing the mainland. Passenger ferries from San Pedro, Long Beach, and Newport Beach dock here, making the town something of a tourist side-pocket on the otherwise empty green billiard table of Catalina Island.

The first person we encountered at the end of the ferry gangplank at the Green Pleasure Pier in Avalon was a bearded son of a gun with a sailor's cap scrunched atop his gnarled web of red hair. With no encouragement from us—we were perfectly content to lug our bags—he pronounced himself "our man." This meant that for a modest fee he'd tote our bags to the hotel, which he warned was "all the way over on the other side of town." Avalon is all of one square mile, and many of its hotels are within easy walking distance of the harbor. Our man no doubt serves some useful purpose here. Just decide before being browbeaten by him or his like whether you can manage for yourself.

There are excellent ways to see other parts of the island without having to trek like a Sherpa. Several different bus tours depart the Avalon Harbor area regularly, and taxis can be hired for private trips. The most reasonable of the bus tours is the Skyline Drive ($39 for adults, $29 for kids), a two-hour trip that ventures 10 miles into the heart of the conservancy. The Inland Motor Tour ($79.50 for adults, $71.50 for kids) is a four-hour version of the trip. Glass-bottomed boat tours ($17.50 for adults, $13.25 for kids) operate out of Avalon Harbor, offering eyewitness proof of the prodigious underwater life teeming in the blue-green waters. Other boat tours sail around the southern tip of Catalina to the western side of the island, where the only other "town," Two Harbors, is located. Two Harbors is a jumping-off point for some of the best hiking trails on Catalina. There are snorkeling tours, too, and buffet cruises. For information on tours, call or drop by the **Catalina Island Visitor Bureau,** on the Green Pleasure Pier (310/510-1520), or **Two Harbors Visitor Services** (211 Catalina Avenue in Avalon and at the foot of the main pier in Two Harbors, 310/510-2800).

Many people travel to the island from the mainland on their own boats, at times turn-ing the channel into a watery version of the Santa Ana Freeway. Some even swim over from Los Angeles. Each year an Ocean Marathon is held; the record time is 7.5 hours.

The salvation of our visit was a golf cart. Everyone on Catalina uses them, and they can be rented for $30–40 an hour, or around $100 for an entire day. After two hours of exhilarating travel into the arrow-marked hills above Avalon, we had seen everything we wanted to see. We also got a sufficiently uplifting feel for the natural riches of the island's interior to make us fantasize about a backpacking expedition at some later date.

Steer your golf cart south out of Avalon on Pebbly Beach Road. This state route hugs the shoreline, revealing placid waters with a rocky bottom—perfect for snorkeling and scuba diving, not so hot for swimming. Quite chilly, in fact. After two miles the road moves inland, up a steep and winding grade that peaks at Mount Ada and the Wrigley Mansion. Incredible as it may seem, Catalina Island used to belong to William Wrigley Jr., the chewing-gum magnate and owner of the Chicago Cubs. Upon his death he deeded the island to the organization that now maintains it as a nature conservancy. Along this route you'll pass the second oldest golf course in the country. It's a nine-holer that was wedged into a rugged canyon in 1892. The road also skirts the now-overgrown field where the Cubs held their spring training from 1921 to 1951 (with four years off for World War II).

The nicest Wrigley legacy is **William Wrigley Jr. Botanical Gardens.** The Wrigley Memorial, set at the top of the gardens, is an imposing structure (232 feet by 130 feet) that dwarfs the surrounding Avalon Canyon like a misplaced Lincoln Memorial. The memorial took a year to build, and plaques attest to its tonnage, craftsmanship, and sturdiness. The plaque at the courtyard entrance reads, "The building is dedicated to William Wrigley Jr., who in 1919 recognized the potential of Santa Catalina as a nature preserve."

The gardens next to the memorial are a

pleasure to stroll. Laid out in sections, they feature Catalina's indigenous plants, as well as oddities from around the world, like South Africa's red-hot poker. The most intriguing part of the garden is the separate wing devoted to cacti, some of which are the strangest and most Freudian we've ever seen.

One other noteworthy attraction is **The Casino,** a Mediterranean-style structure built by Wrigley on Avalon Harbor in 1929. It dominates the waterfront the way Wrigley's memorial overwhelms Avalon Canyon. At one time big bands blew hot and cool in the ballroom of this casino, which has also been used as a backdrop in many Hollywood films. Today, the Catalina Island Museum, featuring historic artifacts of human habitation on the island, is housed in its basement, and first-run movies play on the first floor.

For more information, contact the Catalina Island Chamber of Commerce and Visitors Bureau, 1 Green Pleasure Pier, P.O. Box 217, Avalon, CA 90704, 310/510-1520, www.catalinachamber.com.

BEACHES

First off, just know that you won't be coming to Catalina Island for the beaches—unless you take the trouble to visit the Little Harbor area on the island's backside. **Crescent Beach** (in Avalon) and **Pebbly Beach** (just south of Avalon) provide access to chilly, waveless harbor water. Crescent Beach has a bathhouse at 228 Crescent Avenue with lockers and a laundry. The beach itself is a tiny line of sand upon which you might place towels. A private beach, **Descanso Beach,** can be accessed via the beach club near the casino. Nonmembers must pay for access to this safe, sandy beach and its cabanas. Kayaks can be rented at **Descanso Beach Ocean Sports** (310/510-1226) or **Wet Spot Rentals** (310/510-2229).

Cove beaches can also be found farther up the north side of the island, above Avalon. (Gallagher Beach, Lava Wall Beach, and Starlight Beach are among the ones that have names.) This area is pocked with pebbly or sandy coves,

offering environmental camping on a first-come, first-served basis. **Little Fisherman's Cove** is the site of a campground right on the water close to Two Harbors, where you'll find a restaurant, bar, and dive shop.

The best pure ocean beaches are on the western side of the island, necessitating a long walk or a bus or boat ride from Two Harbors. **Little Harbor Beach** is a wide, sandy, protected beach—a real jewel for swimmers, snorkelers, divers, and campers. Four miles south is **Ben Weston Beach,** a nice sandy cove. Again, this beach requires some advance planning to gain access to it—not to mention an 11.5-mile trek from Two Harbors. For divers, the **Casino Point Underwater Park** sits just off Descanso Beach. Home to a sunken 70-foot schooner and all the squiggly marine life it attracts, the park can be explored via **Catalina Scuba Luv** (126 Catalina Avenue, Avalon, 310/510-2350) or **Catalina Divers Supply** (310/510-0330). For getting around under your own power, try **Catalina Kayak Adventures** and **Wet Spot Rentals** (120 Pebbly Beach Road, 310/510-2229).

❶ DESCANSO BEACH

Location: at Descanso Beach Club, beside the Casino on Avalon Harbor
Parking/Fees: $2 per person entrance fee
Hours: 9 A.M.–sunset
Facilities: concession, restrooms, and showers
Contact: Descanso Beach Club, 310/510-7410

❷ CRESCENT BEACH

Location: Crescent Avenue at Green Pleasure Pier in Avalon
Parking/Fees: no cars allowed
Hours: 24 hours
Facilities: concession, lifeguards, and restrooms
Contact: Santa Catalina Island Conservancy, 310/510-2595

🖪 PEBBLY BEACH

Location: on Santa Catalina Island along Pebbly Beach Road, one mile southeast of Avalon Harbor
Parking/Fees: no cars allowed
Hours: 24 hours
Facilities: none
Contact: Santa Catalina Island Conservancy, 310/510-2595

🖪 BEN WESTON BEACH

Location: on Santa Catalina Island at the end of Middle Canyon Trail, 11.5 miles south of Two Harbors
Parking/Fees: no cars allowed
Hours: sunrise-sunset
Facilities: picnic area
Contact: Santa Catalina Island Conservancy, 310/510-2595

🖪 LITTLE HARBOR BEACH

Location: seven miles south of Two Harbors on the western side of Santa Catalina Island
Parking/Fees: no cars allowed; camping fees $12 per adult, $6 per child per night
Hours: sunrise-sunset
Facilities: restrooms, showers, and picnic tables
Contact: Santa Catalina Island Conservancy, 310/510-2595

🖪 LITTLE FISHERMAN'S COVE

Location: Two Harbors, 12 miles northwest of Avalon, on Catalina Island
Parking/Fees: no cars allowed; camping fees $12 per adult, $6 per child
Hours: sunrise-sunset

Facilities: restrooms, showers, and picnic tables
Contact: Santa Catalina Island Conservancy, 310/510-2595

ACCOMMODATIONS

First, for bicyclists and hikers, the campgrounds on Catalina are among the most secluded in California. Permits are required for bicycles and hiking, and separate permits are required for camping. The best conduit to campground reservations and hiking trails is **Two Harbors Visitor Services** (888/570-2595). For bike permits, contact **Catalina Island Conservancy** (125 Claressa Avenue, Avalon, 310/510-2595). The **Hermit Gulch Campground** (310/510-8368), a mile outside Avalon, is privately run, but the only campground in the vicinity of Avalon ($12 adult, $6 child). Two county-run campgrounds within a reasonable hike of town—**Bird Park Campground** (75 sites) and **Black Jack Campground** (75 sites)—can be reserved through the County Parks and Recreation Department, but neither is anywhere near a beach.

Almost all of the lodgings on the island are in Avalon. In fact, Avalon seems like one large hotel. Our first night in town some years back reminded us of "Duncan," the Paul Simon song: "Couple in the next room bound to win a prize/They've been going at it all night long." We holed up in a Mediterranean-style "villa" that shall remain nameless, the brochure for which promised "a touch of Old World elegance and luxury." By "Old World," they apparently meant a windowless room with cots, tiny shower stall, a sliding glass door for an entrance, and the thinnest walls this side of an eggshell. Moral of the story: Book carefully on Catalina Island.

We have found sane and commodious sanctuary at the **Pavilion Lodge** (513 Crescent Avenue, 310/510-2500 or 800/851-0216, $$). The lodge spreads back from the harborfront street into a landscaped courtyard, replete with a two-ton piece of redwood that drifted from the mainland and was placed here with the aid of several trucks, tractors, and herniated laborers. The rooms are quiet and comfortable, too. Ah, golden slumbers.

The most venerable hotel in town is the **Glenmore Plaza Hotel** (120 Sumner Avenue, 310/510-0017, www.glenmorehotel.com, $$$$). This pastel-tinted beauty is over a century old and has hosted such eminences as Teddy Roosevelt (who hunted on the island) and Clark Gable. The wicker-filled rooms are airy and large, and the room rate includes wine and cheese in the courtyard each afternoon and a continental breakfast. All this starts at a reasonable $204. Avalon's poshest hotel is the **Hotel Metropole** (205 Crescent Avenue, 310/510-1884, www.hotel-metropole.com, $$$), a three-story beauty set in the Metropole Marketplace, overlooking Avalon Harbor. Rooms start at $200 in the summer and can cost $300 or more for even a partial ocean-view room.

Over at Two Harbors, lodging can be found at **Banning House Lodge** (Two Harbors, 310/510-2800, $$$), an 11-room bed-and-breakfast built in 1910 as a summer home for the Bannings, two island-owner siblings. This homey, unpretentious inn looks out over Two Harbors' Isthmus Cove from its hillside perch.

Crowds throng to Catalina Island in the summer, but the island is no less charming during its "undiscovered season," September–April, when the room rates run considerably lower. Oh, and there's nary a chain hotel or motel to be found.

COASTAL CUISINE

Around dinnertime one evening some years back we watched an elderly gentleman with hearing aids and a cane wheezing in front of a seafood restaurant on Crescent Avenue, Avalon's waterfront thoroughfare. Winded from his search for a suitable meal—a stroll that had covered three blocks and several posted menus—he turned on his wife when she sweetly suggested they eat at a place with

a "pot roast and potato pancake" special. "I'm not going to put that junk in my mouth!" he cried in frustration. Propped up by his cane, he turned and shuffled farther down the street, bound and determined to find something more to his liking.

Many visitors to Catalina Island find themselves in the same, ahem, boat. A hungry army, they wander the quaint Mediterranean streets of Avalon at sundown, studying one menu after another for some clue as to the cuisine. Much of the food here is necessarily brought over from the mainland. Even the little pier-side food hut serves a pretty generic paper boatload of fish 'n' chips. It also offers abalone burgers and buffalo burgers, which were described to us by a female buffalo-booster as being "leaner than beef."

The best bet for seafood is **Armstrong's Fish Market & Seafood Restaurant** (306 Crescent Avenue, 310/510-0113, $$$). Believe it or not, lobsters are local to these waters and are served in Catalina Island restaurants during a brief season that starts in late September. You can get local or Maine lobsters at Armstrong's or another popular restaurant, **El Galleon** (411 Crescent Avenue, 310/510-1188, $$$), which also serves prime rib and similar hearty fare. **Steve's Steakhouse** (417 Crescent Avenue, 310/510-0333, $$$) is another surf-and-turf-serving favorite overlooking Avalon Harbor and fairly priced, considering the island setting. Steaks and filet mignons run $25–33, and local swordfish is $27.

One night years ago during our first visit to the island, we settled on **Antonio's Pizzeria & Cabaret** (230 Crescent Avenue, 310/510-0008, $) because of the intriguing sign in the window: "This restaurant has been declared a genuine Catalina bomb shelter—come on in and bask in the ambience of the decaying 1950s while the world passes on." The place has moved from its original Sumner Street haunt to Crescent Avenue, into a building that is not bomb-proof, but where the spirit of the original lives on.

NIGHTLIFE

Unless you know someone at the members-only Catalina Yacht Club or the Tuna Club—the latter of which was founded in 1898 and has boasted Winston Churchill, Richard Nixon, King Olaf, and Hal Roach as members—your night moves will be as humble as the lonely buffalo. The best place is **J. L.'s Locker Room** (126 Sumner Street, 310/510-0258), a sports bar. Rams, Angels, and Dodgers photos adorn the walls, some inscribed to J. L. himself by players who have come all the way to Catalina to quaff a cold one at his pub.

Long Beach

This is a city whose fortunes tend to rise and fall with those of a famous British cruise ship. The *Queen Mary* is to Long Beach what London Bridge is to Lake Havasu City, Arizona: a grand relic of the crumbling British empire purchased and brought to America to confer a borrowed identity upon a place that has little of its own. In 1967, the ailing city of Long Beach welcomed the arrival of the *Queen Mary*. The world's largest ocean liner had itself fallen on hard times, as people had come to prefer the convenience of flying to making the time-consuming passage by water. The old boat was docked in the Port of Long Beach and refurbished into a combination hotel and tourist attraction. More important, perhaps, was the symbolism of the luxury liner. Laid to rest in Long Beach after 1,001 transatlantic crossings, the grande dame of the high seas became the city's beacon for a hopeful future.

It hasn't quite worked out that way. In terms of tourist revenue, the *Queen Mary* has had good years and bad years, and it's been as much of an albatross as a savior. The *Queen Mary*'s one-time companion in tourism—the *Spruce Goose*, a gargantuan wooden airplane that never flew, built by Howard Hughes before he began growing his fingernails—was sold off in 1992 and hauled off to Oregon. A 1993 editorial in the *Long Beach Press-Telegram*

wondered, "Who will save the Queen?" Citing maintenance problems, declining attendance, and the need for massive capital improvements at a time when no funding could be found, the editorial concluded: "The signal coming from the *Queen Mary* isn't all that clear, but it's beginning to sound like an S.O.S." The boat was re-christened on September 26, 1994, exactly 60 years after being launched on its maiden voyage in Clydebank, Scotland. The grandson of the vessel's namesake broke a bottle of champagne on its hull, but only a few hundred people showed up for the occasion.

In 2001, the *Queen Mary* laid off 175 employees. Four auctions of original *Queen Mary* furniture, fixtures, art, and tableware were conducted in 1996 and 1997. In 1997, Joe Prevratil—the *Queen Mary*'s president and CEO—was revealed to be hatching a secret plan to have the ship towed to Tokyo. Many complain of the exorbitant cost of touring the ship ($24.95 for adults, $12.95 for kids 5–15, and $15 for parking) or bunking down in one of the 365 staterooms ($159 and up per night).

During an overnight stay aboard the *Queen Mary*, we found the old ocean liner to be eerily deserted. Our fellow passengers included two elderly couples dancing to a jazz trio playing for an otherwise empty house at the Observation Bar; a smattering of foreigners as confused as we were about the layout of the boat; and a housekeeping staff who could not tell us how to get from one point to another. Admittedly, the *Queen Mary*—like the Long Beach Convention and Entertainment Center and all the surrounding hotels and restaurants that serve business travelers—does most of its business during the August–November "convention season." Even so, the historic vessel—a living museum that served both as a luxury liner "where the rich and famous took their ease" and as a World War II troop carrier—should be hauling aboard at least a moderate catch of tourist business during summer months.

The truth hurts, but Long Beach is simply not a prime vacation destination. Beyond

QUEEN MARY FACTS AND FIGURES

- **Number of workers involved in construction:** 300,000
- **Date work began:** December 1, 1930
- **Date launched:** September 26, 1934
- **Maiden voyage:** May 27, 1936
- **Date retired:** September 19, 1967
- **Number of transatlantic crossings:** 1,001
- **Period of wartime service:** 6.5 years (March 1940 to September 1946)
- **Number of troops transported in World War II:** 765,429
- **Number of miles sailed in World War II:** 569,429
- **Bounty placed on ship by Adolf Hitler:** $250,000
- **World War II nickname:** The Gray Ghost
- **Passenger capacity:** 1,957
- **Officers and crew:** 1,174
- **Number of decks:** 12
- **Number of lifeboats:** 24
- **Number of portholes:** 2,000
- **Number of rivets:** 10 million
- **Length of ship:** 1,020 feet

- **Weight of ship:** 90,985 tons
- **Height of ship (keel to top deck):** 92 feet
- **Cruising speed:** 34 mph
- **Fuel consumption:** 0.0025 miles per gallon (13 feet per gallon)
- **Fuel consumed per crossing (from Southampton, England, to New York City):** 1,267,600 gallons
- **Fresh meat consumed per crossing:** 77,000 pounds (38.5 tons)
- **Capacity of wine cellar:** 15,000 bottles
- **Record number of passengers carried at one time:** 16,683 (during World War II)
- **Record time, Atlantic crossing:** 4 days, 10 hours, 6 minutes (August 24-29, 1966)

The Queen Mary is open daily 10 A.M.–6 P.M. It is at the south end of I-710 (Long Beach Freeway). Self-guided tours cost $24.95 for adults and $12.95 for children ages 5-11.

For more information, contact the Queen Mary, 1126 Queens Highway, Long Beach, CA 90802, 562/435-3511, www.queenmary.com.

the *Queen Mary*, this is a town ruled by its harbor, which primarily exists to serve naval and shipping interests. Away from its harbor, Long Beach has big-city problems but lacks sufficient big-city compensations to make it very tolerable or interesting. Thus, local boosters and PR people are reduced to touting entertainment and recreational options that surround Long Beach—such as Disneyland, Catalina Island, and Knott's Berry Farm—rather than the city itself.

After the *Queen Mary*—which celebrated its 40th anniversary in Long Beach in 2007—has been talked up and talked out, antsy visitors may find themselves in figurative dry dock, their remaining options running to things like driving past the world's largest whale mural, which covers the Long Beach Arena. A local columnist, attempting a feel-good broadside on behalf of downtown Long Beach, wrote the following, which unintentionally confirmed our worst suspicions: "Anything can happen downtown. If it rains, you get wet. If it's hot out, you sweat. Panhandlers may ask you for money. A few people get mugged. Downtown is life."

Well, at least Long Beach—a city of 466,000 that is California's fifth largest and the nation's 36th largest—never stops trying to improve itself. The downtown intersection of Broadway and Pine Avenue has become the center of a gentrified urban island. The concentration of music clubs, restaurants, movie theaters, and coffeehouses is a strategy we saw repeated elsewhere in metropolitan Southern California (such as in Santa Monica). There's safety and strength in numbers, it seems, though sleazy sorts can still violate the permeable borders. The entire neighborhood throbs in hot pink and purple neon, implicitly buzzing the message "class and cool" but instead saying "trendy urban cliché." At least there is good food and music to be had in downtown Long Beach, and it feels reasonably secure.

Also well worth a visit is the **Museum of Latin American Art** (628 Alamitos Avenue, 562/437-1689). Located in the burgeoning East Village Arts District, this beautiful facility features contemporary works by Latin American artists. It is affiliated with **Viva** (644 Alamitos Street, 562/435-4048, $), a nearby restaurant that serves lunch only. The many dishes on the menu come from Cuba, Chile, Peru, Colombia, et al. It's a great way to travel abroad without leaving the table.

Hundreds of millions of dollars have been pumped into redeveloping Long Beach's shoreline and downtown. The **Long Beach Convention and Entertainment Center** (300 East Ocean Boulevard, 562/436-3636) boasts 224,000 square feet of meeting and exhibit space. The complex also includes the 13,500-seat Long Beach Arena (home of the Long Beach Ice Dogs professional hockey team) and the 3,050-seat **Terrace Theater,** a performing arts center. Since 1992, a major waterfront project—first called Disney Sea-Park, then Queensway Bay, next The Pike at Rainbow Harbor, and now simply The Pike Project—has been planned, presented, and battled over (and over). Ten years after Disney was sent packing, the bickering continues. Nevertheless, the **Pike Project** opened in

2003 and has been an unprecedented failure. Though hailed as the largest waterfront development in California history, the $130 million, 369,000-square-foot dining, entertainment, and retail complex essentially turned its back on the harbor and its blandness has not exactly won the hearts of the culturally diverse Long Beach.

Among the most notable arrivals over the last decade is the **Aquarium of the Pacific** (100 Aquarium Way, 562/590-3100). With more than 12,000 maritime creatures and 550 species, it is one of the nation's largest aquariums. Exhibits highlight underwater life in the three regions of the Pacific Ocean: Southern California/Baja Peninsula, the Tropical Pacific, and the Northern Pacific. (Be sure to check out the Shark Lagoon.) Admission is $18.75 for adults, $9.95 for children 3–11. The Aquarium of the Pacific adjoins Rainbow Harbor, a landscaped park with a 2,000-foot public esplanade, a fleet of commercial vessels, and the tall ships *California* and *American Pride*. Still, in typical Long Beach fashion, all is not well with the Aquarium of the Pacific. Attendance has been healthy but not sufficient to allow the aquarium to pay its own way, so Long Beach has had to help out with bond payments, inciting the usual rounds of editorials and citizen grousing in this financially strapped city.

Long Beach has been trying to rebound since taking a direct hit on June 23, 1995—a day referred to as "Black Friday"—when the Defense Base Closure and Realignment Commission announced the 1997 closing of the Long Beach Naval Shipyard. The city lost an estimated 3,000 military jobs and about $757 million a year in lost wages and spending. The announcement came a year after the Long Beach Naval Station and the Long Beach Naval Hospital closed their doors, taking a staggering 17,500 military and civilian jobs from the community.

Though most visitors never see it, there's more to Long Beach than the downtown waterfront. Miles and miles of poor, ethnic neighborhoods roll inland, interspersed with

SHOOTING HOOPS, DRINKING BEER, AND TALKING ABOUT ELVIS

We came to the **Acapulco Inn** (5283 East 2nd Street, 562/439-3517) in Long Beach looking for a Pop-a-Shot machine, a game that allows you to fire little basketballs at a miniature net six feet away. For two guys who'd spent their college years at the University of North Carolina, where basketball is king, an opportunity to shoot hoops was a welcome diversion – even at a scaled-down barroom game. Fortunately, or maybe not – we wasted tons of quarters – these stand-up shooting galleries are found in bars and pool halls all over Southern California.

With a mound of quarters in our pockets and frosty mugs in hand, we prepared to fritter away another five bucks or so feeding our basketball jones in the corner of the Acapulco Inn, a beer joint in Belmont Shore.

We were beaten by a millisecond to the hoops game by a pair of dudes named Greg and Kevin. The former was a construction foreman, the latter a construction worker and one-time marine. They'd just gotten their paychecks and were spending them on draft beer and miniature basketball. They asked us to join them, and we had a night-long round-robin, four-man basketball shootout that grew so noisy we would have been thrown out of any other bar but this one. Kevin wore a baseball cap, smoked fat cigars, made pitchers of beer disappear like magic, and had a wicked set shot. When he found his rhythm, he racked up the points.

A nonstop talker and self-promoter, he would lapse into a deadly accurate Dick Vitale impersonation after scoring a particularly high game. "Oh, bay-bee, he's shooting out the lights tonight! Rock and roll!" He scored an evening-high 46, leaving the rest of us in the dust, and gloated to all within earshot that his score was unbeatable. That is, until one of us entered what is referred to as "a zone," swishing one after another and mounting up a final score of 54. It silenced Kevin for a little while. He gnawed on his cigar, looking annoyed. Then he tried to top it, feverishly popping quarters, game after game, until he bounced a ball so hard in frustration that it hit the ceiling. Then he declared he had finally had enough.

At this point he took a seat at the bar and shared his wisdom on any subject we cared to name. He knew everything about everything, challenging us to stump him. Elvis Presley, surfing, world geography, sports, the fairer sex, bar brawls – you name it. Likable almost in spite of himself, he embodied a good-natured self-centeredness that we'd seen across Southern California. This expressed itself in boundless braggadocio and a glaring lack of curiosity about anything outside his sphere of existence. He also made a blanket offer to drop whatever he was doing at any time to share with us his firsthand knowledge of the coast on behalf of our book. He'd be glad to take us around. In fact, we'd *better* call him, he said, jabbing a finger for emphasis.

As the beer flowed so did his rhetoric.

"You want to know about surfing? I've surfed up and down the coast since I was a kid. You name it: County Line. Oil Piers. Rincon. I finished sixth out of 12 in my first amateur competition. I'll take you anywhere you want to go. I can get you onto places you won't believe. I've got three boards. Used to have four. Sold one of them. Son-of-a-bitch still hasn't paid me for it."

"I don't like fighting, I'm a Christian person, but I won't walk away from a fight. I've been in 14 bar fights and never lost once. You want to try me? *[flexes biceps]* See that bartender? I've taken down guys bigger than him. No problem."

"What do you want to know about Elvis Presley? You wanna know Elvis? I know Elvis. I'm the biggest Elvis fan there is. I'm only 24 and I've got records, actual vinyl records, by Elvis. The Beatles? The Beach Boys? What do you want to know? I know it all."

block-long car washes, hangar-sized topless bars, huge rail yards, and horrific industrial plants that make you understand why British poet/visionary William Blake coined the term "dark satanic mills." One blighted ghetto bears the nickname "Dogtown." A hip-hop hotbed, Long Beach has produced such gangsta rappers as Snoop Dogg and Nate Dogg.

On a brighter note, Belmont Shore, a self-contained neighborhood along the water in south Long Beach, has excellent ocean- and bay-beach access and lively shopping and nightlife along Second Street. If you find yourself priced out of the high-rise hotels near the Long Beach Convention and Entertainment Center, Belmont Shore is a viable place to stay. We prefer it, in fact.

Long Beach, when all is said and done, is really more oriented to convention business than pleasure travelers. It is better described as a jumping-off point for attractions in the surrounding area than a bona fide destination in and of itself.

For more information, contact the Long Beach Area Convention and Visitor Bureau, One World Trade Center, Suite 300, Long Beach, CA 90831, 562/436-3645 or 800/452-7829, www.visitlongbeach.com.

BEACHES

Away from the downtown waterfront redevelopment zone, there are some fine neighborhoods along the water in Long Beach. Heading south along Ocean Boulevard from the Long Beach Freeway to its end at Alamitos Bay in Belmont Shore, you pass miles of beautifully landscaped, architecturally varied homes facing the green, linear Bluff Park that runs along the oceanfront. Long Beach has its own sandy, extensive city beach, but water quality can be poor and the offshore breakwater keeps the waves at bay, so to speak. Yes, the same breakwater that makes Long Beach's man-made harbor the busiest port on the West Coast cuts off the surf completely. The ocean is calmer than a farm pond. No waves roll ashore here, forcing natives to head

to points north and south to surf and swim. Over a Memorial Day weekend, the beach was all but empty. Those who could afford to had high-tailed it out of Long Beach for Santa Catalina Island or the Baja Peninsula. The rest simply threw surfboards and wet suits in the back and pointed their wheels to Huntington Beach.

Long Beach City Beach runs for four miles, between First Place and 72nd Place seaward of Ocean Avenue. It's a nice expanse of sand, but there are much better ocean beaches in the vicinity—for instance Seal Beach or the beaches of the South Bay Peninsula. The city beach is bisected by Belmont Pier, a 1,620-foot pier used by locals who appear not to be fishing for recreation but out of necessity, angling for their dinner. Looking across the rippled waters of Long Beach Harbor, one spies what appears to be a series of small resort islands with 10-story hotels built on them. They are, in fact, oil derricks, dressed up to be more appealing from the vantage point of the shoreline. These artificial islands received their designer look from the Disney organization. Named after dead astronauts (e.g., Island Grissom, Island Chaffee), the derricks are hidden behind high-rise camouflage and bathed in peach and green lighting; Long Beach's offshore oil industry is innovative—at least in its exterior design.

The best beach in Long Beach turns out to be on the bay—specifically, the inner flank of **Alamitos Bay Beach** in Belmont Shore. It's a calm-water strip of sand that runs along Bay Shore Drive between Ocean Avenue and Second Street. Locals refer to this bayside beach by the nickname Horny Corners. Old folks, young kids, hot babes from Cal State Long Beach, scarlet-skinned dudes with yellow hair—all are content to lie prone on a beach towel. Some fling Frisbees, others read or gawk at the flesh parade, and a few rent kayaks. Some even swim in the bay's glass-smooth waters. Bay Shore Drive is blocked off all summer, in deference to walkers, in-line skaters, parents with strollers, and so on.

Belmont Shore also has 15 blocks of ocean frontage along Ocean Boulevard.

7 ALAMITOS BAY BEACH

Location: Bayshore Drive at Second Street in Belmont Shore area of Long Beach
Parking/Fees: free street parking
Hours: 5 A.M.-10 P.M.
Facilities: lifeguards and restrooms
Contact: Long Beach Marine Services, 562/594-0951

8 BELMONT SHORE

Location: in the Belmont Shore area of Long Beach, along Ocean Boulevard between 39th and 54th Places
Parking/Fees: metered street parking
Hours: 5 A.M.-10 P.M.
Facilities: lifeguards and restrooms
Contact: Long Beach Marine Services, 562/594-0951

9 LONG BEACH CITY BEACH

Location: in Long Beach along Ocean Boulevard, from Belmont Pier to Alamitos Avenue
Parking/Fees: metered lot and street parking
Hours: 5 A.M.-10 P.M.
Facilities: concession, lifeguards, restrooms, and showers
Contact: Long Beach Marine Services, 562/594-0951

ACCOMMODATIONS

There are too many high-rise hotels and not enough bodies to fill them in Long Beach. The $80 million, 398-room, 15-story **Hilton Long Beach** (701 West Ocean Boulevard, 562/983-3400, $$$), which opened in 1991, contributed further to what was already a soft, saturated hotel market. Already plans for further new hotel construction have fallen through. Take your pick of the brand names, all of them towering above the action in the area of the convention center, downtown, and waterfront. Other impressive contenders for your lodging dollar include the **Westin Long Beach** (333 East Ocean Boulevard, 562/436-3000, $$$), with rooms starting at $240, and the **Hyatt Regency Long Beach** (200 South Pine Avenue, 562/491-1234, $$$), with rooms starting at $200. If you've got a yen to stay on the beach at a budget price, the **Edgewater Beach Motel** (1724 East Ocean Boulevard, 562/437-3090, $) fits the bill, offering views of Catalina from its deck and five-minute proximity to the downtown hubbub.

Then there's the **Hotel Queen Mary** (1126 Queens Highway, 562/432-6964, www.queenmary.com, $$$). Her 365 staterooms are the largest ever built aboard a ship. Whereas they might have been a blast to stay in on a high-seas voyage four decades ago, today they are substantially less commodious than the rooms you'll find at one of the downtown high-rises (or even at a generic Travelodge). There's but a single porthole in each standard room that faces the water, providing a small, circular shaft of light onto the harbor. The rooms are dark and mildly claustrophobic, the bathrooms are small (and the plastic shower stalls scandalously cheap), yet the beds are comfortable and the unique experience of bunking down aboard a grand old ocean liner compensates for some of the drawbacks. The price is, for the novelty, right, with rooms starting at $159. The ship seems to be particularly popular with large wedding parties, with ceremonies conducted right on deck. To be perfectly honest, however, we'd recommend taking a daytime tour of the *Queen Mary* and laying your head elsewhere in Long Beach.

COASTAL CUISINE

The oldest seafood restaurant in town, **Fish Tale** (5506 East Britton Drive, 562/594-8771, $$), got larger new digs, but the old ambience (fish tales, antique artifacts) is still intact, as are the heaping helpings of fresh fish. There's also an oyster bar on the premises. Downtown, the **King's Fish House** (100 West Broadway, 562/432-7463, $$$) is a terrific choice for grilled or broiled fish served with light, creative, and tasty sauces, such as Chilean sea bass with dill chardonnay sauce (a house favorite) or blackened halibut with corn relish and red pepper coulis. The award-winning cioppino—a tomato-based fisherman's stew with clams, mussels, shrimp, crab, squid, and fish—is another excellent choice.

All manner of varied ethnic cuisine is available in Long Beach, but we were most surprised to find a place that served real Southern-style barbecue. The down-home fare at **Johnny Reb's Southern Smokehouse** (4663 Long Beach Boulevard, 562/423-7327, $$)—pit-cooked barbecue, crackling fried chicken, coleslaw, and hush puppies—sent this pair of erstwhile rebels home happier than hot hogs in cool mud.

We can't quit without mentioning **Joe Jost's** (2803 East Anaheim Avenue, 562/439-5446, $). It's the oldest continuously operating bar in California, and it has been run by three generations of Jost's. Papa Joe, God rest his soul, invented a deli sandwich that has become a local institution. Called Joe's Special, it consists of a hunk of Polish sausage surrounded by a slice of Swiss cheese with a pickle spear stuck into a V-shaped slit, all stuffed between mustard-slathered pieces of rye bread and wrapped in a waxed-paper handle. Joe Jost's serves hundreds of them every day, and just as many of the other house specialty: a basket of pretzels, peppers, and pickled eggs. As for what's on tap at Joe Jost's, they pump ice-cold Blitz beer, brewed in Oregon, in 20-ounce schooners.

NIGHTLIFE

The centerpiece of the Broadway/Pine Avenue downtown renaissance is a 16-screen AMC cineplex at **Pine Square** (245 Pine Avenue, 562/435-4262). Surrounding it is a neon galaxy of munchie parlors, coffeehouses, restaurants, and clubs. **System M** (213-A Pine Avenue, 562/435-2525) is the gathering place for Long Beach's new bohemians, with gentlemen on the outdoor patio affecting pince-nez, goatees, and Kramer-like explosions of hair while sucking contemplatively on cigarettes and watching the smoke curl against the fuchsia glow of the restaurant's neon. Food, drinks, coffee, and art are served within.

In the same vicinity, the **Blue Cafe** (210 Promenade, 562/983-7111) pays homage to the electric guitar along a largely undeveloped pedestrian promenade. Regionally popular blues, rock, and alternative musicians perform here for a modest cover charge. We paid $4 apiece on a Monday night to see a local band called Standard Fruit and had a fine time. Bathed in ubiquitous neon, it is, like every other business on this embryonic scene, an outpost of civility trying to stay afloat in a sea of economic uncertainty.

From there we felt like getting rowdy, so we proceeded down to Belmont Shore, a livelier and more organic community in south Long Beach. We've always had a good time rambling around the bars and taverns of Second Street. They are jam-packed with friendly and fun-loving college kids, neighborhood residents, and navy guys out for a brew. Take your pick and pull up a bar stool. There's **Legends** (5236 East Second Street, 562/433-5743), a sports bar that's always abuzz with folks ogling the action on the big screen; **Panama Joe's** (5100 East Second Street, 562/434-7417), an upscale "meet market" that gets good bands on weekends; and our personal favorite, the **Acapulco Inn** (5283 East Second Street, 562/439-3517). The latter is a collegiate dive bar that's wilder than any toga party John Belushi ever attended. At the "AI," students from nearby Cal State Long Beach cut loose in a party environment so out of control on big nights that it's almost a caricature of hell-raising. The jukebox leans heavily on 1960s party favorites, while an assortment of games—including a Pop-a-Shot concession that nearly cleaned out our wallets—gives you something to do besides clutch a beer. If you can keep up with this crowd, you deserve whatever you wake up with the next morning: a hangover, a fellow party animal, or both.

San Pedro

Tucked behind the protective, ever-changing Palos Verdes Peninsula is San Pedro (population 86,000), the port town for the city of Los Angeles. In 1889, after heavy competition with other bay towns like Redondo Beach, it was chosen to house Los Angeles Harbor, thanks to the good offices of Senator Stephen M. White (after whom a main drag in town is named). Before it was enlarged to its present size, the harbor was so shallow that oceangoing vessels had to be anchored offshore and loaded and unloaded from there. Today it is known as "Worldport L.A." The harbor covers 7,000 acres and 28 miles of waterfront, making it one of the largest artificial ports in the world.

Overlooking San Pedro Harbor is formidable Fort MacArthur, once an integral part of our West Coast defense posture. San Pedro is home to 86,000 people, many of whom make their living on the docks. It was also the home of one of our favorite writers, the late Charles Bukowski. He came to live in San Pedro in 1978, leaving Los Angeles after 58 years of a squalid hand-to-mouth existence. According to biographer Neeli Cherkovski, Bukowski chose San Pedro because "unlike some of the other beach towns, the spirit of the 1960s hadn't settled on it." That much is true. The real lure of San Pedro for Bukowski was its proximity to the freeways, which afforded a quick escape from anonymous middle-class respectability to the racetracks at Hollywood Park and Santa Anita. Bukowski died here in 1993.

Despite the relative lack of beaches, elbowed out by the harbor, there's plenty of waterfront activity in San Pedro. The **Cabrillo Marine Aquarium** (3720 Stephen M. White Drive, 310/548-7562) has 38 aquariums with marine life native to Southern California, as well as a multimedia show for kids, seasonal grunion tours, and whale-watching expeditions. It's only $5 per adult and $1 for children and seniors, and parking costs $1 per hour. Down on the docks is **Los Angeles Maritime Museum** (Berth 84, Sixth Street, 310/548-7618), which presents an assortment of maritime equipment, memorabilia, and historical photographs detailing the construction of the harbor and the old ferry days. Admission is $3 for adults and $1 for kids. In addition, you can take several tours out of San Pedro Harbor, including ferries to Santa Catalina Island and dinner and harbor cruises.

For more information, contact the San Pedro Peninsula Chamber of Commerce, 390 West Seventh Street, San Pedro, CA 90731, 310/832-7272, www.sanpedrochamber.com.

BEACHES

There are a few beaches in San Pedro worth seeking out if you're in the area. The main one—and the only sandy beach in San Pedro—is **Cabrillo City Beach,** east of Point Fermin on either side of the San Pedro Breakwater. The "harbor" side of the beach is protected and calm, with a boat-launching ramp. The "ocean" side, on the other side of the harbor fortification, receives the full force of the ocean—real waves for board surfing and windsurfing. The tidepools are rich in marine life, and in the summer the grunion hold some epic runs here. The Cabrillo Marine Museum elaborates on the local ecology. Attached to the breakwater at Cabrillo City Beach is a 1,000-foot municipal fishing pier. **Point Fermin Park** and lighthouse are on a bluff overlooking the ocean; steep trails lead to the rocky shore below.

West of Point Fermin, the parking lot below the cliffs at White Point is divided into **White Point County Park** (left) and **Royal Palms County Beach** (right). The former is a bluff-top park with playgrounds and overlooks, while the latter is a rugged, rocky shoreline popular with shell collectors and surf casters. Surfers like it, too, in winter.

The most remarkable feature of White Point/ Royal Palms, though, is the presence of mineral springs that lie offshore, which divers explore. When you tire of the beach, you can always wander the grounds of the old Royal Palms Hotel, which was washed away in a storm seven decades ago, though the royal palm trees remain. Tidepoolers and divers go to White Point, at the east end, while picnickers and sunbathers congregate at Royal Palms. The latter, incidentally, has received a $2.2 million sprucing up of its facilities and is really looking sharp.

10 CABRILLO CITY BEACH

Location: Stephen M. White Drive at 40th Street in San Pedro
Parking/Fees: $5 entrance fee per vehicle
Hours: 5 A.M.-10:30 P.M.
Facilities: concession, lifeguards, restrooms, showers, and picnic tables
Contact: Los Angeles County Lifeguard Service, Southern Section, 310/832-1179

11 POINT FERMIN PARK

Location: Gaffey Street at Paseo del Mar, near Point Fermin Lighthouse in San Pedro
Parking/Fees: free parking lot
Hours: 6 A.M.-sunset
Facilities: restrooms and picnic tables
Contact: Los Angeles County Lifeguard Service, Southern Section, 310/832-1179

12 WHITE POINT COUNTY PARK

Location: From Paseo del Mar in San Pedro, turn right on Kay Fiorentino Drive and follow it to the park. On the left side of the parking lot

is White Point County Park, on the right side is Royal Palms County Beach.
Parking/Fees: $2 entrance fee per vehicle on weekdays, $5-6 on weekends
Hours: 6 A.M.-sunset
Facilities: restrooms
Contact: Los Angeles County Lifeguard Service, Southern Section, 310/832-1179

13 ROYAL PALMS COUNTY BEACH

Location: From Paseo del Mar in San Pedro, turn right on Kay Fiorentino Drive and follow it to the park. On the left side of the parking lot is White Point County Park, on the right side is Royal Palms County Beach.
Parking/Fees: $5 entrance fee per vehicle
Hours: 6 A.M.-sunset
Facilities: lifeguards and restrooms
Contact: Los Angeles County Lifeguard Service, Southern Section, 310/832-1179

ACCOMMODATIONS

The **Sunrise Hotel** (525 South Harbor Boulevard, 310/548-1080, $$) happens to be the closest hotel in town to the harbor. Rooms look out on the harbor; amenities include deluxe continental breakfast, pool, and a hot tub. The best, most reliable of the chains in San Pedro is the **Holiday Inn San Pedro/Los Angeles Harbor** (111 South Gaffey Street, 310/514-1414 or 877/865-6578, $$).

COASTAL CUISINE

The **22nd Street Landing Seafood Grill & Bar** (141 West 22nd Street, 310/548-4400, $$$) serves more than a dozen types of fresh fish daily in a dining room that looks out on the harbor. For seafood it's the best choice for miles around. There are also a number of excellent Italian restaurants in the area. Tops among them is **Madeo Ristorante** (295 Whaler's Walk, 310/521-5333, $$$), adjacent to the Doubletree Hotel at Cabrillo Marina.

CROSSTOWN TRAFFIC: DRIVING IN LOS ANGELES

It is nearly impossible to visit Los Angeles without spending a lot of time inside a car. In order to get around the spread-out city, you will have to drive and drive...and drive some more.

There are 200 bus lines in Los Angeles run by the Los Angeles County Metropolitan Transit Authority. They also operate three MetroRail light-rail lines, totaling 74 miles of track. The Metro Blue Line makes 22-mile runs from Los Angeles to Long Beach, with stops in San Pedro, Anaheim, and other communities. The Metro Green Line runs a 20-mile east-west route across southern Los Angeles County, including stops at Redondo Beach, LAX, Long Beach, and Norwalk. The Metro Gold Line travels from Los Angeles' Union Station to Pasadena.

The Metro Red Line, the city's first subway, opened in 1993. Today it runs from North Hollywood through Hollywood to Union Station, in downtown L.A. The Metro Purple Line runs from Union Station to stops along Wilshire Boulevard. There is a total of 17 miles of underground rail in Los Angeles.

For city bus, Metro Line, and MetroRail information, contact the **Los Angeles County Metropolitan Transit Authority,** 425 South Main Street, Los Angeles, CA 90013, 213/626-4455, www.metro.net.

Metrolink is a regional commuter rail system, established in 1991, that serves 56 stations across Southern California from its hub at Union Station. In terms of the coast, it goes as far south as San Clemente and as far north as Oxnard. They own about 256 route miles of track. Unfortunately, on September 12, 2008, Metrolink made national news when one of its trains collided with a Union Pacific freight train near Chatsworth, killing 25 and injuring 135 (40 of them critically). It was the deadliest U.S. rail accident in 15 years and the worst in Southern California in half a century.

For Metrolink commuter rail information, contact **Metrolink,** 700 South Flower Street, 26th floor, Los Angeles, CA 90017, 213/808-5465 or 800/371-5465, www.metrolinktrains.com.

If you are getting around Los Angeles by car, you will notice that the freeways loop into each other like asphalt pretzels. Perversely, the freeway carpool lanes in Los Angeles and Orange Counties are nearly always clear. The number of passengers constituting a High Occupancy Vehicle (HOV) has been dropped. Now you need only two passengers per car. And still the carpool lanes are empty. That is because nearly everyone in Southern California is a "Lindbergh" – a solo driver. So the roads stay jammed.

If you're in the area, it pays to learn the names and numbers of the freeways you'll be traveling:

Highway 2	=	Glendale Freeway
Highway 10	=	Santa Monica or San Bernardino Freeway
Highway 60	=	Pomona Freeway
Highway 90	=	Marina Freeway
Highway 91	=	Artesia Freeway
Highway 110	=	Pasadena Freeway
Highway 170	=	Hollywood Freeway
U.S. 101	=	Ventura, Hollywood, or Santa Ana Freeway
I-5	=	Golden State or Santa Ana Freeway
I-110	=	Harbor Freeway
I-405	=	San Diego Freeway
I-605	=	San Gabriel River Freeway
I-710	=	Long Beach Freeway

Keep track of traffic over the airwaves. Many radio stations offer traffic reports. The stations with the best coverage are KNX (1070 AM) and KFWB (980 AM).

KNX, an all-news radio station, gives traffic reports every six minutes, 24 hours a day. A typical traffic update sounds like this (imagine a fast-talking, mellifluous deejay voice): "It's stop-and-go all the way from Santa Monica to Pasadena, but the good news is there are no accidents blocking the road."

When an explanation for a traffic tie-up is warranted, the tone of the deejay's voice doesn't modulate and his update sounds like this: "There's a bus on top of a car near the Avalon exit on I-405. Ouch, that's gotta smart!"

Further coloring the experience of driving in Los Angeles is the haze of smog, plus vast wastelands of junkyards and salvage lots, oil refineries, and industrial complexes. But Los Angeles keeps on growing and, after each earthquake, roads are rebuilt before homes are, inviting more cars and creating more problems.

So what's the solution? In 2009, with the bottom falling out of the American economy and gas breaking the $5 per gallon barrier for the first time, it's certainly not "drill, baby, drill," as some would have it. In our opinion, the answer is smaller, more fuel-efficient hybrid vehicles, better mass-transit options (especially in sprawling L.A.), and the physical compacting of cities like Los Angeles in order to reduce commutation. One thing's for sure: The old way of driving by depending on cheap gas is history.

NIGHTLIFE

Most of the restaurants on the harbor have cocktail lounges. For a nonalcoholic alternative, duck into the **Sacred Grounds Coffee House & Art Gallery** (468 West Sixth Street, 310/514-0800), where art, live entertainment, and cappuccino are the house blend. Incidentally, if you really want to understand San Pedro, check out native Mike Watt's excellent 1997 CD, *Contemplating the Engine Room.*

Palos Verdes Peninsula

The enormous landmass known as the Palos Verdes Peninsula, in the southwest corner of Los Angeles County, is one that will (as Muhammad Ali used to say) "shock and amaze ya." As is the case in the northern part of the county—with the Santa Monica Mountains, the Malibu Peninsula, and the Hollywood Hills—the Palos Verdes Peninsula is an example of the incredible diversity of landforms found in and around the City of Angels.

This craggy, lunarlike peninsula is no party to the smog dish of the Los Angeles Basin. Even though its jagged, cliff-lined shore embraces 15 miles of Pacific coastline—from San Pedro to Torrance—the Pacific Coast Highway doesn't come near it. Instead, it moves inland, leaving the tough, shifting terrain of the peninsula to the hermitic wishes of the folks who live out here on the edge of the planet.

Driving around this wondrous peninsula entails following a series of small, winding back roads that pass through a quaking, unsettled landscape. Along this Jell-O-like terrain, a road sign warns, Constant Land Movement Next 8 Miles. What could this mean? we wondered. It means that sections of the road, particularly in the vicinity of Portuguese Bend, look like they've just been removed from a waffle iron and have more dips in them than an amusement-park roller coaster. The land here actually moves at a rate of one to six inches a month and has

been doing so since the mid-1950s, when highway blasting caused the top layer of rock to separate from and slip over the lower layer (a phenomenon known as "block-glide"). A prodigious chunk of the peninsula fell into the ocean in May 1999, taking with it a portion of a new golf-course development. (Talk about poetic justice!)

You will find yourself holding your breath for reasons other than fear, however, as one seductive panorama of sky, sea, and headlands follows another until you work your way off the peninsula at Torrance. Depending on how you approach it, the drive is either an unexpectedly nice side trip or the most unusual way to enter the back door of Los Angeles. At one time the entire peninsula was the rancho of the Sepulveda family, until they sold it in 1914 to a company with plans to develop it as a "millionaire's colony." To that end they called in the landscape firm of Olmstead and Olmstead (sons of Frederick Law Olmstead, designer of New York's Central Park). The Olmstead brothers planted trees on the barren lands and built houses among them, and the millionaires dug in for the long haul. They're still dug in out here, although the nerve-jangling land movement has driven many to abandon the sloping Portuguese Bend area. The houses that didn't slip into the drink have been sold off for a song to intrepid souls unafraid to live in them. Yet the neighborhoods behind the falling ridge remain some of the most exclusive properties in Los Angeles.

For more information, contact the Palos Verdes Peninsula Chamber of Commerce, 707 Silver Spur Road, Suite 110, Drive North, Rolling Hills Estates, CA 90274, 310/377-8111, www.palosverdeschamber.com.

BEACHES

The small, sandy coves on the Palos Verdes Peninsula are difficult to get to, but they are among the most prized in the county, due partly to their very inaccessibility. The most visited are Malaga Cove and Abalone Cove

Beach. **Malaga Cove**—also known as RAT (for Right After Torrance)—is the only true sand beach on the peninsula. It's popular with surfers and swimmers who climb down with their boards and towels from the paved access point at Via Arroyo, off Palos Verdes Drive West. There's a small, free parking lot. **Abalone Cove Beach,** which straddles the legendary Portuguese Bend off Palos Verdes Drive South, can be reached via a pay parking lot. Surfers' localism is at its worst on the peninsula, however, where the best surf spots are zealously (and sometimes violently) defended by local gangs. We were told you could avoid the parking fee by parking a block away on the roadside, which we noticed many people doing.

Even if you don't take the plunge to the beaches, the cliff-hugging route along the outer rim of Palos Verdes makes for an exciting afternoon drive. Particularly appealing is Paseo del Mar, a loop road that leaves Palos Verdes Drive and cuts through **Palos Verdes Estates Shoreline Preserve,** which runs for 4.5 miles and comprises 130 city-owned acres above a bluff top. Several precipitous paths leave the bluff top and zigzag down to cove beaches at Lunada Bay, Bluff Cove, and Malaga Cove. On the southwestern corner of the peninsula, the small **Point Vicente Park** offers free parking, restrooms, a whale-watching deck, and displays that interpret local history and ecology. At the park's pullout a dirt trail leads to **Point Vicente Fishing Access.** This magical fishing hole draws skin- and scuba divers as well as anglers. South of Point Vicente Park is the Point Vicente Lighthouse, which was built in 1926 and is now closed to the public.

The splendid architecture on the peninsula is worth checking out from a car window. It is something every developer should witness and learn from. Hidden among the trees and hills, the human habitations don't try to compete with the grandeur of the landscape. This philosophy of architectural noninterference reaches a zenith with the **Wayfarers Chapel**

(5755 Palos Verdes Drive South, 310/377-1650), on the mainland side of the road just beyond Portuguese Bend. Built in 1946 by Lloyd Wright (son of Frank), the predominantly glass edifice allows worshippers (devotees of the theologian Emanuel Swedenborg) to feel as if they're outdoors among the redwoods and gardens that surround the chapel. It is open to the public daily 11 A.M.–4 P.M. A small museum on the grounds has exhibits about "Swedenborgianism" and Helen Keller, a practitioner thereof.

One final note: It was on Palos Verdes that Marineland of the Pacific was built in 1954. Once the home and playpen for a small navy of Flippers, Orcas, and Jaws, the three-ring aquatic circus is long gone. The park's inaccessibility is the reason for its financial demise. The property was sold off, presumably to an eccentric millionaire with a penchant for large swimming pools.

14 ABALONE COVE BEACH

Location: Palos Verdes Drive at Narcissa Drive on the southwest corner of Palos Verdes Peninsula
Parking/Fees: $4 entrance fee per vehicle
Hours: 6 A.M.-sunset
Facilities: lifeguards, restrooms, and picnic area
Contact: Los Angeles County Lifeguard Service, Southern Section, 310/832-1179

15 MALAGA COVE

Location: Paseo del Mar at Via Arroyo on northwest corner of Palos Verdes Peninsula
Parking/Fees: free parking lot
Hours: 6 A.M.-sunset
Facilities: lifeguards, restrooms, and showers
Contact: Los Angeles County Lifeguard Service, Southern Section, 310/832-1179

Redondo Beach

Redondo Beach has fancied itself a vacation destination since the 1890s, when a trio of Spanish sisters sold the sand dunes they inherited to developers. Shipping was an important early industry, but after Redondo Beach unsuccessfully vied to have the Port of Los Angeles located here (San Pedro won), the town turned to tourism. A huge luxury hotel, along with tent cities for the fiscally challenged, drew vacationers to the pristine beach. The Hotel Redondo—which opened in 1890 and was stupidly torn down in 1926—actually was the sister establishment of the splendid Hotel del Coronado down the coast. During Redondo's heyday, folks would ride the fabled Pacific Electric "red cars" from downtown Los Angeles to the beach.

At one time Redondo Beach (population 67,100) had it all: big-band ballrooms, offshore gambling ships reached by water taxis, and a huge, heated indoor saltwater pool called "the Plunge." A Hawaiian native named George Freeth demonstrated the strange new sport of surfing to curious onlookers behind the Hotel Redondo. (Freeth was described biblically by developer Henry Huntington as "the man who could walk on water.") Redondo's glory days are documented in the **Redondo Beach Historical Museum** (320 Knob Hill Avenue, 310/543-3108), operated by the Redondo Beach Historical Commission.

Residents would no doubt like to see those golden days return, but that will take a long reprieve from the forces of nature and economics, and that is one tall order. Of the triumvirate of beach towns that are conjoined in the South Bay area of Los Angeles, Redondo Beach was spiked the hardest by economic recession and natural disaster. Whereas its sisters in sand and sun, Hermosa Beach and Manhattan Beach, are primarily residential communities and only secondarily tourist-oriented, Redondo Beach—at least that part of town seaward of the Pacific Coast Highway—seeks and depends on visitor dollars. The lineup of waterfront attractions in Redondo Beach includes the marinas at King Harbor (there are four of them), the International Boardwalk, the town's famous "horseshoe pier," and several resort hotels. You can gauge Redondo's dependence on visitors by the size of the parking decks. Whether you're berthing a yacht in one of the basins or wheeling a rented Escort into one of the garages, Redondo Beach is glad to have you and your pesos jingling around town. For this reason it is the most outsider-friendly of the South Bay communities.

Redondo is struggling gamely out of the hard times that have befallen it and rekindling some of the spirit that made it a beach-lover's mecca. Having persevered through repeated bouts of storm damage, plus a catastrophic pier fire, the collapse of a parking deck, and the impact of prolonged economic downturns in the early- to mid-1990s and in the present recession, Redondo Beach has a survivor's mentality.

Today, Redondo's waterfront complex is a catacomb of parking decks, food stalls along the concrete boardwalk, and a handful of pier-based restaurants. Still, we can't help but wonder what will happen the next time the Arctic or El Niño sends another unforgiving squall Redondo's way. How long this cycle of destruction and rebuilding can continue is anyone's guess.

On a cheerier note, one of the best-loved features of the waterfront, the **South Bay Bicycle Trail,** endures. A 26-mile paved path that extends from Torrance City Beach (just south of Redondo) to Will Rogers State Beach (in Malibu), it is a two-way concrete freeway for cyclists, in-line skaters, skateboarders, and joggers. Even the odd walker can be spotted, although mere strolling is a little too undemanding for this high-speed crowd. If you're not in shape, this isn't the place to reveal your unseemly bulges. The bike path is part aerobic runway, part fashion runway, and always crowded—the place to see and be seen.

Traveling south from Hermosa Beach, the trail swings onto the streets of Redondo for a few blocks before entering the innards of the

King Harbor-Pier Complex. Once past this maze, through which you're asked to walk your bike, the path resumes a straight and steady course south along Redondo State Beach, giving cyclists a superb view of the rugged bluffs of the Palos Verdes Peninsula. Cruising the South Bay is a popular pastime, and bikes can be rented at local shops, the best of which are in Hermosa Beach. The local climate almost mandates outdoor activity. The mercury rarely falls below 45 degrees in January or rises above 75 degrees in July. Los Angeles's chronic halo of smog doesn't choke the beaches of the South Bay. Cooling offshore breezes ensure that the air is generally clean and the skies blue.

And so Redondo Beach sits at the edge of the Pacific like a tarnished jewel in a splendid setting. It has been knocked around by Mother Nature and is still somewhat punch-drunk, yet its residents doggedly regroup, rebuild, and persevere.

BEACHES

The beach at Redondo Beach maintains a respectable width south of the pier, but it is narrow and eroded north of it. Erosion is the result of harborfront construction, including a breakwater that diverts sand into a submarine canyon just offshore. The same canyon causes wave crests to refract in a way that concentrates their energy onto the beaches north of the canyon, occasionally wrecking beaches and the houses built along them. In severe storms, the breakwater has been overtopped and damaged. Signs warn people away from what's left of the beach in the vicinity of the harbor, where the ocean angrily slaps walls of riprap that have been erected to protect the construction behind it.

The beach scene improves markedly on the south side of the pier along the strand encompassing **Redondo State Beach** and **Torrance City Beach**. Redondo State Beach runs for about 1.5 miles from the pier south to some restrooms, on the other side of which it becomes Torrance City Beach, continuing down to the Palos Verdes Peninsula for three-

quarters of a mile. It's the same beach—a flat swath of sand that widens between pier and peninsula, a nice place to come for a little more nature and a little less in the way of crowds than you'll find at Hermosa or Manhattan Beaches. To the delight of surfers, this stretch is serviced by the west swells of winter. Incidentally, though it's now called Redondo State Beach, this beach is lifeguarded and maintained by Los Angeles County. Similar city/county arrangements and nomenclature apply throughout the county.

For more information, contact the Redondo Beach Chamber of Commerce & Visitors Bureau, 200 North Pacific Coast Highway, Redondo Beach, CA 90277, 310/376-6911 or 800/282-0333, www.redondochamber.org.

16 TORRANCE CITY BEACH

Location: along Paseo de la Playa in Torrance
Parking/Fees: $4 entrance fee per vehicle
Hours: 6 A.M.-sunset
Facilities: lifeguards, restrooms, and showers
Contact: Los Angeles County Lifeguard Service, Southern Section, 310/832-1179

17 REDONDO STATE BEACH

Location: Torrance Boulevard at Esplanade in Redondo Beach
Parking/Fees: metered street and lot parking
Hours: 6 A.M.-sunset
Facilities: concessions, lifeguards, restrooms, and showers
Contact: Los Angeles County Lifeguard Service, Southern Section, 310/832-1179

ACCOMMODATIONS

To oversimplify, Redondo Beach has the hotels, Manhattan Beach has the restaurants, and Hermosa Beach has the nightlife. Numerous chain motels are located along and west of the Pacific

Coast Highway, only one-third mile from the beach. Down along the harbor are the two top choices: the **Portofino Hotel and Yacht Club** (260 Portofino Way, 310/379-8481, www.hotelportofino.com, $$$) and the **Crowne Plaza Redondo Beach Hotel** (300 North Harbor Drive, 310/318-8888, www.cpredondobeachhotel.com, $$$). The latter is an especially attractive property, an airy and spacious five-story resort hotel overlooking King Harbor from the dry side of Harbor Drive. Room rates are $180 a night and up in season. Private balconies, outdoor heated pool and sundeck, exercise facilities, sports bar, piano bar, on-premises restaurant, and more make this a prime place to lie in when visiting Redondo Beach.

Another option is the **Palos Verdes Inn** (1700 South Pacific Coast Highway, 310/316-4211 or 800/421-9241, www.palosverdesinn.com, $$$), only three blocks from the beach along a curve on the coastal highway, where it begins to skirt the uplands of the Palos Verdes Peninsula. The hotel is a self-contained city, with an excellent Continental restaurant (**Chez Mélange,** 310/542-1222, $$$), gourmet deli (**Chez Allez,** $), live-music venue (**Club Caprice,** 310/316-1700), and half-acre pool, spa, and gardens on the premises. Rooms are comfortably furnished, and many come with ocean-view balconies.

COASTAL CUISINE

In Redondo Beach, restaurants don't always go out of business due to bad reviews or word of mouth. Big waves wreck them. Several pier restaurants have been washed into the big drink over the years. Still, the harborside restaurant scene survives, particularly the **Blue Moon Saloon** (207 North Harbor Drive, 310/373-3411, $$$), a casual seafood eatery in the Redondo Beach Marina that has endured wind and wave to emerge as a long-lived institution on the waterfront. The International Boardwalk is home to **Quality Seafood** (130 South International Boardwalk, 310/374-2382, $$), a seafood market and snack bar that displays and

prepares all manner of fresh, colorful seafood: local crab and fish, plus Louisiana crawdads and New Zealand eel. Cooks will steam a crab for you on the spot, which you can take to a table and crack to your heart's content.

NIGHTLIFE

There's a **Hennessey's Tavern** (1710 South Catalina Avenue, 310/316-6658) in Riviera Village, a shopping area set back from the beach. Come to think of it, there's a Hennessey's in each of the three South Bay beach towns: Redondo, Hermosa, and Manhattan. You can also find a decent cocktail lounge at one of the seafood restaurants in King Harbor: the old reliable **Chart House** (231 Yacht Club Way, 310/372-3464) or the **Blue Moon Saloon** (207 North Harbor Drive, 310/373-3411). You might wander into a decent jam at **Papa Garo's** (1810 South Catalina Boulevard, 310/540-7272), a Mediterranean restaurant and music club where you'll find live blues music in a smoke-free environment, as incongruous as that might seem. What was formerly the Strand Supper Club is now **Club Caprice** (1700 South Pacific Coast Highway, 310/316-1700), the best music venue in town. On Pacific Coast Highway, a few blocks from the beach, **Coyote Cantina** (531 North Highway 1, 310/376-1066) leaves them howling with their 60-label tequila list.

Hermosa Beach

In Spanish *hermosa* means "beautiful," and it's an apt description of this unpretentious community, which seems light-years removed from the smoggy hubbub of Los Angeles, against which it brushes. The more things change around it, the more Hermosa Beach (population 19,400) remains the same. It is the most relaxed and laid-back of the South Bay communities, a town full of coffee bars and shops catering to the healthful prerogatives of a physically fit populace. Living beside

EAVESDROPPING IN HERMOSA BEACH: "I'M VERY THERE"

The following is a real-life play in one act. All conversation is reported verbatim. (Yes, we eavesdropped and took notes.)

Scene: The bright stucco interior of the Hermosa Beach Post Office on a summer afternoon.

He: A slouching, unshaven male who looks like he's just rolled out of bed. His face is stubbly, his hair unkempt. He is wearing soiled cutoffs, sandals, and a T-shirt that has grayed from one too many unsorted washings.

She: A former California beach queen now gone to seed in middle age. Her skin has been worn to alligator hide by the sun, her face is creased with age and worry lines, and her thighs sag with cellulite. Her hair is dirty blonde, and she wears Spandex bike shorts and a loose-fitting T-shirt. Her eyes are concealed by designer sunglasses.

[They meet at a counter in the front room of the post office, where he is addressing a package.]

He: You look great!

She: Thanks. I feel great. *[Pauses.]* But it just ain't enough. *[She cackles ruefully, then continues.]* People are so goddamned superficial out here. Everybody is chasing that big white cloud, and I don't know what it is.

He: Yeah, I know. I'm so busy, I'm just running around all the time. This is what my day looks like: I get up, go to work, look for a place to park, and work for eight hours. I don't even have time to eat. I'll call to have some food delivered then shove it down when I can grab a moment. Then it's off to classes. Then I get home and call for more takeout food while I'm doing my homework and whatever *work* work I've had to take home. I'm beat all the time. The harder I work, the more I fall behind. I just don't know what's wrong.

She: I know what you mean. I spent six years in therapy, and all I wanted to know was how to find peace. Now I've found it, but I'm in the minority.

He: I'm very there.

She: I just don't need it anymore.

He: Good for you!

She: I'm going to Costa Rica to look for work. I've had it with L.A. It's just too crowded for me. Everyone running around, getting in each other's way. You know what I mean? No one wants to admit it, but it's over. L.A. is over. I've had it.

He: Are you going to Costa Rica with your mate?

She: No. *[Thoughtful pause.]* We're taking a second look at where we're at right now. If it happens, it happens. We'll see.

He: I was talking to my mate about this. A relationship starts out with a certain amount of mass, and once that mass begins falling away, you're forced to interface with one another. *[Pauses to reflect.]* You know, I like that phrase.

She: That's so true. Well, gotta go. Gotta get back to work. We'll hook up sometime.

He: Bye.

She: Bye-bye.

[Both walk away.]

the ocean in an almost perfect climate tends to make people look after themselves. Even a place like the Rocky Cola Cafe, a 1950s-style burger-jukebox joint, offers a healthy menu, analyzing its food items in terms of fat grams and calories; the café leaves things like egg yolks out of its omelets and serves black beans and brown rice as side dishes.

Hermosa Beach has a solid sense of itself and has plotted its destiny well. In 1901 the beach was surveyed for a boardwalk, in 1904 the first pier was built, and in 1907 the town of Hermosa Beach was incorporated. At that time the city gained ownership over its two-mile oceanfront in a deed mandating that it be held in perpetuity as "beach playground, free from commerce, and for the benefit of not only residents of Hermosa, but also for the sea lovers of Southern California." Those ideals remain in force today. It is an aesthetically attractive town with a gleaming, well-maintained beach.

What's most magical about Hermosa Beach is the descent down Pier Avenue toward the ocean. Rounding a curve, the road yields a spectacular view of the ocean. The light sea breeze is constant, the air feels clean and continuously refreshed, and you just can't help but stroll around Hermosa Beach in a state of grateful rejuvenation. If you want to get out of the sun, you can always duck into Nations Travel Bookstore, a shop specializing in travel guides, maps, and videos.

While you're there, rent a bike or a pair of in-line skates at one of the shops down on the Strand, then take off for a spin along the bike path up to Malibu, down to Redondo—anything's possible. And the unfolding beach scenery is worth the legwork.

Parking remains the one big bugaboo in Hermosa Beach. There's barely enough of it for those who live here, much less for visitors. Street parking is hard to find and expensive, and parking-meter charges are enforced 24 hours a day. Hotel guests are covered, but day-trippers be advised: Come via rapid transit, on foot, or via bicycle, if possible. Otherwise you might find yourself incurring some degree of expense and/or hassle. To quote from a letter to the editor of the *Easy Reader,* a free local paper: "The nemesis of Hermosa Beach that there's just no getting around is parking." We can second that emotion. Still, we like everything else about Hermosa Beach and recommend it highly.

BEACHES

Hermosa City Beach stretches for two unblemished miles, part of the continuous strip of sand that runs along the Santa Monica Bay before slamming to a halt at the Palos Verdes Peninsula. The 1,328-foot-long Hermosa Pier is its centerpiece, offering year-round angling in the waters of Santa Monica Bay. At the foot of the pier is a statue of a surfer poised in mid-ride. Beneath the frozen surfrider's impassive gaze, swarms of people whiz by on the South Bay Bicycle Trail. Although everyone moves at different speeds and in different directions, this complex symphony of motion somehow plays through without a lot of serious spills or collisions.

In addition to all the hell-on-wheels aerobicizing along the South Bay Bicycle Trail, sand rats play volleyball and paddleball out here on the ample beach, which we have yet to see in a condition that could be described as overcrowded. One pastime that's not too big, oddly enough, is surfing. Apparently the breakwater that protects Redondo Beach's harbor knocks the waves here down to a size for which only novices and locals have much use.

For more information, contact the Hermosa Beach Chamber of Commerce, 1007 Hermosa Avenue, Hermosa Beach, CA 90254, 310/376-0951, www.hbchamber.net.

18 HERMOSA CITY BEACH

        BEST (

Location: Pier Avenue at Hermosa Avenue in Hermosa Beach
Parking/Fees: metered street parking
Hours: 6 A.M.–sunset

Facilities: concessions, lifeguards, restrooms, and showers
Contact: Los Angeles County Lifeguard Service, Southern Section, 310/832-1179

ACCOMMODATIONS

The best place to stay in Hermosa Beach is the **Beach House** (1300 Strand, 310/374-3001, www.beach-house.com, $$$$). It's perched right on the beach, with 96 "loft suites" overlooking the ocean in the vicinity of the pier. It doesn't get any better (or better situated) than the Beach House, but $300–430 a night for a room is a bit rich for our blood, at least in funky Hermosa. We're also fond of a funky, down-to-earth place called the **Sea Sprite Motel** (1016 Strand, 310/376-6933, www.seaspritemotel.com, $$) that's perfect for a true beach lover. The Sea Sprite is an informal yet well-tended motel that rents rooms and apartment-style cottages. From the second-floor pool deck you can watch the world skate by on the bike path below or just enjoy the misty breezes rolling off the ocean. The hotel has even managed to shoehorn in a parking space for every room, a perk that's worth its weight in parking tickets. There's nothing fancy about the Sea Sprite, but when you're right on the ocean—and you couldn't be any closer except on a surfboard—who needs marble bathrooms and turn-down service?

Hotel Hermosa (2515 Pacific Coast Highway, 310/318-6000, www.hotelhermosa.com, $$), an attractively landscaped property five blocks away from the beach, has a more upscale feel. A recent arrival, it's a Spanish-style three-story hotel with a heated pool, Japanese garden, workout facilities, and comfortable rooms, many with ocean-facing balconies. We also got a nice room for a fair price at the **Quality Inn** (901 Aviation Boulevard, 310/374-2666, www.qualityinn.com, $$). A large room with two beds that was spacious, well appointed, and clean for only $125 at the height of summer qualifies as a deal in our book—and you're only a bracing, 10-minute walk from the beach.

COASTAL CUISINE

Restaurants are abundant in Hermosa Beach. Boasting the highest per capita income in the South Bay, the town is sufficiently cosmopolitan to support a high-quality, ethnically diverse restaurant scene. You can take your pick of Thai, Italian, Mexican, French, Peruvian, Greek, Japanese, Indian, Cajun, Middle Eastern, macrobiotic, and more in this village. The crowds really seem to gravitate to the Italian eateries, such as **Buena Vita** (439 Pier Avenue, 310/379-7626, $$), a popular restaurant serving a broad variety of creative pasta dishes befitting a restaurant whose name translates to mean "good life." Prices are very reasonable.

Sushi just might be the favorite food of all. There are more sushi bars in Hermosa Beach than you can shake a chopstick at. **Sushi Sei** (1040 Hermosa Avenue, 310/379-6900, $$) is the consensus choice of raw-fish fans in the South Bay, offering sushi and comedic sushi chefs. **California Beach Rock 'n' Sushi** (844 Hermosa Avenue, 310/374-7758, $$) is another good place to eat it raw. But just exactly what is the connection between rock and roll and sushi here? Beats us.

We had a hearty, healthy lunch at **Rocky Cola Cafe** (1025 Pacific Coast Highway, 310/798-3111, $), a combination 1950s-style diner and health-food restaurant. Amid the standard fare of burgers, floats, and onion rings is a "bodybuilder fitness menu," including such things as ahi tuna tacos (dolphin-safe, of course) and egg-white veggie omelets. Close by, we dropped into **El Pollo Inka** (1100 Pacific Coast Highway, 310/372-1433, $$) to sample the Peruvian-style grilled chicken. It's a good, inexpensive, rotisserie-style plate of chicken, served with salad and rice or French fries. If you're feeling a bit more adventurous, you can ante up for one of the seafood dishes, such as *saltado de camarones* (sautéed shrimp, onions, tomatoes, and red pepper). Excellent!

Coffeehouses are big in the South Bay (as they are all over California). At a place called **Java Man** (157 Pier Avenue, 310/379-7209, $), we sipped on big mugs of the coffee of the day (macadamia nut) and munched pastries with the other clientele, who were similarly absorbed in the *Los Angeles Times*. One serious and sensitive fellow, though, was drawing psychedelic swirls onto paper with colored pencils, attentively rendering paisley blobs in an abstract, Romper-Room-on-acid style. He accompanied these with poetic thoughts and lyric fragments. When he made a trip to the bathroom, we sauntered over to inspect his drawing pad. Sample verse: "I am looking for my vision/A sight to set me free." We returned to our java, muffins, and newspapers, burying our beaks in the latest revelations about Republican politicians' pasts.

NIGHTLIFE

We've rarely seen a row of bars and clubs as entrenched as the one in Hermosa Beach. It can be found on the south side of Pier Avenue before it ends at the Strand. Such constancy is almost unheard of at the beach. Like a stack of dominoes, four clubs are arrayed in a row. It might be you, however, that's falling over by the end of the evening. Your choices are **Hennessey's Tavern** (8 Pier Avenue, 310/372-5759), a franchised Irish-themed bar/restaurant; the **Lighthouse Cafe** (30 Pier Avenue, 310/376-9833), a once-legendary jazz club that traffics in contemporary sounds, though a change in ownership has returned jazz to the mix; **Patrick Molloy's** (50 Pier Avenue, 310/798-9762), yet another would-be Irish bar; and **Aloha Sharkeez** (52 Pier Avenue, 310/374-5668), a faux surf bar that is the most popular spot in town.

Around the corner from Pier Avenue's string of watering holes, facing the beach itself on the Strand, is the old reliable **Poop Deck** (1272 Strand, 310/376-3223), a well-worn and unfancy place where well-worn and unfancy types come to slake their thirsts on a daily basis. It's a good hangout for a celebratory brew at sundown.

Then there's the back-alley institution known as **Bestie's** (1332 Hermosa Avenue,

310/318-3818). Once owned by British soccer legend George Best, a player second only to Pele in the annals of the sport, Bestie's faithfully re-creates a friendly British pub atmosphere. The menu is filled with staples of British cuisine like lamb stew and bangers and mash. Bartenders will pull you a long, cool mug of inky Guinness draft, and you can play pool, toss darts, or watch sports on one of a dozen or so TVs strung up around the premises. On weekends a back room miraculously metamorphoses into BBC, a hip dance club. Though the address is on Hermosa Avenue, Bestie's is entered from an alley behind it. Because you must know what you're looking for, Bestie's/BBC is popular with locals and all but unknown to outsiders.

Manhattan Beach

The view of the sand in either direction from Manhattan Beach Pier is enough to convince anyone that living in Los Angeles is worth every hassle—meteorological, seismic, automotive—just to have access to such splendor. Volleyball nets are strung out to the south as far as the eye can see. Surfers bob in the water, waiting for the wave that will carry them shoreward. Hot, hard-bodied babes oil down and catch rays on the beach. Weather-beaten anglers stand poised against the pier railings, their poles and lines an excuse for sitting all day in the golden sun.

You could almost flip a coin when choosing among the three beach towns—Redondo, Hermosa, and Manhattan—strung out along the southern edge of Santa Monica Bay. The three have more similarities than differences. For starters, they're linked by the South Bay Bicycle Trail, which also serves as a boardwalk, and they all strive to cultivate as low-key a personality as possible, given their proximity to Los Angeles.

If there is any difference between Manhattan Beach and the others, it is evident away

THE ART OF SURFING

Charles Lynn "Chick" Bragg is obsessed with surfing. Ever since he walked away from the baseball diamond – where his Little League teammates included future major-leaguers Robin Yount, Pete LaCock, and Rick Dempsey – he has fallen head over heels for surfing. Now in his mid-50s, Bragg has surfed virtually every day of his life since he was 18. When he is not in Fiji, Java, or Hawaii searching for the perfect wave, he can be found hopping over the wall in front of his tiny Manhattan Beach studio and dashing toward the water.

"I'm not really a beach guy," says Chick. "I just surf. The beach just happens to be where the ocean is."

He is also abundantly blessed with artistic talent. The skill runs in the family. Chick's father is Charles Bragg, the painter, etcher, and sculptor best known for his satiric takes on the legal profession and America's right-wing pomposities. Chick Bragg has nurtured his own vision, which has gotten his artwork displayed all over the planet.

You've seen Chick Bragg's work without realizing it, on posters, prints, coffee mugs, and T-shirts in seaside gift shops from here to Timbuktu. You've even owned some of his work without knowing it. His paintings of undersea life – inspired by his secondary passions, scuba diving and underwater photography – were used by the U.S. Postal Service for a series of first-class stamps run off in "limited editions" of 255 million. He has also achieved the prominence of a rock star in Japan. His paintings are filled with the wonders of the water, a sort of Henri Rousseau meets Jacques-Yves Cousteau.

Bragg surfs right across from where he lives, in the El Porto section of Manhattan Beach, about a mile north of the town pier. He does not surf farther north, toward Playa del Rey, because the water is too polluted for his liking. A truly gentle spirit, he is a throwback to the civilized days of surfing. As such, he's disturbed by the combative nature of today's wave riders.

"That stereotype of the sweet-natured surfer boy is all wrong," he said. "There is nothing sweet or gentle about these younger guys. They'll fight you over a wave. I'll share a wave, but when it gets to be a hostile situation, I just get depressed and can't enjoy the rides. Young surfers have less respect for everything, and they're really impatient. I still have to compete with them, as much as I dislike it."

If you want to learn more about the point at which art and surfing intersect, point your browser to www.surfart.com. It is one of the more handsomely designed, useful, and fun sites to, uh, surf that we've run across.

from the water. Manhattan Beach is the most moneyed, family-oriented, and residential of the three. Its 2,300 acres are as developed as a suburban community can be, crowded with smallish homes and yards that typically consist of a square foot of bleached pebbles and a dark green bush. The line of natural dunes hasn't been bulldozed away, and building heights have been held down to a bearable level. These facts, coupled with the town's sudden roller-coaster plunge toward the ocean, allow nearly all who live here an invigorating view of the Pacific Ocean. You feel the ocean in Manhattan Beach. It's like a permanent drive-in movie to help relieve the stress of the gridlock to the east.

Inside the snug city limits of Manhattan Beach (population 36,500) are 13 churches, five parks, and two libraries; one of the parks provides the setting for Sunday afternoon concerts during the summer. Most of the commerce is concentrated around the intersection of the two main drags, Manhattan Beach Boulevard and Highland Avenue.

"CATCH A WAVE": A BRIEF HISTORY OF SURF MUSIC

In the early 1960s, the state of California infiltrated rock and roll with a sound that could have come from nowhere else: surf music. The Beach Boys, Jan and Dean, and Dick Dale launched a nationally popular music scene out of the sun-dappled wonderland of Southern California. It was a movement that was well established before the Beatles made their first stateside splash with "I Want to Hold Your Hand."

The Beach Boys are principally deemed responsible for popularizing the California myth – a harmony-rich musical outlook based on the holy trinity of sun, surf, and girls – although Jan and Dean (with "Surf City") and the Mamas and the Papas (with "California Dreamin'") certainly warbled a few anthems of their own. The promise of a beatific adolescence in the Golden State transcended the foursquare suburban reality of cow towns like Hawthorne and Torrance. As Brian Wilson, the Beach Boys' founder, explained in a 1976 interview: "It's not just surfing; it's the outdoors and cars and sunshine; it's the society of California; it's the *way* of California."

Southern California was the wellspring of the California myth. For those plowing acreage in the Plains states or buried to their knees in winter snows in the Northeast, it was a potent come-on. The California myth promised everything: health and longevity beneath a bountiful sun that shone warmly year-round; prosperity in a job-filled environment catering to the burgeoning aeronautics and communications industries; and, finally, a relaxed approach to life that had "fun, fun, fun" as its first commandment.

Until the Beach Boys came along, surf music was the domain of instrumentalists such as Dick Dale, the "king of the surf guitar." According to Dale, "Real surfing music is instrumental, characterized by heavy staccato picking on a Fender Stratocaster." A surfer could listen to one of his solos and feel the surging power of the ocean as it hurtled him toward shore. Such numbers as "Let's Go Trippin'," "Surf Beat," and "Miserlou" promoted a sense of identity within the surfers' ranks.

Although surf music primarily functioned as party music for surfers in this locale, the genre left its mark on the national charts with songs by the Surfaris ("Wipe Out") and the Chantays ("Pipeline"). Both were released in 1963. The Chantays, a five-man garage band from Santa Ana, rode "Pipeline" all the way to #4. The Surfaris, a quintet from Glendora, saw "Wipe Out" soar to #2. A tumbling wave of tom-tom rolls and

---

The local businesses squeezed in here are the sort of nonfranchised shops that obsessive consumers love to believe they've discovered for themselves, bearing such names as Pour Moi! La Boutique, Foote Fetish, and Le Chat. Parking isn't necessarily a problem, but it isn't cheap and it isn't easy. Street meters run 24 hours and cost $0.25 for 15 minutes, with a five-hour limit. They take quarters only. Where is somebody supposed to come by that many quarters?

There are some nagging signs that Manhattan Beach may be losing its grip on growth. A 187-acre business park has been relegated to the eastern edge of town in the flight path of Los Angeles International Airport and next to a smoke-belching power plant. With it has arrived an army of nouveau riche who have driven up land values with their real estate schemes. This has caused longtime residents to skirmish with developers.

A young woman who lives in Manhattan Beach told us that the town has developed an attitude that is lacking in the more laid-back Hermosa Beach. That attitude, one supposes, comes from the money it costs to live here. One local realtor—whose slogan is "I have the right energy to sell your house"—advertised

frenzied guitar breaks, "Wipe Out" remains the premier instrumental surf hit of all time. The Marketts made their mark with "Surfer's Stomp" and "Balboa Blue." Then there were the Pyramids, from Long Beach, who recorded the surf classic "Penetration." These gonzo freaks performed with shaved heads and arrived at shows in helicopters and atop elephants.

However, it was the Beach Boys who triggered a nationwide mania for surf and hot-rod music. The Beach Boys spread the gospel of surfing "even in places where the nearest thing to surf is maybe the froth on a chocolate shake!" (to quote the liner notes of *Surfin' USA*, their second album). With their earliest songs, "Surfin'" and "Surfin' Safari," the Beach Boys made a magical, intuitive leap – bridging Chuck Berry and the Four Freshmen and adding their own libretto about surfing and the California way of life.

Jan (Berry) and Dean (Torrance) were the other major minstrels in the car-and-surf-song sweepstakes. With "Surf City," a tune cowritten by Brian Wilson, Jan and Dean had the first #1 surfing song in 1963. The real-life "surf city" they had in mind was Huntington Beach, which has taken to promoting itself with that handle in modern times.

Other singing surf and car groups from the 1960s included the Fantastic Baggys ("Tell 'Em I'm Surfing," "Summer Means Fun"), the Rip Chords ("Hey Little Cobra," "Three Window Coupe"), and the Sunrays ("I Live for the Sun"). At mid-decade a new wave of Southern California-based acts swept the Top 40. Among them were the Turtles, Gary Lewis and the Playboys, Paul Revere and the Raiders, the Mamas and the Papas, the Byrds, the Monkees, and the Grass Roots.

In 1967 California would enter a whole different stage when psychedelic music would become all the rage during the "summer of love." The seeds of this revolution can be traced back to five Pendleton-shirted Beach Boys and their idea to sing about surfing. As the late Carl Wilson of the Beach Boys once told us, "People wanted to hang out at the beach. It was really an early hippie thing." In a way, it still is.

If you want the best possible overview of California surf music, then lay your hands on Rhino Records' *Cowabunga! The Surf Box*, a lovingly assembled various-artists box set that tells the story perfectly. Incidentally, the Beach Boys are scattered about, and only Brian Wilson is alive among the three Wilson brothers who formed the core of the band. In late 2008 he released a concept album, entitled *That Lucky Old Sun*, an affectionate ode to Southern California and all that makes it special.

---

this bargain: "A classic beach home on the walk streets with fabulous ocean views." Translation: A modest wooden box with an upstairs balcony located blocks off the ocean. Asking price: $699,000. Of the mega-mon-eyed set that has just about displaced the beach bums, one longtime resident said, "The vibe here is spoiled, arrogant, impatient…as if their pampered lives are so pressured. Oh yes, and greedy."

Still, as you near the beach, all pretensions disappear in a blaze of tanned, libidinous glory. Relaxed bars, taverns, and restaurants near the pier on Manhattan Boulevard help sustain the friendly cacophony that is at the heart of the Southern California beach experience.

For more information, contact the Manhattan Beach Chamber of Commerce, 425 15th Street, Manhattan Beach, CA 90266, 310/545-5313, www.manhattanbeachchamber.net.

BEACHES

Manhattan Beach's two-mile oceanfront is completely residential (i.e., no motels, few affordable rentals). The clean, sandy **Manhattan County Beach** is bisected by a 900-foot pier (at the west end of Manhattan Beach Boulevard) and backed by a seawall adorned with tasteful murals and less tasteful graffiti. The water is subject to occasional rough currents but is well patrolled by a bevy of lifeguards. Beach volleyball is not just a sport, it's a religion here. From the pier, sand volleyball courts and nets extend down toward Hermosa Beach. North of Manhattan Beach is **El Porto Beach.** You can walk to it from Manhattan Beach or park near the ramps at 41st and 44th Streets. El Porto has full facilities and volleyball nets, but the scene here tends to be loud and uninviting.

19 MANHATTAN COUNTY BEACH

Location: the Strand at Manhattan Pier in Manhattan Beach
Parking/Fees: metered street and lot parking
Hours: 6 A.M.-sunset
Facilities: concession, lifeguards, restrooms, and showers
Contact: Los Angeles County Lifeguard Service, Southern Section, 310/832-1179

20 EL PORTO BEACH

Location: end of 45th Street in Manhattan Beach
Parking/Fees: metered street parking
Hours: 6 A.M.-sunset
Facilities: lifeguards, restrooms, and showers
Contact: Los Angeles County Lifeguard Service, Southern Section, 310/832-1179

ACCOMMODATIONS

Lodging isn't Manhattan Beach's strong suit. The closest you can get to the beach is three steep uphill blocks away from the action on Highland Avenue. The **Sea View Inn** (3400 Highland Avenue, 310/545-1504, www.seaview-inn.com, $$) is the most appealing of a handful of choices. It has only eight rooms, but these surround a swimming pool away from the noise of the busy thoroughfare.

COASTAL CUISINE

The most celebrated restaurant in town was H$_2$O, but the award-winning nouvelle cuisine venue has evaporated. One that is garnering

Manhattan County Beach

© PARKE PUTERBAUGH

similar raves is **Rock 'N Fish** (120 Manhattan Beach Boulevard, 310/379-9900, $$), where the healthy preparations of seafood are as impressive as the extensive wine list. **Fonz's Steak and Seafood** (1017 Manhattan Avenue, 310/376-1536, $$$) seems to get the spillover from Rock 'N Fish.

NIGHTLIFE

A clear sign of the upscaling of Manhattan Beach is the fate of La Paz, once considered to be the "king of the beach bars" and "Animal House at the beach" by the usual reliable sources of surfers and local beach bums. It was a sloppy, wonderful, ramshackle place that we feel privileged to have visited on a previous trip. La Paz is gone now, replaced by a municipal parking lot beside the pier. Bars picking up the slack include **Beaches** (117 Manhattan Beach Boulevard, 310/545-2523), which used to be the rowdy Sunsets and is more restaurant than bar now, though it has won "best dance club" honors from a local weekly; **Manhattan Beach Brewing Company** (124 Manhattan Beach Boulevard, 310/798-2744), with designer home brew; and the **Shellback Tavern** (116 Manhattan Beach Boulevard, 310/376-7857), which is the closest in spirit to La Paz you'll find on the beach. It serves pretty good tacos and burgers, too. Just two blocks up a steep hill from the beach is **Baja Sharkeez** (3801 Highland Avenue, 310/545-6563), the most popular surf bar in town. "If I were single," one surfer confided, "this is where I'd come. At night you can't move without knocking someone with an elbow." Sawdust on the floor, surf videos and sports on screens, old flotsam hanging from ceilings, and the best fish taco and veggie burrito within five miles—Baja Sharkeez has it all.

El Segundo

Like San Pedro, El Segundo (population 16,300) is an integral part of Los Angeles, but it is mostly overlooked or ignored. It is home to a sprawl of oil refineries, oil piers, the Hyperion Sewage Treatment Plant (the Grand Coulee Dam of sewage plants), and the Scattergood Steam Generating Station. Hyperion is the "largest activated sludge plant in the world," its 330 million gallons of sewage a day treated and dumped, as sludge, in off-shore canyons. El Segundo is also directly beside Los Angeles International Airport. This bathes the town in a toxic-industrial-aeronautic cacophony that blends perfectly with the boom boxes that reign along the shore.

For more information, contact the El Segundo Chamber of Commerce, 427 Main Street, El Segundo, CA 90245, 310/322-1220, www.beach-web.com.

BEACHES

In spite of the surrounding environment, El Segundo has two of the broadest beaches in the Los Angeles area: **Dockweiler State Beach** and **El Segundo Beach.** Together they comprise a six-mile stretch of sand that would make any other beach town sorely envious. Although there's beach access and large parking lots off El Segundo Boulevard and at the end of Grand Avenue, the best way to see El Segundo and Dockweiler State Beaches is by bicycling along the shoreline-hugging South Bay Bicycle Trail. Almost anywhere along this stretch you can pull off the bicycle trail and the beach is all yours.

It's an odd sensation to be on a beach so huge on a picture-perfect summer day, all of five miles from the center of Los Angeles, and find the place nearly deserted. As long as you don't look shoreward at the oil refineries and sewage plant, or fret too much over the gangsta rap blaring from the direction of the parking lot, you'd swear this was as perfect a beach as you could hope to find. Dockweiler State Beach has the added incentive of a 117-site campground, for RVs only, at its south end. Dockweiler is so long that it encompasses the oceanfront in both El Segundo and neighboring Playa del Rey. To make things even more disorienting, Dockweiler is considered a state beach, though it is leased to the City of Los Angeles and operated by the County of Los Angeles.

21 EL SEGUNDO BEACH

Location: Grand Avenue at Vista del Mar Boulevard in El Segundo
Parking/Fees: $7 entrance fee per vehicle
Hours: 6 A.M.-10 P.M.
Facilities: lifeguards and restrooms
Contact: Los Angeles County Lifeguard Service, Southern Section, 310/832-1179

Playa del Rey

Playa del Rey is a largely residential town built along streets that dead-end into a lagoon at sea level and run on top of towering bluffs that look out over the beach. The chief calling card is Dockweiler State Beach, a wide, white-sand beach extending from Del Rey Lagoon south to the RV campground in El Segundo. Across the lagoon lies Venice Beach; behind it, along constructed waterways, Marina del Rey. It is due west of Los Angeles International Airport.

The drive out to Playa del Rey, west from Lincoln Boulevard through the last unblemished wetlands in Los Angeles, is relatively pleasant. It might not have been, however, had Steven Spielberg and pals had their way with the proposed (and now abandoned) Dream-Works SKG project, which would have defiled 1,087 acres of this oasis for their studio. However, the massive Playa Vista development has a bright side: despite all the new homes and office space, 70 percent of the property has been dedicated to open space.

For more information, contact the LAX Coastal Area Chamber of Commerce, 9100 South Sepulveda Boulevard, Suite 210, Westchester, CA 90045, 310/645-5151, www.laxcoastal.com.

BEACHES

The word "wide" does not even begin to describe the sandy expanse at **Dockweiler State Beach,** which is shared by Playa del Rey and neighboring El Segundo. Dockweiler and adjacent beaches in Los Angeles County have been extended seaward with sand dredged from the site of the Hyperion Sewage Treatment Plant and the Scattergood Steam Generating Station. They can handle all eager beachgoers, all summer long. Even with all of mighty Los Angeles knocking at the back door, such beaches as Dockweiler, Venice, and Santa Monica seldom reach the saturation point. Not that they're terrifically attractive, but they are indisputably large. They are also prone to closure when the waters of Santa Monica Bay become polluted with storm-drain runoff.

22 DOCKWEILER STATE BEACH

Location: Vista del Mar Boulevard at Imperial Highway in Playa del Rey
Parking/Fees: $7 entrance fee per vehicle; camping fees $16.35-26.35 per night
Hours: 6 A.M.-10 P.M.
Facilities: concession, lifeguards, restrooms, showers, and picnic tables
Contact: Los Angeles County Lifeguard Service, Southern Section, 310/832-1179

Marina del Rey

Marina del Rey can be summed up in two words: *yachting* and *eating.* It is the world's largest recreational small-craft harbor, consisting of eight basins that collectively contain 6,100 boat slips. It also claims to have the greatest concentration of restaurants in a single square-mile area this side of New York City. The place is a magnet for money.

It's hard to imagine that until the mid-1950s

WANT TO BE AN L.A. COUNTY LIFEGUARD?

If week after week of watching the flesh parade on reruns of *Baywatch* has you eager to join the ranks of Los Angeles County lifeguards, then bear in mind that the reality of landing the job is a little tougher than showing up with a Screen Actors Guild card. In fact, to make it into rookie school at the Lifeguard Training Academy, you must meet the following conditions right off the bat: 1) you must have uncorrected vision of 20/30 or better; 2) you must be able to complete a 1,000-meter ocean swim race (approximately three-fifths of a mile); 3) you must be 18 years of age or older; and 4) you must have a valid California driver's license and high school diploma.

There is a difference between pool and beach lifeguards. In order to become a beach lifeguard, one must first accumulate 600 hours of experience as a pool lifeguard. Candidates for beach lifeguard positions must undergo a 60-hour training program.

Lifeguard trials are held once yearly in September and draw roughly 250 applicants. If chosen, new recruits begin as part-timers, making $19.32 per hour, and attend a hundred hours of "rookie school." They learn first aid and safety and rescue techniques. Recertification is required every year. The county employs 132 year-round lifeguards and hires 650 seasonal lifeguards. It hires roughly a hundred pool lifeguards a year, as they move up or out of the system.

For more information, call the **Los Angeles County Lifeguard Administrative Headquarters** (323/881-2411) or the **Lifeguard Training Academy** (310/939-7200). Los Angeles County lifeguards earn their pay, collectively making 10,000 ocean rescues a year along the 72 miles of the county coastline. There are four section headquarters (at Hermosa Beach, Marina del Rey, Santa Monica, and Zuma Beach), 158 lifeguard stands, and ten Baywatch boats.

However seriously you may or may not take it, *Baywatch* has indirectly saved lives. According to the Guinness Book of World Records, *Baywatch,* which aired from 1990 to 2001, was the most widely watched TV show around the world. (How else would Borat have become so enamored of Pamela Anderson?) Its influence, then, has been positive, raising the level of lifeguard competence in cities all over the world. Case in point: Barcelona, Spain. After city officials flew Los Angeles County lifeguards over for consultations, the beaches of Barcelona were demonstrably safer. On one weekend in 1993 (before the consultations), there were 14 drownings on its beaches. During the first nine *months* of 1994 (after the consultations), there were none.

the area was a swampy lagoon at the mouth of Ballona Creek. Progress, you say? Well, maybe. The construction of the marina has not been without problems. Although the East Coast has an abundance of natural harbors, the California coast has few of them, necessitating the construction of harbors, involving jetties, breakwaters, and the dredging of marinas. After opening, Marina del Rey faced a series of design-related problems. First, under a certain set of wave conditions outside the marina, the original design enabled the spread of destructive standing waves inside the marina, resulting in damaged boats and lawsuits. To rectify this, designers hastily added a 1,200-foot, detached offshore breakwater in 1962. The marina has also seen the recurring problem of sand shoaling up against the north jetty and forming a bar across the southern entrance channel, which has required expensive dredging on a regular basis.

All the same, the marina generates more money than it costs to maintain, so most everyone is happy, especially L.A. boat group-ies. Like a hand with eight fingers, the yacht basin at Marina del Rey reaches inland, grab-bing Los Angeles by the seat of the pants. In addition to the 6,100 boat slips in the water, it can store another 3,000 vessels in dry dock. There are nearly as many boats in Marina del Rey as there are residents. Admiralty Way runs in a semicircle around the harbor. It con-nects with Via Marina (on the west side) and Fiji Way (on the south side) to form a great horseshoe around the octet of boat basins. It is in this watery world-within-a-world that the moneyed heart of Marina del Rey can be heard to beat. Some people live on their boats. A few have died on them. Dennis Wilson of the Beach Boys drowned here while diving for discarded souvenirs in a boat slip where he used to live with a former wife.

Over the past three decades, Marina del Rey (population 8,900) has blossomed like a cac-tus flower out of its desert-like surroundings. An impressive retail industry of waterfront restaurants, luxury hotels, dance clubs, and specialty shops has grown around the harbor. In Marina del Rey you can, as a brochure pro-claims, browse for everything "from socks to solid gold." Signs heralding one's arrival in Ma-rina del Rey offer this menu of options: Apart-ments, Berths, Chandlery, Hotels, Launching, Maintenance, Moorings, Motels, Restaurants, Shops, Sportfishing, Town Houses, Yacht Sales. As you spiral closer to Admiralty Way from the outside world—passing through the buffer zones that isolate Marina del Rey from the less glamorous neighboring com-munities of Culver City, Playa del Rey, and Venice—an oasis of boats, buildings, and greenery emerges out of nowhere. If you look and listen closely, you might even hear ducks quacking and waddling around a large lake that's part of a nature preserve. Off-road bike paths wind around the marina. The South Bay Bicycle Trail leaves the beach at the mouth of Ballona Creek and passes through the ma-rina, reemerging by the ocean at Venice Pier. Four small parks within the marina add a note

of greenery and tranquility. **Burton Chase Park,** at the end of Mindinao Way, is a six-acre green space from which one can watch boats enter and exit the marina. The retail area known as **Fisherman's Village** is one of the more convincing of the nautical-themed, New England–style shopping complexes we've seen, right down to its cobblestone walks. The whole of Marina del Rey has the privileged, dream-like aura of a mirage. It's a great mirage, if you've got the monetary means to enjoy it.

For more information, contact the LAX Coastal Area Chamber of Commerce, 9100 South Sepulveda Boulevard, Suite 210, Westchester, CA 90045, 310/645-5151, www.laxcoastal.com.

BEACHES

In this case the proper heading would be the singular *beach*. Because it is a protected in-land harbor, Marina del Rey by definition has no ocean beaches. The marina does have one beach at the end of Basin D: **Mother's Beach,** where water-lovers can swim, wind-surf, and sail on a sandy, lifeguarded stretch of sand where no waves roll ashore. Maybe that's why choosy mothers choose Mother's as a place to bring their kids to frolic in rela-tive safety. In any case, this mushroom-shaped lagoon enables both calm-water swimming and wind-free sunbathing. The drawback is water quality. Would you want to swim in a man-made lagoon routinely fouled by boat fuel, bilgewater, and storm runoff?

23 MOTHER'S BEACH

Location: Basin D on Panay Way in Marina del Rey

Parking/Fees: $6

Hours: sunrise–10 P.M.

Facilities: lifeguards, restrooms, showers, and picnic tables

Contact: Marina del Rey Parks, Beaches, and Harbors, 310/305-9503

ACCOMMODATIONS

The selection of hotels and restaurants in Marina del Rey makes it the Neiman-Marcus of beach communities. Starting from the top, the vaunted **Ritz-Carlton** (4375 Admiralty Way, 310/823-1700, $$$$) brings a touch of Old World elegance to the land of new money. This 14-story masterpiece affords a choice of harbor or ocean views, swaddling guests in comfort (for a price) in a veritable island of first-class amenities: lighted tennis courts, heated outdoor pool, yacht charters, and so on.

The **Marina Beach Marriott** (4100 Admiralty Way, 310/301-3000, $$$$) offers comparable upscale accommodations in a 10-story tower that looks like a giant sand dune from the street. The balcony views—of the Malibu coastline to the north, of Palos Verdes Peninsula to the south—are majestic, especially around sunset. With a ninth-floor cocktail lounge, ground-floor California-cuisine restaurant (Stones), outdoor garden café and pool, and sumptuous rooms decorated in muted pastels and accented with brass and marble, you won't lack for pampering here.

If money is a consideration, nearby Culver City is loaded with cheaper chain motels. You'll save a bundle, which you can blow on dinner and nightlife in the marina.

COASTAL CUISINE

A few years back one of us had Sunday dinner with rock 'n' roll pioneer Little Richard at **Aunt Kizzy's Back Porch** (4325 Glencoe Avenue, 310/578-1005, $$), a soul-food eatery in the Villa Marina Shopping Center. Not only can Richard sing and pound the piano, the man knows how to pick a restaurant. The culinary style is Deep South and down-home: mounds of fried chicken, pork tenderloin, homemade mashed potatoes and biscuits, stewed vegetables, fruit cobblers, and other fresh desserts. Aunt Kizzy's food is so good it's enough to give you religion, if you haven't got it already.

On the waterfront **Edie's Diner** (4211 Admiralty Way, 310/577-4558, $) does a big business in burgers, fries, and pie. It's done up in diner chic, from the gleaming ceramic tile to the retro rock tunes on the booth-side jukeboxes, and the burgers are everything you'd want in a slab of ground cow: big, sloppy, and good. Edie's does breakfast as well.

Coffee-holics will want to head over to **Joni's Coffee Roaster Cafe** (552 Washington Boulevard, 310/305-7147, $$), a favorite gathering place of Venice-Marina bohemians and wealthy mavericks. One leather-clad wannabe biker casually ordered a glass of chardonnay and an Anchor Steam beer before the sun was up. "What the heck," he told the nonplussed clerk, "it's Monday morning." In addition to espresso, cappuccino, and pastries, the café offers healthful breakfasts, lunches, and dinners. Hit **Noah's Bagels** (548 Washington Boulevard, 310/574-1155, $) next door, and you're good to go.

NIGHTLIFE

A night on the town in Marina del Rey begins with a fruitless search for a parking space. The way they've got it rigged, there's next to nothing in the way of legal street parking, leaving one with no choice but to hand the keys to a valet at the club or restaurant of your choice. We despise valet parking.

In this vexatious spirit we drove around Marina del Rey looking for parking. After cruising for a while, we tried the lot at a shopping center just outside the marina, but it was filled with signs warning that all cars belonging to non-customers would be towed. We took our chances all the same and left the car, hiking to a place called—it hurts just to type a name this stupid—Moose McGillycuddy's. Moose's is now called **Waikiki Willies** (13535 Mindinao Way, 310/574-3932), but is essentially the same animal as before. It's an indoor/outdoor pub, grub, and disco venue that claims the same sort of crowd that used to jam the Red Onion, a now-defunct singles-bar chain that, in its own way, helped further the 1980s population boom in Southern California.

At Willies, a young crowd hopped to the

fascistic beat of the latest synthetic dance hits. Some lined up to be plastered with free temporary tattoos, which was that evening's big promotion. A salty dog who looked like the Skipper on *Gilligan's Island* circulated with a wicker basket full of plastic-wrapped Moonie roses, cutting an odd figure. In the bathroom a guy removed the sweaty T-shirt in which he'd arrived and changed into a trendier leisure-wear ensemble, looking like a discofied Clark Kent who'd come to dazzle the ladies with his sartorial Kryptonite. At one table a mutually infatuated couple took turns grooming each other, like Rhesus monkeys, with combs and brushes. We stationed ourselves at the Pop-a-Shot concession, vainly trying to impress the locals with our shooting ability and finally retreating to the outdoor patio.

The **Baja Cantina** (311 Washington Boulevard, 310/821-2252) was hopping all night long. Maybe hot chilies were warming up the patrons in this popular Mexican restaurant and watering hole. You come in, put your name on the list, belly up to the bar, grab a Mexican beer, and wait for a table in tight quarters with what seems like half of Los Angeles. The Baja Cantina is noisy and fun, with its socio-cultural ambience best suggested by two of the celebrities whose framed, autographed pictures hang on the wall: actor Tony Danza and porn star Christy Canyon.

Venice

In the 1993 film *Falling Down,* the Michael Douglas character—an everyman driven to psychopathy by the stress of living in Los Angeles—cuts a swath westward across the city to Venice, committing a rash of demented crimes on his way. The police track him down, forcing a final stand at the end of Venice Pier. As he dies, falling over the pier railing after absorbing a point-blank blast from Robert Duvall's service revolver, he gives Venice a last befuddled backward glance and then splashes into the beautiful blue Pacific.

In Venice, life doesn't just imitate art. It defines it. If it's cutting edge, chances are it started in Venice—and it probably will end here, too. Venice is many things: fascinating human zoo, nasty urban war zone, and just about everything in between.

Take the hard-luck Venice Pier, for instance. Built in 1997, it had to be closed down for several years due to structural concerns. (It reopened in 2006.) Like the Michael Douglas character, many alienated people gravitate to Venice to make an escape. On the other hand, many who come here—us, for example—have given it a befuddled backward glance as they headed out of town.

It's easy to trash Venice. Not for nothing is it known as the home of $2 sunglasses, $3 T-shirts, $4 Tarot readings, and $5 stress massages. New Age prophets walk shoulder to shoulder with the old-age homeless. Runaway children seek shelter in group houses, and gangs bring their hideous territorial squabbles to the shore. Cops walk the beat, half amused and half afraid.

It's easy to allow preconceptions to unfairly blind a first-time visitor to Venice's peculiar appeal. The source of that appeal goes right back to the town's roots. Venice began as the dream of a man named Abbot Kinney, who made his millions on cigarettes and spent them all in 1900 purchasing 160 acres of marshland south of Santa Monica. For some reason (nicotine frenzy perhaps), he saw similarities between his new property and the site on which Venice, Italy, was built. He commissioned two architects to design a "thoroughly equipped" city with streets, hotels, houses, and canals—15 miles of cement-bottomed canals. By June 1905, the canals were filled with water. All Kinney needed for his new Venice was people to build their dream homes beside his waterways.

Like any good businessman, Kinney lured folks here with a gimmick: gondolas and gondoliers. He imported some of Italy's finest oarsmen and had them serenade prospective buyers while rowing them up and down the canals to inspect the empty lots. He persuaded merchants to build hotels, restaurants, and shops in the architectural style of the Venetian Renaissance. He also oversaw the construction of a lecture hall, pavilion, and theater. Provocative speakers were brought in, first-rate plays were staged, and blue-ribbon orchestras performed. All the while, the gondoliers kept singing.

Kinney's noble experiment failed, culminating in a poorly attended and abbreviated run of *Camille* starring Sarah Bernhardt, the greatest stage actress of her day. Visitors to Venice, it turned out, preferred sand and sidewalks to the interior of a concert hall. To salvage his enormous investment, the dauntless Kinney did an about-face, filling in a number of his festering, plant-choked canals and bringing in sideshow freaks, street theater, and a roller coaster. A miniature railroad was built to run along with the Ocean Front Walk, turning the town into an amusement park by the sea. In 1925 the little town became part of Los Angeles. By 1939 Kinney's conversion was complete, with Venice known as "the Playland of the Pacific" and "the Coney Island of the West."

Venice has since undergone other transformations. It was covered with oil wells, low-income housing, and boarded-up slums in the 1940s. It was adopted by beatniks in the 1950s, hippies in the 1960s, artists and fitness freaks in the 1970s, and gentrified homeowners—the original audience Kinney had dreamed of for Venice—in the 1980s and 1990s. Venice still lives in a dream, as it always has, perceiving itself as some sort of impervious Left Bank, but one beset by problems.

Granted, certain aspects of Venice's surreal sideshow are real and fascinating. There's the endless parade of oddballs who entertain for spare change along Ocean Front Walk, the cement boardwalk that runs along the backside of Venice Beach. Although this pedestrian thoroughfare is only seven-tenths of a mile long, it is light-years beyond whatever else passes for cutting edge elsewhere in America. The best place to start a walk-through is at the Windward Avenue access, the halfway point in the human parade. Here you'll find the classic *Venice on the Half Shell* mural, which captures the spirit of the procession. It may sound like a cliché, but you really are likely to see anything out here. The following are just some of the things we've witnessed: guy in a turban chewing glass; guy on a unicycle juggling knives; another unicyclist juggling chainsaws; legless, armless dwarf dancing on his stumps to Latin disco music; assortment of Michael Jackson impersonators, with proud mamas pocketing the donations; "post tribal artist"; cabalistic Tarot reader; a village shaman offering a spoken "love revival"; a gypsy performing "three-day dissolving marriage ceremonies"; folk performers with purple hair; ancient black woman shrieking incoherent blues while strumming an electric guitar lent her by a well-meaning college kid; body piercers; hair braiders; X-rated comedians; conceptual artists; mural artists; caricaturists; acrobats; animals performing stupid pet tricks; transvestites; leather freaks; Rastafarians; punks, drunks, and punch-drunks; and some people who are really and truly insane.

Along this same route you'll find a few passable bars, some decent take-out food stalls, a good book shop, and a museum of Native American art. Hang around long enough and you'll also absorb the prevailing Venetian outlook: a healthy and well-cultivated disregard for chicness, big money, and normal ways of doing things.

Away from the curious clamor on Ocean Front Walk, Venice reveals another side of itself—a pleasant residential community of 50,000 filled with proud homeowners who casually enjoy the placid life along the town's back canals. In the past few years, the more secluded canals have been cleaned up, and fish are even seen in the no-longer-murky waters. The Canal Walk—between Washington Boulevard and Rose Avenue—is part of the Venice Canal Historic District, which is listed on the National Register of Historic Places. Walking here is an enjoyable and quiet diversion as you observe the fascinating and eclectic architecture and the commendable lengths that the residents have gone to turn the tiniest plots of land into gardening masterpieces.

THE DANDELION UNDER THE PILLOW

Tell someone to put a dandelion under their pillow to cure dandruff and they'll elect you President...of anything.

Henry Morgan, interviewed in *The Realist,* 1960

Some years back, a local news story captured the nation's imagination. A Los Angeles woman lost her cat on a flight from New York's La Guardia Airport to LAX. A California psychic was called in for the cat hunt. The psychic picked up some feline vibes – our theory is litter-box odor – in the cargo bay. Tracking the vibes, the psychic pinpointed the cat's location. That is, the psychic pointed to the section of the cargo bay where the cat was later found. With that, California's booming alternative industry racked up yet another success story.

California is the holy land for spiritual, medical, personal, and political alternatives. This is the state that gave us the Summer of Love and the Monterey Pop Festival – but also the Altamont disaster and the Manson family. It has produced great alternative literature and groundbreaking music. It has also given rise to taxpayer revolts and Pebble Beach. It has coughed up Jim Jones and Ronald Reagan, the Black Panthers, Jerry Brown, the SLA, Patty Hearst, and cults too numerous to name. One of them committed mass suicide one night, believing they would all thereupon hitch a ride upon a comet as it passed closest to earth's orbit. And who can forget former First Lady Nancy Reagan, whose reliance on a California astrologist directed the fate of the country for a spell.

A veritable smorgasbord of healers, shamans, counselors, holistic therapists, ministers, colon irrigators, foot reflexologists, and other assorted gurus make their homes in California. This is especially the case along the coast, where the sea breezes and unchanging weather help foster a meditative, anti-mainstream turn of mind. Every single one of these alternative healers is an expert on something. Some are quacks, while others have legitimately helped people beyond the reach of mainstream medicine while also serving to loosen the fascistic grip that the medical establishment has on our nation's health care system.

One way to get a handle on available alternative services is to consult the myriad free weekly publications devoted to this subject. How can so many people, we wondered, ply their trade in this alternative market? And if indeed they do find enough customers to make a lucrative living, why is the state still so bedeviled? If Los Angeles, for instance, is filled to bursting with self-actualized, self-empowered, and healthy people with their chakras in a row who eat the right organic foods and sip healing herbal teas all the livelong day, why is the city such a dysfunctional smog-choked sprawl that its saner citizens can't wait to flee when a better opportunity elsewhere comes along?

It's not our intent to knock alternatives. In fact this guide is intended to be an alternative to the fulsome, skin-deep prose that fills most travel books and virtually all travel websites. Still, as one peruses the alternative reference tools, the notion begins forming that many of these experts are peddling false hope. At their most innocuous, however, they provide an entertaining sideshow.

Here's a random sampling of those doing business in the alternative healing arts along the California coast:

- "OPENING TO THE GODDESS ENERGY: Explore and heal the denied feminne (sic) within...$80 advance, $100 at the door."

- "SINGING, MOVING THROUGH THE FEAR, FOR NON-SINGERS WHO MUST SING: reasonable rates." (Don't karaoke bars provide this service free of charge?)

- "ENHANCED SEXUALITY TRAINING: Sexual meditation. Extended orgasm. Soul union and enlightenment. No overt sexual activity." (What a tease!)

- "PAST LIFE REGRESSION. Explore past lives for: Curiosity, Removing Blocks, Soul Cleansing. Affordable sessions. Sessions led by a metaphysical minister."

- "CLEAR KARMA NOW: Commander A_ S_ offers 'Karma clearings by phone.'"

- "TRAVEL AROUND THE NATIVE AMERICAN AND CELTIC MEDICINE WHEEL...different journeys each week...$20 session."

- "AN EVENING WITH XANDO, channeled by G_. Donation. XANDO is a composite of six angelic beings."

- "POWER NEGOTIATION SKILLS. You will learn to: Formulate and dovetail outcomes for Win-Win results. Preserve the relationship while achieving your outcome. Apply these skills to business, personal, and family issues...$250 at the door." (In other words, learn to manipulate others blind.)

- "GRANDFATHER OF THE NEW AGE REVEALS MYSTERIES: Now nearing 70 years of age, N_ is considered the leading expert on crystal skulls...They are thought to be at least 10,000 to 20,000 years old. A three-day retreat will cost $149, plus transportation to and from Arizona, plus $25 a night at the Healing Center, plus $5 for breakfast and lunch, plus $7 dinner."

- "LOVESTAR INSTITUTE. Holistic Health Psychologist Thanatologist (grief) Counselor." (Good grief!)

- "I AM A CLAIRVOYANT CHANNELER OF MULTIDIMENSIONS: Sit in the presence of Ascension and Dolphin energy attunement while receiving important messages and answers to your delicate and urgent questions."

Heard enough? If not, contact Whole Life Times, P.O. Box 1187, Malibu, CA 90265, 310/317-4200. Tell them Xando sent you.

Community leaders regularly organize cleanups, and ad hoc action, block parties, and neighborhood watches have made inroads on crime prevention. Venice is not about to let the town go to seed as it did in the past.

The best way to see the full tableau that Venice has to offer is to book a walking tour through the **Venice Historical Society** (310/967-5170). The tour costs around $7.50, and reservations must be made ahead of time.

Although the fear of crime is less intense now, and neighborhood pride and vigilance is at an all-time high, Venice still has a ways to go. There are parts of town that even the police have been hesitant to patrol. During one of our visits, a group of Los Angeles's finest staged a protest at being transferred to the Venice beat.

We were warned repeatedly about a trend in urban crime that has been particularly prevalent in Venice: bike-jacking. Meanwhile, a beachside pavilion smells of human waste and is so thick with graffiti that you have to look closely to make out this sign: Notice—Defacing Park Property May Result in a Maximum Penalty of $500 Fine and Six Months in Jail. At the south end of Venice Beach, the gazebos along Ocean Front Walk have not been closed down but might as well be to anyone who doesn't regularly urinate outdoors. We met a Dutch fellow who had a word for the less savory side of Venice: *onguur*. Though he claimed it was untranslatable, his facial expression told us all we needed to know. Venice can be real *onguur* sometimes.

None of this stems the flow of onlookers in Venice. Perversely, the sense of forbidden danger seems to add to its appeal. And so goes Venice, into the setting sun of the California dream, once delicious and golden, and now… Well, we'll close with a quote from one of Venice's stellar residents, Orson Bean, who wrote in *Venice* magazine: "Venice of America dares you to be happy. Someone once wrote that the most revolutionary act possible might be three straight days of continuous happiness. People walk in Venice. They roller-skate and bicycle and skateboard. They rally to save ducks. They don't mind looking like fools. They figure everyone else enjoys it when they look like fools, so why shouldn't they?"

For more information, contact the Venice Chamber of Commerce, P.O. Box 202, Venice, CA 90291, 310/822-5425, www.venice.net.

BEACHES

Venice City Beach has never looked better. It is an amazingly wide sheet of sand, running for two miles north from Venice Pier to Santa Monica Pier. People use this beautiful, wide porch of sand for all the normal activities—swimming, sunning, hanging out—but the dimensions of the beach are so large that their numbers seem deceptively small.

The beach itself is spiked by three enormous jetties and was widened by sand dredged from the site of the massive Hyperion Sewage Treatment Plant. The most intriguing area is at the north end, where a weightlifting area attracts body freaks and has earned the name "Muscle Beach." Some incredible games of basketball are played on the nearby blacktop, with occasional visits from pro stars. The paddle-tennis games are as intense as any matches at Wimbledon. The beach can be accessed from any of the main east–west streets in Venice (Washington Street, Venice Boulevard, Rose Avenue, Windward Avenue, Park Boulevard) or from anywhere on the Ocean Front Walk promenade. Metered parking is available along any of these thoroughfares as well.

24 VENICE CITY BEACH

Location: Washington Boulevard at Ocean Front Walk in Venice

Parking/Fees: $7-10

Hours: 5 A.M.-10:30 P.M.

Facilities: concession, lifeguards, restrooms, showers, and picnic areas

Contact: Los Angeles County Lifeguard Service, Central Section, 310/394-3264

ACCOMMODATIONS

No matter how cutting edge you feel, you do not want to stay in Venice. For one thing, it's unpredictable and sometimes unsafe after dark. For another, there's really not much to choose from in the way of accommodations, unless you rent a beachfront villa by the week (and that is shockingly expensive). Visit for the day and buy a T-shirt, hot dog, and a slab of pizza. Watch the street performers, then quietly take your leave, preferably back to the hotels of Marina del Rey.

All things considered, we fared okay the one time we did stay in Venice. We found a room at the **Venice Beach Cotel** (25 Windward Avenue, 310/399-7949 or 888/718-8287, $). "Cotel" is short for "community hotel," and it is primarily for international travelers on a tight budget. A hostel, if you will, only a notch nicer. The rooms are spartan but clean, with shared bathrooms and no TV or air-conditioning, and the security is reassuringly tight (you must be buzzed in). Most of the foreigners we met at the hotel claimed to be afraid to leave it. They weren't shrinking violets, by any means; we're talking hale and hardy Europeans in their 20s who had seen their share of world travel. After experiencing Venice at night, though, they preferred the hotel's hospitality room—now expanded into "the Interclub"—to the bars and clubs on the streets below. After a few night moves of our own around Venice, we saw their point and gladly joined them.

The best compromise between Venice access and a safe and quiet stay is the **Inn at Venice Beach** (327 Washington Boulevard, 310/821-2557, $$). The rooms are clean and cheerful, and continental breakfast is served in an airy courtyard. Europeans are smitten with this place. And it's just three blocks from Venice Pier.

COASTAL CUISINE

In Venice you take the bad with the good. And some good old reliables are still around. During the day the **Sidewalk Cafe** (1401 Ocean Front Walk, 310/399-5547, $) is the best vantage point from which to observe the human circus. The items on the menu have been given literary names, because the café adjoins the excellent Small World Bookstore. Breakfast, for example, can consist of an omelet named after Gertrude Stein, Carlos Castaneda, or Jack Kerouac. Lunch could be a burger named for Charles Dickens, Pablo Neruda, or James Michener. (The latter, logically enough, features pineapple and ham.) The best place for coffee and conversation is **The Cow** (34 Washington Boulevard, $), a local hangout.

Two arrivals in Venice worth considering are the **West Beach Cafe** (60 North Venice Boulevard, 310/823-5396, $$$) and **Nikki's** (72 Market Street, 310/450-3010, $$$). The former is a crowded, casual establishment specializing in California cuisine. Nikki's has developed a more hip-hop vibe than it used to have as its former incarnation, 72 Market Street.

NIGHTLIFE

We first read about aromatherapy, a New Age form of healing, in a Venice weekly devoted to planetary health. This therapy is based on the belief that your nose takes in "essential oils" vital to your well-being. When unhealthy, you simply need to inhale the proper mix of oils until you're good as new. Depression, for example, can be cured by inhaling the following herbs: basil, bergamot, chamomile, clary, lavender, marjoram, rosemary, and ylang-ylang.

After sampling Venice, both by day and night, we have devised our own form of aromatherapy, which we'd like to share with anyone who has grown sick and tired of life back home. Go to the south end of Venice City Beach at the end of a long, hot summer day. Stand anywhere along Ocean Front Walk and breathe deeply, keeping your mouth closed so as to maximize the essential oils your nose takes in. We promise that you'll be exclaiming, "There's no place like home" in short order.

If you wish to pick through the olfactory minefield of Venice after dark, the **Town House** (52 Windward Avenue, 310/392-4040) is the place to rock out. Large and loud enough for the rowdiest bike gang, the Town House features live rock and roll most nights in summer. If you're looking for a more civilized alternative, amble up Washington Street in the direction of Marina del Rey, where you'll find coffeehouses, sports bars, and cantinas galore.

Hinano (15 Washington Boulevard, 310/822-3902) is a "brasserie de Tahiti," a fancy way of saying "friendly beach bar." Pool tables in one room, booths in the other room, Hinano is what a locals' hangout ought to be. Help yourself to free popcorn out of an old machine, order a pitcher of beer, and sit a spell.

Santa Monica

The most "urban" of Los Angeles's beach communities, Santa Monica (population 87,500) is a showcase for much of the best, and some of the worst, that the city has to offer. The town has a temperate, even climate—perfect for those who live outdoors or play so much in it that they might as well be living outdoors. After the "June gloom" has run its course, the weather in Santa Monica is dependably good the rest of the year.

Santa Monica's beach is where the heart and soul of Los Angeles comes to have fun in the summer. It serves as the steam-release valve for Los Angeles's vast and diverse population, a no-frills playland that attracts close to 15 million visitors a year. That's about a quarter of the total load borne by all the beaches in Los Angeles County. Santa Monica is easily accessible to all. Perhaps for this reason it suffers in comparison to its more glittery neighbors up toward Malibu and down by Manhattan Beach. At Santa Monica it's just good people having a high old time at the beach, many of whom speak English only as a second language. Without Santa Monica in the summertime, Los Angeles would be one big, smog-laced pressure cooker.

In the process of serving as the city's back door to the beach, Santa Monica somehow manages to maintain a character and charm all its own. Grandeur and squalor are mixed here in unequal proportions, creating an appealing blend of tropical rot and urban cool that Raymond Chandler captured in his detective novels. (His fictional "Bay City" was modeled after Santa Monica.) Chandler's subterranean noir universe is but a flickering image now, seen in the architectural splendor of some of the older apartment buildings and the art deco facades of the theaters. The city is in what might be called a period of transition, as it has been for several years. Many buildings are boarded up, some are being torn down, and other marginal properties await the inevitable.

An attempt has been made to revive downtown Santa Monica, adding pedestrian shopping malls and multi-screen cinemas in hopes of bringing back the healing plasma of money that fled to the hills in the 1980s. It seems to have worked. At last count we found over 70 museums and galleries, 12 book shops, and more coffee shops than Dublin has pubs in Santa Monica's 8.3 square miles. The epicenter of this downtown renewal is the Third Street Promenade. This brick pedestrian walkway courses through four blocks of storefronts, from Colorado Avenue to Wilshire Boulevard, running parallel to the beach from three blocks back.

Though this mall dispenses the usual trendy consumer flotsam, the experience of walking through it is spiced by some unique street performers. In fact, these performers lend the promenade a flavor more distinctive than the shops. The Third Street brigade is more talented, and less scatological and dangerous, than the ragtag army in Venice. A string quartet composed of conservatory students plays Vivaldi beautifully. A small ensemble cranks out a huge big-band sound. A lonely jazzman offers mournful blues on the vibes. An old man with an ashen face sings Willie Nelson's "On the Road Again" and yodels while standing on his head in a chair. Awesome! An atheist and a born-again Christian rant at each other through microphones; it is hard to decide who is the more repellent. Two silver-painted characters do coordinated, robotic choreography to hip-hop blaring from their boom box. Weird!

The overwhelming feeling one gets while strolling Third Street is nostalgia for the grandeur that Santa Monica once represented. Many of the promenade businesses trade on nostalgia, re-creating the 1950s and 1960s. The most popular eatery is a faux 1950s diner. The hippest clothier is a thrift shop manqué that sells used clothing at boutique prices. (Ragged-looking T-shirts for $18—what a concept!) The bars are upscale pool halls filled with yuppies slumming as bikers. The nicest theater is a beautifully restored 1940s film palace. Third Street is ultimately a mirage of fake evocations: The upscale, chrome-railed pool hall serves gourmet pizza, the 1950s diner gleams with an antiseptic aura, and the mock-bohemian coffeehouses collect 18 dimes (instead of one) for a cup of coffee.

Only the presence of the homeless milling about soils the mood of sentimental yearning (unless you're nostalgic for the Great Depression). The collision of Santa Monica's downward mobility with its last-ditch attempts at creating an urban island of crime-free consumerism makes for an odd mélange on the streets. We saw some strange scenes indeed. An executive in a designer running outfit was spitting orders into a mobile phone while roller-skating past a haggard woman on a bench who was flicking at invisible bugs, her belongings arrayed in bulging bags at her feet. It was hard to tell which of these two characters was more insane. Then there was the wraithlike, barefoot woman who punched the air like Fred Sanford, intimidating a striding stream of Dockers shorts and Polo shirts into stepping out of her way. At a yogurt café she walked in, looked around, and snatched some food right off the plate of a startled German tourist. To curb such excesses in the city once known as "People's Republic of Santa Monica," stiff new laws on vagrancy, loitering, and overnight sleeping on the beach have been instituted.

In many ways Santa Monica remains the most appealing and unique place in Los Angeles. Certainly it is among the last bastions of kindness, egalitarianism, and liberalism. Still, it is life lived at its extremes. On the one hand homeless occupy the parks and promenades, and proletarian hordes roam the beach and pier. On the other, luxury hotels overlook the ocean, and stores cater to people with too much disposable income. As is the case in most American cities these days, there is no longer much in the way of a middle class or a happy medium.

For more information, contact the Santa Monica Convention and Visitor Bureau, 1400 Ocean Avenue, Santa Monica, CA 90405, 310/319-6263, www.santamonica.com; or the Santa Monica Chamber of Commerce, 1234 6th Street, Suite 100, Santa Monica, CA 90401, 310/393-9825, www.smchamber.com.

BEACHES

Santa Monica State Beach is easily accessible from downtown Los Angeles via the Santa Monica Freeway (I-10) or one of several primary east–west arteries (Pico, Wilshire, Santa Monica). Any number of bus lines start and end here as well. The dimensions of this beach are amazing: It is 3.3 miles long and several football fields wide. Generally it attracts a close-packed crowd of Hispanic families who bring beach towels and picnic baskets. South of Santa Monica Pier the blankets and bodies thin out. Two concrete walkways run parallel some distance back from the ocean. One ferries pedestrian traffic, while the other transports those on wheels. An army of mobile twenty- and thirty-something cyclists and in-line skaters can be seen leaving vapor trails on the South Bay Bicycle Trail. You can park

BEACH FLICKS

Endless Summer II, released in 1994, didn't capture the imagination of young America the way the original *Endless Summer* did in 1966. Of course the Beach Boys, the Ventures, Dick Dale, and Jan and Dean had musically paved the way for Bruce Brown's first documentary on surfing.

Even before Brown's watershed flick, there were several attempts to capture the burgeoning surf culture on celluloid. Most were stilted and hokey, though these movies did help infuse California and Hawaii with a sort of mythical, siren-like power. In hindsight, these California "beach flicks" – think Frankie Avalon (who was actually from New Jersey) and Annette Funicello (a former Mouseketeer) – have a so-bad-it's-good kind of appeal. The great majority of them were released in 1964 and 1965, after which point a rising countercultural tide would wash away all traces of Frankie, Annette, and their ilk. But thanks to them, everyone who came of age in that time wanted to live beside a California beach – and many, in fact, took pains to make it happen.

Here are capsule summaries of some of the best and worst of the beach flicks, arranged by year:

- *Blue Hawaii* (1961) – Elvis Presley stars in this sandy epic, the most intriguingly perverse aspect of which is the soundtrack, boasting winners like "Slicin' Sand," "Beach Boy Blues," and "Ito Eats." Angela Lansbury plays his mama.

- *Beach Party* (1963) – The first in the Frankie and Annette beach sagas, this had the redeeming presence of Dick Dale & the Del-Tones, plus some of the world's first surf punks, led by notorious Erich Von Zipper. This movie also had an original plot idea: An anthropologist studies surf culture through a telescope. Maybe this is where Tom Wolfe got his inspiration for *The Pump House Gang!*

- *Beach Ball* (1964) – A hokey rip-off of *Beach Party* with a threadbare plot having to do with a music-store owner and a band called The Wigglers, it stars Edd "Kookie" Byrnes and features performances by the Walker Brothers, Jerry Lee Lewis, the Four Seasons, the Nashville Teens, the Righteous Brothers, and the Supremes.

- *Bikini Beach* (1964) – Here's another Frankie and Annette vehicle lacking a full tank of gas, although it turns on a potentially hilarious idea – spoofing the Beatles via a teen idol named the Potato Bug. Little Stevie Wonder performs "Fingertips."

- *Muscle Beach Party* (1964) – Frankie and Annette (again) meet bodybuilders and

in state-run fee lots or take your chances feeding the meters on the streets.

The center of the action is **Santa Monica Pier,** which is among the best in the Golden State. The pier, originally built in 1874, is an antiquated slice of Americana, a West Coast Coney Island stocked with gaming arcades, T-shirt vendors (four for $10, rivaling Venice for, uh, value), fast-food stalls, and incongruously chic restaurants. This incarnation of the pier was built in 1909 but underwent a full-scale $12 million renovation completed in 1997. Tiny arcades flare off from the main concourse, creating an atmosphere not unlike the midway at a state fair. All the ingredients are here for kids to have a good time and for parents to get nostalgic about their own gloriously misspent youth: Skee-Ball, basketball shoots, Wedges/Hedges, bumper cars, rocking horses, an antique carousel, and a gift shop where one can purchase a plaster cast of Elvis stranger than any to be found in Memphis.

Once part of a huge playland, replete with a glamorous ballroom and famous "Blue Streak

an Italian countess. Dick Dale & the Del-Tones and Little Stevie Wonder provide musical context.

- *Surf Party* (1964) – Set in Malibu, with songs by the Astronauts, the Routers, Bobby Vinton, and Jackie DeShannon.

- *Beach Blanket Bingo* (1965) – Buster Keaton makes an appearance, rescuing this Frankie Avalon and Annette Funicello farce, based on the latter's reaction to the former's crush on a bimbo named Sugar Cane.

- *How to Stuff a Wild Bikini* (1965) – Frankie, Annette, and Erich Von Zipper reprised. Frankie hires a witch doctor to keep an eye on Annette while he is in the Navy Reserves. Mickey Rooney and Buster Keaton make cameos.

- *Girls on the Beach* (1965) – A sorority tries to raise funds with a rock concert. They want the Beatles to perform, but they settle for the Beach Boys, with equally happy results. It also includes songs by the Crickets and Leslie Gore.

- *Wild on the Beach* (1965) – The best thing about this lame beach-sploitation flick is the music: songs by Colorado's Astronauts ("Little Speedy Gonzalez," "Rock the World," "Snap It") and "Drum Dance," by the great Sandy Nelson.

- *Ghost in the Invisible Bikini* (1966) – Monsters go to the beach, with Boris Karloff and Basil Rathbone trading spooky taunts amidst the beach blankets.

- *Paradise – Hawaiian Style* (1966) – Although the hula dancers were required by film code to cover their navels under their hula skirts, the movie does have Elvis singing "Queenie Wahine's Papaya."

- *It's a Bikini World* (1967) – Tommy Kirk is a poor man's Frankie Avalon. The Animals play "We Gotta Get Out of This Place." We assume they meant this film.

- *Catalina Caper* (1967) – Set on the island off the coast of Los Angeles, this soundtrack's most improbable moment: Little Richard singing "Scuba Party."

- *Clambake* (1967) – Elvis Presley bakes some clams, makes some clams, and goes to Las Vegas afterward to make even more. He's a water-ski instructor in this turkey.

- *Back to the Beach* (1987) – Frankie, Annette, and the gang, which now included the likes of Bob Denver (a.k.a. Gilligan) and Pee Wee Herman (a.k.a. "mud"), attempt to re-create the spirit of their early-1960s beach flicks in the late-1980s. They should've heeded the words of author Thomas Wolfe when he wrote, "You can't go back to the beach again." Or words to that effect.

Racing Coaster," the old outlying structures fell to the wrecking ball some years ago, and all that remains is the pier. New cafés are planned for the future. For now, the fast-food stands are guaranteed to bring back memories of indigestion. Step right up for tacos, hot dogs, cotton candy, fried dough, and fish 'n' chips. Then head home for a large, cool drink of Alka-Seltzer.

We took our Skee-Ball prizes (two tiny plastic rats and a thimble-sized trophy) and headed to Back On the Beach. Yes, that's the name of a wonderful piazza on the sand, an invigorating half-mile hike north of the pier. A former private beach club and now a café with a seating capacity of 200, **Back On the Beach** (445 Palisades Road, 310/393-8282) is a quintessential L.A. beach experience. You can eat a salad as an antidote to the pier food or simply sit back with a beverage and watch the passing parade on the South Bay Bicycle Trail. President Clinton chose this spot for his morning jog when he was in the city, and Al Pacino is regularly seen here. Even more telling is the fact that several episodes of *Beverly Hills 90210* were filmed here. Volleyball nets and playground equipment are nearby, for further diversions.

As for swimming, the waves at Santa Monica State Beach are sufficient to excite the tiny tots on their Styrofoam boards but not large enough to attract serious surfing. Several hundred yards south of the pier is the original **Muscle Beach,** where, since the 1930s, Conan-like men and women have been hoisting barbells all day long while lesser mortals stand around in the sand and applaud. Jack LaLanne and Steve Reeves flexed their pecs here, and Mr. America and Mr. Universe contests have been held here. Down toward Venice you'll come to a sprawl of basketball and paddle-tennis courts, with grandstands beside them. Rest a spell and marvel at the athleticism of the men and women sweating in the sun.

The physical setting of the beach is almost as muscular as the weight lifters. Backed by a long, undeveloped bluff, Santa Monica's beach somehow seems tranquil even when thousands are jammed on the sand below—a glorious sight! Atop the bluff is Palisades Park, a shaded 26-acre jewel that runs for 14 city blocks from Colorado Avenue to Adelaide Drive. This green, shady buffer between the sand and the city is filled with benches and shuffleboard courts, and it's popular with Santa Monica's large contingent of senior citizens. It is also popular with the homeless. The two groups seem to coexist peacefully, though.

Given a city the size of Los Angeles, there are bound to be problems with its most popular beach. In the late 1980s Santa Monica Bay became a colostomy bag for the city's then sick body. The Hyperion Sewage Treatment Plant, a gargantuan facility that serves four million people and was once the pride and joy of Los Angeles (earning rapturous accolades from Aldous Huxley, of all people), broke down. Millions of gallons of raw sewage poured directly into Santa Monica Bay. This set off a chain reaction that brought the county sewage

system and city government to near collapse. The mayor called for voluntary water conservation, but the filthy rich in Westside and the San Fernando Valley didn't go along with it, filling pools and watering lawns in protest. Water became even scarcer, exacerbating tensions with Arizona and Northern California. But, on the bright side, the pollution of the Santa Monica Bay provided the impetus for a slow-growth and eco-minded grassroots movement that has gained strength ever since. An organization called Heal the Bay has gone a great distance toward doing just that through environmental education and direct action.

25 SANTA MONICA STATE BEACH

Location: Ocean Avenue at Colorado Avenue in Santa Monica

Parking/Fees: $5-8 entrance fee per vehicle, or metered street parking

Hours: 6 A.M.-sunset

Facilities: concession, lifeguards, restrooms, showers, and picnic tables

Contact: Los Angeles County Lifeguard Service, Central Section, 310/394-3264

ACCOMMODATIONS

It is possible to stay near the beach in Santa Monica. Many hotels and motels, large and small, line Ocean Avenue a block or two from the pier and a pedestrian bridge away from the beach. Staying here also solves your biggest beach problem, which is parking. Leaving your wheels in a hotel garage sure beats battling experienced, have-you-hugged-my-bumper-today natives, who will beat you to any available slot. There's only one drawback: Ocean Avenue can be loud, even at night. We learned this the hard way one year when we were younger and poorer, taking a room at the least expensive motel on the strip: a $40 jobbie. The price was cheap because it was a four-walled cell with rancid bedcovers and thin, lifeless pillows. Caveat emptor. These fleabags litter the roadside like yesterday's papers.

A money transfusion in recent years has transformed the beachfront. Along with the older, dependable **Holiday Inn at the Pier** (120 Colorado Avenue, 310/451-0676, $$$), high-rise luxury hotels now tower over the Santa Monica Beach south of the pier. The cream of the crop is the **Loews Santa Monica Beach Hotel** (1700 Ocean Avenue, 310/458-6700, $$$$). It's an attractive, upscale tower that somehow exudes a casual sort of class. (The additional parking charges aren't classy or casual, though.) The lobby alone is worth a look-see. You can hear the waves roll in from your balcony and watch the human parade roll by on the bike paths. At night milk and cookies are brought to guests' doors, providing a nice bedtime touch worthy of Mom.

Another recent arrival at Santa Monica Beach is **Le Merigot** (1740 Ocean Avenue, 310/395-9700, www.lemerigothotel.com, $$$$), a J. W. Marriott Beach Resort. It's an opulent resort done in neutral tones. You're a block back from the beach, which is easily accessible via the pool area. The rooms and furniture are upscale and functional. A lobby bar and terrace make a good place to hang out and eavesdrop on conversations. One afternoon we heard a bartender carry on about the way things are in Los Angeles: "Unlike back home, it's not enough just to say that you like a movie out here," he animatedly told an attentive imbiber while cleaning wine glasses. "You have to know the director and his previous work, who the key grip was, who cut the deal, how many theaters it opened at, and on and on. That's just the nature of the business out here. Everybody knows all the smallest details." We wondered how many hundred times he had jovially imparted this memorized speech, these same pearls of wisdom, to other strangers at the bar.

The spa at Le Merigot is not to be missed. A roomful of bikes and cardio machines, another full of free weights, and locker areas with eucalyptus steam room can all be used free of charge by guests. There's also an extensive menu of spa services. For a great workout, warm up on a stationary bike, use the Cybex machines and free weights, finish with an off-property run on the South Bay Bicycle Trail (down to Venice and back is about three miles), and then sit in eucalyptus-scented steam for as long as you can stand it. We did exactly that and had a very pleasant chat with Bill Bridges, a former pro basketball player for the L.A. Lakers. Known as a tough defender who snagged a lot of rebounds, Bridges talked hoops with us for half an hour—a great guy, and this was just one of those encounters that seems to happen in Los Angeles.

The **Bayside Hotel** (2001 Ocean Avenue, 310/396-6000, www.baysidehotel.com, $$) earns the honor of being closest to the beach, which sits just across from it on a quiet loop road in an otherwise residential neighborhood. Nearby, the **Santa Monica Travelodge** (1525 Ocean Avenue, 310/451-0761, $$) offers the usual mid-scale chain amenities.

The retro-coolest place is **Hotel Shangri La** (1301 Ocean Avenue, 310/394-2791, www.shangrila-hotel.com, $$$$), a seven-story art deco landmark built in 1939. It's gracefully anonymous, which is probably why people like Bill Murray and Diane Keaton stay here. Straight out of Miami's Art Deco District, the **Georgian Hotel** (1415 Ocean Avenue, 310/451-3374, www.georgianhotel.com, $$$) is an architectural wonder.

COASTAL CUISINE

The Lobster (1602 Ocean Avenue, 310/458-9294, $$$$) has one of the finest settings anywhere, overlooking the Santa Monica Pier, the Pacific Ocean, and the Santa Monica Mountains. It goes without saying that you want to be here at sunset. But that's far from the only reason you'd come here. The food is sensational. The namesake lobster preparations cannot be beat. One of us ordered a pan-roasted 1.5-pound lobster served atop a bed of tomato risotto. The dish was not inexpensive ($45), but the splurge was worth it. You might get Pacific spiny lobster when they're in season (usually September through February); otherwise, your crustacean will be from Maine. Another of us had seared ahi served atop lightly sautéed greens, mushrooms, artichoke slivers, and more. Aside from being an incredible blend of flavors, it makes one feel instantly healthier.

It's hard to make a rational choice from a menu that is so appealing from top to bottom. The clams and mussels, served in a tasty, briny broth that can be eaten like soup or sopped up with bread, is a top entrée. And the desserts! After eating heartily, we recommend something fruity and fresh like Ciao Bella sorbet (a homemade strawberry sorbet served with berries) or blueberry cobbler. Beyond the superb food and view, the people-watching is not to be missed. Pay attention and you'll get a sense of how Los Angeles ticks: movers and shakers on the make, either sealing deals via cell phone or charming their consorts at the table. The energy level at the Lobster is high, the experience of dining here memorable.

The best quick bite is down at **Back On the Beach** (445 Palisades Road, 310/393-8282, $$), and a convenient quick morning hit can be had at **Starbucks** (Third Street Promenade, 310/260-9947, $). At the latter, Charles Bukowski wannabes nurse bottomless mugs and work on their angst. Dinner is another matter. Santa Monica is home to some of Los Angeles's finest dining. Famed chef Wolfgang Puck's **Chinois On Main** (2709 Main Street, 310/392-9025, $$$$) is a celebrated bastion of haute cuisine blending French, Chinese, and Japanese elements. **Rocken Rolls,** chef Hans Rockenwagner's fast-food kiosk at the Third Street Promenade, is as popular as the French contemporary cuisine at his **Rockenwagner** restaurant and bakery (2435 Main Street, 310/399-6504, $$$$).

But we wanted seafood. We found it, sort of, at **Chez Jay** (1657 Ocean Avenue, 310/395-1741, $$). It's a longtime popular beach hangout run by a guy who once hunted pirate treasure. His signature dish is "spuds

fried with bananas"—real surfer food that, along with his steaks, chops, and seafood, has been pleasing palates for 35 years. Nearby, another oceanfront landmark, **Ivy at the Shore** (1535 Ocean Avenue, 310/393-3113, $$$), serves American fare in a tropical setting adjacent to the ocean. Down toward Venice, two blocks from the ocean, is **Enterprise Fish Company** (174 Kinney Street, 310/392-8366, $$), housed in an impressive ivy-covered warehouse. All the entrées, especially the local catches, are nicely prepared.

We couldn't resist a drive inland for some stargazing and schmoozing, so we did as the Clampetts did, loading up our wallets and going to Beverly...Hills, that is. The Elysian Fields of schmoozing is **The Palm** (9001 Santa Monica Boulevard, 310/550-8811, $$$), in West Hollywood. It's a piece of Manhattan at the end of California's rainbow, and we were told, "If you sit at the bar for a week in the Palm, you will meet anyone you care to know." We didn't have a week, but we did lunch and met Sandy Koufax. Enough said.

One of our old favorites from Malibu, the **Reel Inn** (1220 Third Promenade, 310/395-5538, $$), has opened what to our taste buds is the best food joint on Third Street Promenade. You order at the front, picking your fresh line-caught fish from the display case (try the Cajun-blackened halibut or the simply grilled ahi tuna), then retreat to a picnic table until your name is called. They slop some good stuff, like Cajun rice, home fries, and coleslaw, next to it, and you're in business. Entrées start at $7.95, making the Reel Inn a real bargain. Real upscale seafood is found at Shutters on the Beach Hotel, which has the stylish **One Pico** (1 Pico Boulevard, 310/587-1717, $$$), as well as the pleasant **Pedals Cafe** right on the bike path. Pedals is a great brunch spot on weekends, with indoor and outdoor dining areas and menu choices that range from creative omelets to grilled salmon. Look both ways before crossing because the path narrows in front of Pedals, and bikers and skaters rarely slow down.

NIGHTLIFE

Santa Monica is only one boulevard (Sunset, Wilshire, or Santa Monica) away from Hollywood. Pick up the latest copy of *L.A. Weekly*, *L.A. Reader, Rave!*, or the *Los Angeles Times* to find out what's doing in town. The detailed listings for each night of the week will give you some idea of what the term "free will" means. It's difficult to comment in much detail about a scene as extensive as the one in Los Angeles. To a pair of beach bums who have been denied good music in more beach towns than we care to count, Santa Monica and Los Angeles are almost too much of a good thing. If only it could be spaced out evenly over both coasts . . .

The biggest musical waves on the beachfront can be ridden at **Rusty's Surf Ranch** (256 Santa Monica Pier, 310/393-7437), which offers "alternative funk," "masterful power pop," and other hip goodies (as well as pool tables and a full menu) nightly. When we were in town, an adult musical comedy called "Butt Pirates of the Caribbean" was also being presented, no doubt starring a bunch of very jolly Rogers.

We next direct your attention to the vicinity of upper Santa Monica Boulevard, where the old guard clubs are still rocking the City of Angels—**Club Lingerie, Whiskey a Go-Go, the Roxy, McCabe's,** the **Palomino.** We unhesitatingly recommend the **House of Blues Sunset Strip** (8430 Sunset Boulevard, 323/848-5100), less exuberantly the Johnny Depp–owned **Viper Room** (8852 Sunset Boulevard, 310/358-1880). Every night in Los Angeles is a who's who of musicians. Closer to the beach, your main alternative is to stroll the Third Street Promenade (between Colorado Avenue and Wilshire Boulevard). Nondrinkers will dig the outdoor cafés, used book shops, street musicians, cinemas, and dessert places. Imbibers flock to **Yankee Doodles** (1410 Promenade, 310/394-4632), a sports bar that epitomizes all that is faux-gettable about going out these days: overpaid yuppies affecting pirate kerchiefs and $1,000 leather jackets while playing pool and scarfing gourmet pizza. The drinks are overpriced. One large draft Fosters and a cranberry juice cost almost $10! We retreated to a corner and shot at the electronic basketball concession until our quarters ran out. You would do better to walk a little farther and seek solace at **Anastasia's Asylum** (1028 Wilshire Boulevard, 310/394-7113), a hip coffeehouse in the best sense. There's no cover charge, the local atmosphere is genuine, and there's live entertainment and a vegetarian menu.

Pacific Palisades

This community, nestled in the foothills of the Santa Monica Mountains from Chautauqua Boulevard to Malibu, is not a beach town, but it does look down on one of the loveliest stretches of the Pacific coast. Originally populated in the 1920s by Methodists who founded it as their "new Chautauqua," Pacific Palisades (population 23,000) is now the exclusive domain of the very rich. The streets, most of which branch off Sunset Boulevard, are winding, shaded routes, many ending in cul-de-sacs. Parts of Pacific Palisades are included on Hollywood celebrity bus tours.

We had another reason for visiting Pacific Palisades—a motive not unlike our quest for the ghost of Charles Bukowski in San Pedro. Henry Miller retired here after Big Sur became too unnavigable for his aged body. He spent his happiest golden days riding "his best friend" (a bicycle) around these lovely streets. It was while pursuing the vision of this sweet old man that we stumbled upon the **Self-Realization Fellowship Lake Shrine** (17190 Sunset Boulevard, 310/454-4114), a 10-acre "wall-less temple," bird sanctuary, sunken garden, and altar to the "five major religions of the world." Fitting, somehow, that Henry Miller spent his final days nearby.

For more information, contact the Pacific Palisades Chamber of Commerce, 15330 Antioch Street, Pacific Palisades, CA 90272, 310/459-7963, www.palisadeschamber.com.

BEACHES

Pacific Palisades puts its ocean frontage to good use. It is the site of a state beach named after our most famous cowboy-philosopher. **Will Rogers State Beach** is a sandy swath three miles long that's a favorite of sun-bronzed locals who are serious about their volleyball game and their tans. Its proximity to Hollywood makes it one of the more popular beaches in Los Angeles County. Furthermore,

it is the starting point for the South Bay Bicycle Trail, which ends 26 miles later down at Torrance County Beach. That said, we'd take Zuma State Beach, up in Malibu, over Will Rogers any day. The scenery is better and the distance from the highway madness makes Zuma more appealing.

Incidentally, if you want to dig further into the life of the man who never met a man he didn't like, Rogers's 187-acre ranch is open to

THE CITY GETS AN (L)A FOR EFFORT

The State of California is ahead of the rest of the nation on many things, good and bad, but mostly good. And the city and county of Los Angeles, California's largest population center, finally seem to be walking the walk. In addition to a massive tree-planting campaign, communities in the 462-square-mile area are taking stands that should be emulated nationwide. To wit:

- Malibu and Manhattan Beach banned businesses from using plastic carryout bags, in May and July 2008 respectively. Other beach communities will likely follow suit. The Los Angeles County Board of Supervisors, however, bowed to lobbyist pressure, voting for a half-baked measure to delay plastic-bag bans in the Greater LA area. The City Council, perhaps in an effort to shame the county, unanimously approved a ban of all plastic bags by 2010 and, until then, imposed a $0.25 surcharge per bag. Hooray.

- The California Coastal Commission and Heal the Bay, an exceptionally active nonprofit based in Santa Monica, led the 24th annual California Coastal Cleanup Day on September 20, 2008. Lots of plastic bags were found, of course.

- In March 2008, the Los Angeles Water Board put 20 coastal towns on notice that they would be fined $10,000 until they stopped "continually" surpassing federally mandated daily limits of bacterial discharge into the ocean. Among those put on notice were Santa Monica, Long Beach, and Malibu. Malibu has exceeded bacteria limits at its beaches since September 2006. The importance of the Water Board's action can not be overstated. It is the first time in the nation that an oversight body has threatened fines to ensure compliance with beach bacteria limits and clean water standards.

- In February 2007, the California Coastal Conservancy funded the removal of a disused and harmful roadway, aptly named Texas Crossing, from Malibu Creek, freeing a previously blocked mile of new habitat for fish.

- Santa Monica installed three monofilament fishing-line recycling bins on Santa Monica Pier to reduce the damage done by fishing line in the ocean waters. The bins are a prototype for those that will, we hope, soon be appearing up and down the state's coast. Fishing line is virtually invisible in the water, lasts 600 years in the environment, and is responsible for virtual maritime genocide. Derelict fishing gear (nets, rods, traps, hooks, etc.) that has been pitched into the ocean is another problem that is being addressed.

the public as **Will Rogers State Historical Park** (1501 Will Rogers State Park Road, 310/454-8212). Tours of the main house and grounds are offered daily, and one can also hike through the vast natural area or ride on equestrian trails.

26 WILL ROGERS STATE BEACH

Location: 16000 block of Highway 1 in Pacific Palisades
Parking/Fees: $7 entrance fee per vehicle
Hours: 8 A.M.-7 P.M.
Facilities: concession, lifeguards, restrooms, and showers
Contact: Los Angeles County Department of Beaches and Harbors, 310/305-9503

COASTAL CUISINE

Pacific Palisades has got little, if anything, to offer travelers in the way of accommodations and nightlife, being a predominantly ritzy and privacy-hoarding residential community. However, it's got a dandy restaurant on the beach that ranks among the best on the coast. **Gladstone's of Malibu** (17300 Pacific Coast Highway, 310/459-9676, $$$$) is indeed the place to go "4 fish" in Los Angeles County. It's worth the drive, worth the wait, and worth the price. Barrels of peanuts are set out for waiting patrons to crack open and munch, and the oceanside location makes for superb sunset-watching. The portions are huge and the menu expansive at Gladstone's. Prime seafood entrées run in the $25 and up range and include such items as mesquite-grilled sea bass and ahi rolled in Cajun spices, then seared and cooked rare. Appetizers include plump, cold Pacific oysters, as well as ceviche salad and marinated calamari. A sashimi dinner offers a filling platter of raw seafood delights. King and queen crab legs (the latter are slightly saltier and smaller, though still huge) are worth the $30 or so you'll plunk down for

them. What you can't eat at Gladstone's will be wrapped by your server in gold foil and twisted to resemble a seabird or fish—a signature touch that completes a very satisfying dining experience.

Malibu

Malibu might seem to the outside world to be some ultra-chic celebrity enclave accessible only to camera crews from *Lifestyles of the Rich and Famous,* but nothing could be further from the truth. The fact is, there are really two Malibus. The better known of these is the "inner" Malibu—the film colony, the celebrity sandbox, the glamorous private world behind locked gates about which the rest of the world likes to fantasize. The "outer" Malibu is a 27-mile stretch of rugged coastline, plunging canyons, and towering mountains, running along the Pacific Coast Highway from Coastline Drive to the Ventura County line. Local boosters refer to the PCH through Malibu as "the longest main street in America." We like to think of it as Little Big Sur. This side of Malibu—a wild, winding corridor physically bounded by the Santa Monica Mountains and Pacific Ocean—is accessible to all and yet is generally less familiar than the minuscule world of celebrity intrigue that makes Malibu an instant buzzword with readers and viewers of tabloid media.

The reality of Malibu (population 13,000) is very different from popular conceptions of it. Much of it is unforgiving and desolate. Steep mountains plunge to the sea, which crashes angrily against the rocks. The elements hang in precarious balance here, not infrequently tilting over into destructive chaos. Malibu is particularly subject to what native Southern Californians wearily refer to as their four seasons: fire, flood, mudslide, and earthquake. One must drive through Malibu ever vigilant for fallen rocks. Some of the cliff faces along the Pacific Coast Highway are raw where mighty chunks have torn loose and crashed

© PARKE PUTERBAUGH

Malibu Pier

onto the roadway. Narrow ridgetops zigzag northward. Houses are hidden in the canyons between them. The hills are covered with dry, brown vegetation that turns green only when the winter rains come. The threat of fire is constant. Lightning, arson, or a careless match can ignite a blaze that, propelled by hot Santa Ana winds, is capable of racing toward the seaside colony at speeds of 100 miles per hour. The other calamity is mudslides: slow, brown waves of muck, rock, and debris that swallow up everything in their path, houses included. The elements play no favorites here. No matter how much clout they may have in Hollywood, those who live in Malibu have no control over the periodic disasters that plague the seaside colony. Nature does not obey directors' cues.

Still, those who make their residence here derive a perverse sort of pleasure from the challenges of living on the edge. Writer Joan Didion captured its allure in her 1978 essay "Quiet Days in Malibu," in which she wrote: "I had come to see the spirit of the place as one of shared isolation and adversity, and I think now that I never loved the house on the Pacific Coast Highway more than on those many days when it was impossible to leave it, when

fire or flood had in fact closed the highway." A dissenting opinion was rendered in a *People* magazine cover story, which averred: "The plain truth is that [Malibu residents] are getting a noisy, shabby, perilous, and polluted pseudo-paradise."

The extent of the affront includes fecal pollution of the ocean (from untreated sewage and overflowing septic tanks) and not-infrequent offshore oil spills. Damaging waves from winter storms flood homes along eroded beaches in Malibu Colony. There is no beach out back of the Malibu Beach Inn.

Beach closures along Malibu's coast are not uncommon, due to high bacterial counts from human-generated sources of pollution. Breaches of Malibu Lagoon following heavy storms often send ribbons of foul, dark-stained water streaming into the waters near Surfrider Beach, causing mini-epidemics of nausea, vomiting, and diarrhea among surfers. One 21-year-old wave-rider—Erik Villanueva, a student at Pepperdine University, on the hills above Malibu—contracted Coxsackie B virus after paddling through a "dark stain" of pollution off Surfrider Beach in 1992. He has had two heart-transplant

THE PALMS HAVE GOTTA GO

Los Angeles will soon be a city without its most famous visual icon: the palm tree. Since at least the 1940s, tourists have associated palms with the relaxed wealth of sunny Southern California. Image may be everything in the make-believe world of Hollywood, but in the real world, palm trees are an ecological and budgetary disaster.

To begin with, they were never indigenous to Southern California. Not only do palm trees provide little, if any, shade, they do not remove carbon monoxide from the city's car-polluted air as well as other, shadier trees do. They also require frequent expensive maintenance, and their fronds become dangerous spears during winter's Santa Ana winds, bashing windshields and even injuring pedestrians.

Consequently, the city of Los Angeles is planting very few new palm trees once an old one dies off — which they are doing in abundant numbers these days. Instead, sycamores, crepe myrtles, and other indigenous species are being planted throughout the city. The only exceptions will be the relatively few palms that line such tourist routes as Sunset Boulevard and Hollywood Boulevard. In other words, just enough palms will remain to fake out the tourists.

operations and is convinced ocean pollution is to blame. Such events have led to a frenzy of heavily funded studies looking for sources of pollution in the Malibu Creek watershed, studying illness among beachgoers throughout the bay, and monitoring the genetic material of pathogens found in the lagoon. This is another way of saying that life is not always a beach in Malibu. Surfrider Beach receives failing grades when tested for bacterial contamination.

All of this is in large part a consequence of the accelerating pace of development in Malibu. The colony has changed considerably since the late 1970s, when author Joan Didion wrote (in the essay cited earlier): "In a way it seems the most idiosyncratic of beach communities, 27 miles of coastline with no hotel, no passable restaurant, nothing to attract the traveler's dollar." Now, like every other conquered corner of America, there are plenty of hotels, tons of passable restaurants, and lots of places to spend your money, including sprawling malls that would have been unthinkable a decade ago.

In 1986 the California Coastal Commission adopted a land-use plan for Malibu that

permitted significant retail growth in three areas: the Malibu Civic Center, the Point Dume/Paradise Cove area, and Pepperdine University. The same plan also okayed the construction of up to 6,582 new dwellings, nearly doubling the number that existed at that time. Many Malibu natives fought the plan, and one local activist griped, "They want to allow undisciplined, unbridled growth in Malibu." That seems to be what they're getting. In 1990 Malibu officially approved its incorporation as a city, something that had been rejected in ballot initiatives dating back to 1950.

The Malibu of today is a collage of the upscale and low-rent, plain and fancy, old and new. In certain ways Malibu still has an Old California feel to it, a wayback-machine aura evident in the unpretentious taverns and food stands that squat by the road, refusing to bend to trends. At the same time recent arrivals on the scene, most evidently the flashy Malibu Colony Mall, have altered the landscape so that it looks more like a Los Angeles suburb than the Malibu of old.

The real appeal of the place remains the elemental collision of geological opposites: ocean basin and mountain ridge. A drive up

POLLUTION REPORT CARD:
L.A. COUNTY BEACHES

So you've made it to Malibu and would love to lay eyes on one of the many celebrities from the entertainment community who make their home here. But you discover that their exclusive Malibu Colony is a gated and off-limits fortress. There's just no way for an ordinary peon from Pasadena or Peoria to slip past security. Not to worry! Just head on over to Surfrider Beach, one of Malibu's most popular spots to surf and swim, and hop in the water. You may wind up indirectly having a close encounter with a celebrity, or a whole bunch of them, when fecal coliform bacteria from overflowing septic tanks in the private colony washes into the ocean and travels with the currents to the beaches due south.

Gross as it sounds, this is exactly what happens in the waters off Surfrider Beach, where a combination of sources that the government hasn't the time, money, or inclination to untangle has been fouling the water with bacteria and sickening those who swim there with a variety of ailments that range from ear and eye infections to gastrointestinal bugs. The city of Malibu has exceeded bacteria limits on its beaches for roughly 500 days since September 2006, according to Los Angeles Water Board, which has threatened fines of $10,000 a day until they cease. The chief culprit is outflow from Malibu Lagoon, which serves as a catch basin for all sorts of disgusting muck. In addition to the septic tanks of Malibu Colony, culprits include excrement from waterbirds, urban runoff from the 110-square-mile watershed that drains into Malibu Creek, runoff from soil tilling and animal waste, and refuse from homeless encampments near Malibu Civic Center. Unlike the vast majority of beaches that border Santa Monica Bay, bacterial levels at Surfrider generally remain high during both wet and dry weather. A new water treatment facility was installed at the mouth of Marie Canyon in Malibu in October 2007, but the city of Malibu continues to exceed federal limits on bacterial discharge into the ocean.

The picture improves somewhat down the coast. Will Rogers State Beach, in Pacific Palisades, had always been another pollution hot spot. For many years industrial operations such as the Chevron oil refinery and Hyperion Sewage Treatment Plant were to blame. But under pressure from environmental groups like Heal the Bay, they've gone a long way toward cleaning up their act. Chevron voluntarily extended its wastewater discharge pipes from 300 to 3,000 feet offshore and also provided funding for a pilot epidemiological study to determine the causes and prevalence of illness among bay-area beachgoers.

The guiltiest contributors to the bay's bacterial stew these days are the citizens of Los Angeles themselves. Fertilizer runoff from lawns, oil and antifreeze dumped into sewers, and garbage tossed into streets and gutters all find their way into the bay via storm drains during periods of rain. Piers are another source of human-generated contaminants that stress the bay. Eight native species of fish have been found to be contaminated with DDT and PCBs, severe and persistent toxins dumped into the bay during the 1960s. They are slow to break down in the cold, mucky bay bottom where they reside, and consequently are still working their way up through the food chain.

National organizations such as the Natural Resource Defense Council (NRDC) and Oceana have joined California-based advocacy groups like Heal the Bay and the Surfrider Foundation in calling for solutions to ocean pollution. As an attorney for NRDC noted, "A relaxing day at the beach may actually be a hazard to your health." If you're concerned, take a stand and get involved. By law the beaches belong to everybody and, by God, everyone should be upset about what's happening to them.

Heal the Bay

1444 9th Street
Santa Monica, CA 90404
310/451-1500
www.healthebay.org

Heal the Bay is an increasingly powerful foundation that started out in a living room and grew to an organization with 10,000 volunteers, all upset with the condition of Santa Monica Bay. Their goal is to achieve a "fishable, swimmable, surfable" bay, and they do it by lobbying, educating the public, and barraging the media with facts, figures, and photographs. They have proven that you can indeed "fight city hall" and win the battle. They were responsible for stopping the county of Los Angeles from dumping sewage sludge into the bay and they have pressured the city of Los Angeles to ban plastic bags and begin treating the bay as a vital source of life and health for the entire community. This is a remarkable group, worthy of your donations of money and time.

Surfrider Foundation

P.O. Box 6010
San Clemente, CA 92674
949/492-8170
www.surfrider.org

In 1984 this environmental action group was founded in Malibu by surfers who saw their beloved ocean growing filthier by the day. As former executive director Jake Grubb told *Rolling Stone:* "When I started surfing these waters in the early 1960s, they were green and blue. Today, they're gray or brown." Their ranks have swelled to 35,000 members in 60 chapters, with headquarters in San Clemente. Their high-profile victories have included successfully suing pulp mills for polluting Humboldt Bay and halting plans to construct a mile-long breakwater off Imperial Beach. Their Blue Water Task Force collects ocean samples for water-quality testing. They'd rather be surfing (who wouldn't?), but they've responded to the mandate for action.

Oceana

1350 Connecticut Avenue, N.W., 5th floor
Washington, DC 20036
202/833-3900
www.oceana.org
Pacific Office: 99 Pacific Street, Suite 155C
Monterey, CA 93940
831/643-9266

In 1987, after successfully fighting oil companies on offshore drilling, Ted Danson founded American Oceans Campaign. The Santa Monica-based organization warned people about ocean and beach pollution and educated policymakers and the public about the need to preserve and restore our shorelines. "Oceans and beaches used to be visually pleasing," Danson said in a 1995 interview. "They took your breath away and made you feel good about being alive. Now they're lined with wall-to-wall condominiums. Because of the sheer number of people, water supplies are overburdened and breaking down." Danson's American Oceans Campaign merged with the Washington-based Oceana. This larger international advocacy organization exists "for the sole purpose of protecting the world's oceans to sustain the circle of life." Global in scope, they now have 300,000 members in 150 countries. Oceana's West Coast office is located in Monterey.

ART AND HISTORY IN OLD MALIBU

In search of art and history? There are two Malibu-area attractions to satisfy your hunger. The first is the J. Paul Getty Museum at the **Getty Center** (1200 Getty Center Drive, 310/440-7300, www.getty.edu). The much-hyped Getty Center, a cultural mecca, opened in 1997. This 110-acre "campus" is nestled in the Santa Monica foothills, overlooking Brentwood. The museum reflects Getty's lifelong interests as a collector of Greek and Roman antiquities, Renaissance and Baroque paintings, and European decorative arts. The museum building is a re-creation of the Villa dei Papiri, an ancient Roman country house, and the gardens are filled with plants and trees that might have been found there 2,000 years ago.

Since our last visit, the provenance of many Getty antiquities have been at the center of a legal case that has roiled the international art waters. Marion True, the former chief antiquities curator, was indicted in Italy on charges of conspiring to acquire artifacts that were illegally removed from that country's soil. The Greek government pressed similar charges against True but dropped them when the Getty agreed to return four artifacts. The criminal charges in Italy against True are still active. Visitors are advised to visit the Getty Museum ASAP in case any more of their collection is deemed ill-gotten cultural booty. The museum is open 10 A.M.–6 P.M. Tuesday–Thursday, 10 A.M.–9 P.M. Friday–Saturday, and 10 A.M.–6 P.M. Sunday. Admission to the museum is free, but parking costs $10.

Another curious diversion worth checking out is the historic **Adamson House and Malibu Lagoon Museum** (23200 Pacific Coast Highway, 310/456-8432, www.adamsonhouse.org), located a quick left turn north of Malibu Pier. The house and grounds formerly belonged to the Adamson family, daughter and son-in-law of the last owners of the Malibu Spanish Land Grant. Built in 1929, the house is a classic Moorish-Spanish Colonial Revival–style residence that serves as a museum of ceramic art and design. The fantastic flower gardens on the premises were created by covering the natural dunes with a layer of humus.

History buffs should note that a historical marker commemorates this establishment as the probable site of explorer Juan Rodríguez Cabrillo's New World landing in 1542. He disembarked to greet the canoe-paddling Chumash and to claim all the lands of "Alta California" in the name of the king of Spain. Large-scale real-estate transactions such as this one were apparently a simple matter back then. You just stepped up to the counter, so to speak, and ordered. The Adamson house and Malibu Lagoon Museum are open to the public 11 A.M.–3 P.M. Wednesday–Saturday. Admission is $5 for adults and $2 for children ages 6-16.

the Pacific Coast Highway through Malibu—particularly above Point Dume, where the development subsides—is a stunning and humbling encounter with nature in the raw. The unfolding panorama of beaches yields one remarkable vista after another.

As for the highway, it's something of a bane in Malibu. At various points, especially along a four-mile stretch north of Topanga Canyon, it is subject to mass movements (falling rocks, landslides) from the unstable cliffs that were cut to build it. Traffic tramples through town on the four-lane Pacific Coast Highway like a stampede of cattle. On weekends the road jams to a standstill with carloads of Angelinos headed to their favorite north county beaches or to play with the boats they keep in Ventura County's yacht basins. Beach parking lots fill up quickly, and the overflow lines the highway shoulders in both directions. For pedestrians, dashing across the highway is a bit like playing Russian roulette.

A beach access point we attempted to reach during one such crossing nearly rendered us roadkill. All that risk to check out a cement walk between buildings—one of the narrow accesses the California Coastal Commission has waged costly battles to establish, much to the chagrin of Malibu residents. Officially it is known as the Zonker Harris Accessway, after the *Doonesbury* cartoon character. Malibu is a thorn in the side of the Coastal Commission, as it is the most privatized stretch of California's coast and one near its largest population center.

On either side of it lies private property. You're reminded not to trespass, although California law does grant citizens the right to walk along the beach shoreward of the mean high-tide line. We did just that, ambling in the direction of the Malibu Pier past all manner of sunbathers (including some seminude beauties) who paid us no mind. The pier at Malibu is an old, broad-planked affair with a restaurant on the shore end. You can buy bait and tackle, obtain a fishing license, and charter a sportfishing boat at **Malibu Sport Fishing Landing** (23000 Pacific Coast Highway, 310/456-8030). At one time the modest commercial heart of Malibu, the pier area has been overtaken by all the new commercial development several miles north, near the fabled and private Malibu Colony.

The canyons of Malibu are cut with tortuous roads that wind through the Santa Monica Mountains. A drive up one of the canyon roads is a great way to pass a few hours, offering a mix of ocean vistas and mountain scenery as you make the jagged ascent. We went up Topanga Canyon Road and returned via Malibu Canyon Road, passing in a short time from cool sea level to broiling higher altitudes. Lay hands on a map of Malibu and design your own up-and-back route.

Beyond these suggestions you are more or less on your own in Malibu. Sometimes you can be made to feel as unwanted as a stray dog shuffling along the side of the road. Unless you have a ton of money or know someone who lives here—say, Brad Pitt or Goldie Hawn—you'll have a hard time fashioning any sort of extended vacation on the Malibu coastline other than a camping trip. But we'd rather be tenting beneath a stand of sycamores at Leo Carrillo State Park than attempting celebrity sightings at Paradise Cove any day. When we think of Malibu, we think of the land, not the famous landowners.

For more information, contact the Malibu Chamber of Commerce, 23805 Stuart Ranch Road, Suite 100, Malibu, CA 90265, 310/456-9025, www.malibu.org.

BEACHES

Because the terrain is so rugged, with the Santa Monica Mountains plunging steeply into the sea, the geography of the coastline makes for some amazing beaches along Malibu's 27 miles. About half of the Malibu coast (12.5 miles) is given over to state and county beaches, while the rest is under development. Surfrider, Zuma, and County Line are all names familiar to beachgoers and surfers worth their sea salt. But there are literally two dozen or so named beaches in Malibu. We'll hit the highlights.

Malibu's beach-erosion problems along the more developed areas southeast of Point Dume continue to worsen, as the ocean chomps hungrily at some of the most expensive real estate in the country. Out behind Gladstone's 4 Fish Restaurant, straddling the line between Pacific Palisades and Malibu, breakers tenaciously whittle away the beachfront. A rock jetty built to keep the vanishing beach from retreating is fighting a losing battle as the sea steadily advances upon the establishment.

The first real beach in Malibu is **Topanga County Beach,** at the south end of Malibu, which runs for just over a mile. Like many in the area, it is narrow and rocky, set at the base of steep, eroding bluffs. Surfing is popular at the mouth of Topanga Creek, but there are too many rocks to allow for safe swimming along most of the beach. Above it is **Las Tunas County Beach,** a narrow, unimproved beach beneath the bluffs that holds a special attraction to surf casters.

Surfrider Beach is right up from the Malibu Pier. The beach covers 35 acres, including nearly a mile of ocean frontage. Its waves are perfectly formed and, even when small, carry surfers a good distance. The waves we've seen in summer are unspectacular in size but fascinating in form. Riding them, the surfers look as if they're walking on water, almost moving in slow motion, gliding in on perfectly shaped, long-cycle waves for what seems like an eternity. The beach is at the head of a dramatic, U-shaped cove. Kiddies, bronzed Adonises, and big-bellied men, plus the usual crew of noble surfers, pack the place. Ravishing California girls watch the guys work out on the volleyball courts or in the waves, which are fought over and claimed by the most skillful surfers. The only bum note is water quality, with bacterial contamination making wave-riding here tantamount to surfing in a Petri dish. Adjacent to Surfrider is the small Malibu Lagoon Museum and Adamson House. The museum, Malibu Lagoon (at the mouth of Malibu Creek), Surfrider Beach, and the 700-foot Malibu Pier all fall within the boundaries of **Malibu Lagoon County Beach.** The lagoon is subject to contamination, and though the warm, protected waters are attractive to young children, it can be pretty scummy. Not for nothing does the county post advisories against swimming here.

Between Malibu Lagoon and Point Dume lie several small beaches worthy of mention. **Paradise Cove** is a private fee beach in the heart of Malibu Colony, offering the likeliest chance of celebrity sightings. Unlike whale-watching expeditions, however, a sighting is not guaranteed. The entrance fee lands you on a beach with a short pier and a wonderful view of the opposing sandstone bluffs of Point Dume and the Santa Monica Mountains. **Escondido Beach,** at the mouth of Escondido Creek, can be reached via a stairway near Malibu Cove Colony Drive; it's a good diving area but otherwise not worth the trouble. Close by is **Dan Blocker County Beach** (formerly Corral State Beach), a lifeguarded beach (in season) that draws some surfers and divers. The beach is narrow and rocky, there are few facilities, and only roadside parking. But it's a great spot for scuba enthusiasts.

Much like the coastline in Laguna Beach and La Jolla, Malibu's is intercut with coves, many of them accessible by stairways and paths if you know what you're looking for. Keep your eyes open for some of these spots between Topanga Beach and Paradise Cove (they are numerous). Also, be prepared to park on the highway and deal with hazardous crossings. Just for the record, there are public-access stairways to the beach on the following numbered blocks of the Pacific Coast Highway: 20000, 20350, 24318, 24434, 24602, 24714, 25118, 31200, and 31344.

Around the tip of Point Dume is **Point Dume County Beach** (a.k.a. Westward Beach), on Westward Beach Road. Nearby **Zuma County Beach** is the ultimate Southern California beach: wide, wild, extending for miles, and inhabiting a stupendous natural setting. It is the largest county-owned beach, with no fewer than eight parking lots and a $6 parking charge, avoided by many who use the shoulders of the Pacific Coast Highway. The beach here deserves its reputation for danger, as the waves form close to shore, rising out of nowhere to back-breaking height before crashing noisily and sending tongues of seawater and foam scurrying up the sloping beach face. It's the perfect recipe for rip currents, necessitating frequent heroics from the lifeguard stands. Contrary to notions that primo Malibu beaches such as this one are peopled only with perfect specimens awaiting casting calls from soap-opera producers, Zuma is chock full of families and normal-looking folks on summer weekends. With the invigorating clean air, the azure ocean's churning fury, and the breathtaking backdrop of steep-sided, brushy mountains, Zuma County Beach makes it possible to understand why residents risk life, limb, and earthly possessions to live in Malibu. Zuma comes equipped with food stands at both ends of its four-mile expanse along the Pacific Coast Highway, from the western side of Point Dume to Broad Beach Road. There is also a huge area given over to volleyball courts. West of Zuma, stairways along Broad Beach Road lead to secluded **Broad Beach.**

Next up is **Robert H. Heyer Memorial State Beach.** In fact, it is a trio of small cove beaches accessible by path and stairway. Moving west, the three beaches are **El Matador, La Piedra,** and **El Pescador,** occupying 18, 9, and 10 acres, respectively. The attraction is isolation from the madding crowd. Parking is by the honor system; you're asked to stuff $2 into a collection box. Switchback paths are carved into the crumbly cliffs. No wonder Malibu has mudslides in the rainy season; the hills are nothing more than loosely consolidated dirt clods. The beaches and offshore waters are strewn with sizable, steep-sided sea stacks. Come here for a taste of the wild side of Malibu's coastal geology. Approximately two miles west of El Pescador is **Nicholas Canyon County Beach,** slightly larger (at 23 acres) than the trio preceding it. Keep your eyes out for the turnoff down to the fee parking lot, which is directly across from the Malibu Riding and Tennis Club. You can also hike down from Leo Carrillo State Park, which adjoins it. Formerly known as Nicholas Beach—surfers referred to it as Point Zero— it is less crowded than many Malibu beaches and relatively free of wave-hogging surf punks. It is informally used as a nude beach, though authorities try to discourage it.

27 TOPANGA COUNTY BEACH

Location: 18500 Pacific Coast Highway in Malibu
Parking/Fees: $7 entrance fee per vehicle
Hours: 6 A.M.-sunset
Facilities: concession, lifeguards, restrooms, showers, and picnic tables
Contact: Los Angeles County Lifeguard Service, Northern Section, 310/394-3264

28 LAS TUNAS COUNTY BEACH

Location: 19400 Pacific Coast Highway in Malibu
Parking/Fees: $7 entrance fee per vehicle
Hours: 6 A.M.-sunset
Facilities: lifeguards and picnic tables
Contact: Los Angeles County Lifeguard Service, Northern Section, 310/394-3264

29 SURFRIDER BEACH

Location: Pacific Coast Highway at Malibu Pier
Parking/Fees: $7 entrance fee per vehicle
Hours: 6 A.M.-sunset
Facilities: concession, lifeguards, showers, and restrooms
Contact: Los Angeles County Lifeguard Service, Northern Section, 310/394-3264

30 MALIBU LAGOON COUNTY BEACH

Location: Pacific Coast Highway at Malibu Creek
Parking/Fees: $7 entrance fee per vehicle
Hours: 6 A.M.-sunset
Facilities: lifeguards, restrooms, showers, and picnic tables
Contact: Los Angeles County Lifeguard Service, Northern Section, 310/394-3264

31 DAN BLOCKER COUNTY BEACH

Location: 26000 Pacific Coast Highway in Malibu
Parking/Fees: limited free roadside parking
Hours: 6 A.M.-sunset

Facilities: lifeguards and restrooms
Contact: Los Angeles County Lifeguard Service, Northern Section, 310/394-3264

32 ESCONDIDO BEACH

Location: path at Escondido Creek near Malibu Cove Colony Drive in Malibu
Parking/Fees: limited free roadside parking
Hours: sunrise–sunset
Facilities: none
Contact: Malibu Division of the Angeles District of the California Department of Parks and Recreation, 310/457-8140

33 PARADISE COVE

Location: 28128 Pacific Coast Highway in Malibu
Parking/Fees: $25 entrance fee per car
Hours: sunrise–sunset
Facilities: concession, lifeguards, and restrooms
Contact: Paradise Cove, 310/457-2511

34 POINT DUME COUNTY BEACH

Location: end of Westward Beach Road, on the north side of Point Dume, in Malibu
Parking/Fees: $7 entrance fee per car
Hours: 6 A.M.–sunset
Facilities: lifeguards, restrooms, and showers
Contact: Los Angeles County Lifeguard Service, Northern Section, 310/394-3264

35 ZUMA COUNTY BEACH
     BEST (

Location: four miles north of Malibu at 30000 Pacific Coast Highway

Parking/Fees: $7 entrance fee per vehicle
Hours: 6 A.M.–sunset
Facilities: concession, lifeguards, restrooms, and showers
Contact: Los Angeles County Lifeguard Service, Northern Section, 310/394-3264

36 BROAD BEACH

Location: stairways lead to the beach from Broad Beach Road at Highway 1 in Malibu
Parking/Fees: limited free street parking
Hours: 6 A.M.–sunset
Facilities: none
Contact: Los Angeles County Department of Beaches and Harbors, 310/305-9503

37 EL MATADOR STATE BEACH

Location: six miles north of Malibu at 32350 Pacific Coast Highway
Parking/Fees: $2 entrance fee per vehicle
Hours: 6 A.M.–sunset
Facilities: restrooms
Contact: Malibu Sector, Angeles District, California State Parks, 310/457-8143

38 LA PIEDRA STATE BEACH

Location: seven miles north of Malibu at 32700 Pacific Coast Highway
Parking/Fees: $2 entrance fee per vehicle
Hours: 6 A.M.–sunset
Facilities: restrooms
Contact: Malibu Sector, Angeles District, California State Parks, 310/457-8143

© PARKE PUTERBAUGH

El Matador State Beach

39 EL PESCADOR STATE BEACH

Location: 7.5 miles north of Malibu at 32900 Pacific Coast Highway
Parking/Fees: $2 entrance fee per vehicle
Hours: 6 A.M.-sunset
Facilities: restrooms
Contact: Malibu Sector, Angeles District, California State Parks, 310/457-8143

40 NICHOLAS CANYON COUNTY BEACH

Location: nine miles north of Malibu at Nicholas Canyon Road and Highway 1
Parking/Fees: $7 entrance fee per vehicle
Hours: 6 A.M.-sunset
Facilities: lifeguards, restrooms, and picnic tables
Contact: Los Angeles County Lifeguard Service, Northern Section, 310/394-3264

ACCOMMODATIONS

Malibu has exactly one luxury ocean hotel along its 27 miles, the fabulous **Malibu Beach Inn** (22878 Pacific Coast Highway, 310/456-6444, www.malibubeachinn.com, $$$$). This three-story, pink-stucco wonder is perched beside—and, at high tide, directly above—the ocean. When they say oceanfront, they're not exaggerating. You can open the balcony doors of your room and let the sounds of the churning, crashing ocean lull you to sleep. The complimentary breakfast buffet includes wonderful pastries, fresh fruit, cereal, and coffee. You can carry it to an outdoor sundeck and enjoy the morning meal over a copy of the *Los Angeles Times*. The rattan furniture and contemporary California decor enhance the sense of a relaxed getaway at the ocean's edge. And rooms are a princely $490–675, with suites going for $875–1,350. Oh yes, for that extra touch, you can pay $20 to get a "rose petal turndown."

If you're going to pay top dollar for a place at the beach, you will find no nicer spot to do it than the Malibu Beach Inn. We have our own homemade souvenirs of the visit, incidentally: cassettes of waves breaking on the beach below, made with our portable recorders. The inn has won Robin Leach's seal of approval (check out the handwritten note just inside the lobby), and who better knows about refined lifestyles than he? Situated a short distance down from Malibu Pier, the inn can, incidentally, arrange delivery of a meal from Alice's Restaurant, a long-standing landmark at the base of the pier.

COASTAL CUISINE

Granita (23725 West Malibu Road, 310/456-0488, $$$) is the hands-down standout on the Malibu dining scene. This star attraction in celebrity chef Wolfgang Puck's arsenal of California restaurants has won over even jaded Malibu natives, who are wowed by its beachside proximity, its underwater fantasy decor (done in handmade ceramic tile and etched glass), and such dishes as Mediterranean fish soup, lobster club sandwich, spicy shrimp pizza, and seared scallops over black-pepper fettuccine. Dress is Malibu casual: informal but neat. You may need to call up to a week in advance for a reservation, especially on weekends.

Another popular hangout is **Coogie's Beach Cafe** (23750 Malibu Road, 310/317-1444, $$), a spacious, high-ceilinged restaurant in a shopping center. Coogie's serves Malibu-style cuisine (indulgent and creative but healthy) at fair prices. All the salads are good, as are items like fresh Alaskan salmon patties with dill, served with a plate of eggs any style. It's a very Malibu kind of place, and you're likely to be surrounded by any number of Hollywood notables slumming in their casual wear. No one pays them (or you) any mind; that's part of the unspoken code of civility in celebrity-thick Malibu.

You can't get anything you want at **Alice's Restaurant** (Malibu Pier, 23000 Pacific Coast Highway, 310/456-6646, $$$), but your choices range to such satisfying selections as red snapper or shrimp sautéed with garlic, shallots, and tomatoes. And, of course, the B52 cocktail, for which the bartenders are famous; it apparently gets you "bombed." The **Reel Inn** (18661 Pacific Coast Highway, 310/456-

8221, $$) is a favorite of locals (especially surfing locals) who step up to the counter for everything from fresh fish to tacos.

Up at the opposite end of Malibu, directly across the street from County Line Beach, is a restaurant and fresh-seafood shop with the promising name **Neptune's Net** (42505 Pacific Coast Highway, 310/457-3095, $). It's the kind of place that we tend to romanticize—off the beaten track, filled with local color, offering fresh, nonfranchised food. In reality, much more could be done with it. Still, the location is unsurpassable.

NIGHTLIFE

Nightlife has never been a big proposition up in Malibu, the whole idea being that it is an enclave for people who prefer not to be recognized. Nonetheless, a good time can be had at the **Malibu Inn** (22969 Pacific Coast Highway, 310/456-6060), a riotously fun restaurant and saloon. Its ceiling is bedecked with a bizarre collage of metal wheels, surfboards (one serrated with shark-teeth indentations), baseball mitts, and bric-a-brac. You can order food, if you wish, through a huge, red pair of plastic lips. There's a pool table, bar, some tables, and a sawdust-strewn wood floor in the main part of the saloon. The Malibu Inn is as down to earth as it gets. Lest you think Malibu is all reclusive celebrities and pricey cafés, duck in here for a brew with the surfing clan.

Finally, in the interest of cultural history, we recommend a visit to **Moonshadows** (20356 Pacific Coast Highway, 310/456-3010). It was here, in August 2006, that Mel Gibson got so sloshed that, when pulled over by the police on his way home, he felt duty-bound to lecture them on Middle East history, biblical ideas, and female anatomy. He excoriated "the Jews," called one of the arresting officers "Sugar Tits," and then went into rehab, as they all do after behaving abysmally.

The tabloid press and paparazzi would go into a serious tailspin without celebrities to trail in Malibu—making note of hard and flabby bods on its beaches, monitoring the latest drunk-driving arrests on Pacific Coast Highway, and stalking their prey's every move, including the most banal daily visits to Starbucks. How boring our world would be without celebrity cellulite to cluck about, new serpentine tattoos to ogle, rumored affairs to lose sleep over, and, of course Britney Spears's latest outrage, right? Wrong. Get a life, America.

Leo Carrillo State Park

Malibu's marvelous procession of beaches reaches its crescendo with Leo Carrillo State Park. The 3,000-acre park encompasses two sections of beach, separated by Sequit Point, and a 139-site campground arrayed along a loop road in a scenic, fragrant canyon on the landward side of the Pacific Coast Highway. Nestled amid eucalyptus and sycamore groves, the campsites here are absolutely enthralling. Few other parks in the country can offer access to beach and mountains in such proximity. You are on the geological cutting edge of California's tectonic assembly line here.

For more information, contact Leo Carrillo State Park, 36000 Pacific Coast Highway, 818/880-0350. www.parks.ca.gov.

BEACHES

Leo Carrillo State Park's 1.5 miles worth of beaches are steeply sloped with coarse brown sand. When we visited, little kids were getting waxed on the beach by crashing breakers, while big kids who bobbed in the offshore kelp beds atop surfboards were also being slammed to the mat by the waves' decisive crashes. The surf here is not for the inexperienced or faint of heart, but the setting is as magnificent as any you'll find on either coast, offering sea

caves and tidepools to explore, acres of sand to spread out on, and a scenic mountainous backdrop to gaze upon. For surfers there are good southerly swells, though the offshore and onshore rocks are intimidating.

Up by the Ventura County line vans and cars line the road, and surfers scamper down the steep, reddish-brown bluffs. **County Line Beach** is a favorite of Southern California surfriders, accorded a status on par with such legendary breaks as Rincon and Windansea. And this is where Malibu and Los Angeles County finally come to an end.

41 LEO CARRILLO STATE PARK

BEST

Location: one mile south of the Ventura County line at 36000 Pacific Coast Highway
Parking/Fees: $10 entrance fee per vehicle; camping fees $20-25 per night, plus $7.50 reservation fee
Hours: 8 A.M.-sunset
Facilities: concession, lifeguards, restrooms, showers, and picnic tables
Contact: Leo Carrillo State Park, 818/880-0350

42 COUNTY LINE BEACH

Location: Pacific Coast Highway at Ventura County line
Parking/Fees: limited free roadside parking
Hours: 8 A.M.-sunset
Facilities: none
Contact: Leo Carrillo State Park, 818/880-0350

ORANGE COUNTY

Although the oranges are mostly gone and the county embodies the worst aspects of America's addiction to cars, shopping malls, suburban sprawl, right-wing politics, environmental despoliation, corporate wheeling-dealing, and youth-culture narcissism, the glorious beaches of Orange County are here (we hope and pray) forever. They start with pleasant understatement at San Clemente, an almost quaint community that's lifted into the present tense mainly by its world-class surfing scene. And they work their way up to Seal Beach, a charming town sandwiched between the hulking Goliaths of Huntington Beach and Long Beach.

Most of Orange County's oceanfront was similarly low-key only decades ago. Many beaches singled out by name in the Beach Boys' 1963 classic "Surfin' USA" are in Orange County. But in the years since they celebrated Southern California in song, a major real-estate land rush has effectively walled off much of the prime beachfront in Orange County for the private enjoyment of...God knows who. Nobody we consort with, that's for sure! The worst sins were committed at Dana Point and Huntington Beach—great surfing spots where those who most love the shore (and who have the least impact upon it) are now persona non grata. They're the ones with living memories of how these places used to be.

Orange County's mid-1990s fiscal meltdown, the entire state's turn-of-the-millennium dot-com collapse, the stock market slide and corporate accounting scandals of 2002, the subprime mortgage meltdown and recession of 2008 have all revealed the viciously destructive end results of the greed agenda. Perhaps these revelations will pave the way for a more environmentally and socially responsible mind-set that will spare Orange County's lovely shoreline further developmental

© PARKE PUTERBAUGH

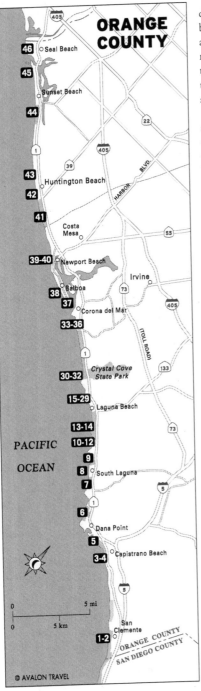

ORANGE
COUNTY

Seal Beach

Sunset Beach

Huntington Beach

Costa
Mesa

Newport Beach

Irvine

Balboa

Corona del Mar

Crystal Cove
State Park

Laguna Beach

PACIFIC

OCEAN

South Laguna

Dana Point

Capistrano Beach

San
Clemente

ORANGE COUNTY
SAN DIEGO COUNTY

0   5 mi

0   5 km

© AVALON TRAVEL

desecration. Granted, it's a far-fetched theory, but we're not above grasping at straws. In reality, we know full well that in a place where money and its materialistic flaunting function as a surrogate religion, any changes to the status quo will be slow in coming and staunchly resisted.

The legendary reputation of Orange County as a bastion of starchy conservatism is well deserved. In this decade, the progeny of all these filthy rich Republican Party donors have become the subjects of several highly successful fictional and "reality"-based TV shows: *The O.C., Laguna Beach,* and *The Hills.* The last of these, which tracks the lives of a few mindless skirts and their party pals, is enough to dissuade a thinking person from ever even visiting Orange County. Here are brief synopses of a few episodes: "Lauren receives flowers and another phone call from Jason." "Heidi gets her big chance to work in the nightclub scene." "Heidi finds out the results of her pregnancy test while Lauren and Whitney are asked to cover a major fashion show."

Orange County's world of political conservatism, social vapidity, and gas-guzzling consumerism has also given rise to its attitudinal opposite: a subculture of punk-rock and hardcore bands who loathe all forms of authority, stupidity, and conspicuous consumption. It's quite a mix of sensibilities going on here in "O.C.," once you start scratching beneath the surface. But we're beach writers first and sociologists second, so we'd simply advise ignoring this mindless cacophony and heading to the shimmering sand beaches of Orange County. Many of its beaches are succulent treasures that will lift the spirit and body like fresh oranges plucked right off the tree. Two of its beach towns—Laguna Beach and Newport Beach—are among our all-time favorites.

San Clemente

Nestled in the hilly contours of the California coast halfway between San Diego and Los

BEST BEACHES

◖ **Doheny State Beach,
page 85**

◖ **Main Beach, page 96**

◖ **Los Trancos, page 102**

◖ **Newport Beach Municipal
Beach, page 107**

◖ **Huntington City Beach,
page 116**

Angeles, San Clemente (population 62,000) is fully removed from the sprawl that slithers toward it from all directions. It has little in common with the harried metropolitan world that bears down upon it. Rather, San Clemente is an entity unto itself, rather like a small-scale Santa Barbara.

Promoting this sense of cozy self-containment is the layout of city streets, which take their cue from the area's geography. San Clemente's roads meander in awkward semicircles, following topographical contours. This confuses one's sense of direction and forces visitors to pay closer attention to their surroundings than they would if driving some boring old grid. And pay attention you do: to beautiful houses, verdant shrubs and gorgeous flowers, and surrounding hills that plunge dramatically to the sea.

The town is built above some striking beaches, with weathered bluffs and scantily vegetated hills rising behind it. Avenida del Mar links El Camino Real (the main drag, which parallels I-5) with the municipal pier and beach. It passes through the heart of town, a shopping and business district that could pass for Anytown, USA. For every cutesy boutique there's a plain old mom-and-pop store serving some basic community need for things like prescription drugs, camera equipment, stationery, and "notions." (When was the last time you heard that word used?) You can sip a civilized cup of coffee at an outdoor café and watch folks amble by, evincing none of the stressful hysteria that sends the rest of us to shrinks, doctors, and an early grave.

Perhaps it is this restful calm that inspired a sitting U.S. president to acquire a second home in San Clemente. The late Richard Nixon put this small town on the map in 1969 by turning Casa Pacifica—a Spanish-style, red-roofed estate at the south end of town—into the Western White House. Built in 1927 by one Hamilton Cotton, Casa Pacifica served as Nixon's home away from the White House during the tumultuous era of Vietnam and Watergate. Coincidentally, the estate faced one of the best surfing spots in all of California (Cotton Point, informally known as "Cotton's"), and surfer lore is filled with tales of trying to outfox the Secret Service in an effort to get to it. Though the way to the waves is more easily negotiated these days, it's still no picnic. Surfers face a half-mile hike down paths of scalding sand and asphalt with boards atop their heads. There's nothing to suggest the Prez attempted the feat himself, but maybe he was actually hipper than anyone knew. During a tape-recorded tour of the Nixon Library (40 miles from San Clemente, in Yorba Linda), the late president allows that "if there had been a good rap group around in those days, I might have chosen a career in music instead of politics." Would he have called the act Tricky Dick and DJ Watergate?

The return to pre-presidential calm after Nixon left office suited San Clemente just fine. It's a lovely, unassuming town that looks much as it did when it was advertised to prospective buyers in 1925 as "a village done in the fashion of Old Spain." Named in 1602 by the

THE ORANGE COUNTY THEME SONG

(sung to the tune of "Green Acres")

male voice:
Orange County is the place to be
Golf and tennis is the life for me
Fairways spreading out so far and wide
Suburban sprawl
To hell with the countryside!

female voice:
Newport is where I come to play
I try on clothes and shoes all day
Shopping binges are what I adore
Darling, I love you
But give me Fashion Island's stores.

he:
Golf balls!

she:
Huge malls!

he:
Corvettes!

she:
Credit debt!

both:
We are alike
We love our moneyed life!
Orange County
We are there!

explorer Sebastian Vizcaino in honor of Saint Clement—whose feast day coincided with the date of discovery—San Clemente was one of California's first planned communities. The founder was Ole Hanson, a former mayor of Seattle. In 1925 Hanson and three partners purchased and designed a 2,000-acre parcel in the classic Spanish style, hoping to attract folks who'd grown tired of big-city living to "San Clemente by the Sea." More of an aesthetic visionary than today's barf-it-up developers, Hanson rhapsodized, "San Clemente is just a painting five miles long and over a mile wide...its foreground the sea, its background the hills. We use for our pigments flowers and shrubs and trees and red tile and white plaster." Some 75 years later, the painting remains sufficiently impressive to make an art lover out of any visitor.

For more information, contact the San Clemente Chamber of Commerce, 1100 North El Camino Real, San Clemente, CA 92672, 949/492-1131, www.scchamber.com.

BEACHES

San Clemente is a town so full of civic pride that it has its own city song, "On the Beach of San Clemente." We can't warble that little ditty, but we'll happily sing the praises of San Clemente's beaches. Avenida del Mar slams to an end at **San Clemente City Beach,** where a historic 1,200-foot pier dates from the 1920s. There's a municipal parking lot, restrooms and showers, and all the usual amenities of a well-tended city beach. The beach is accessible from the west end of Avenida del Mar and numerous street ends and paths along the two-mile stretch from San Clemente State Beach to Ole Hanson Beach Club (a public pool and playground), with the city beach at the center.

A small, hut-like Amtrak station sits next to railroad tracks so close to the ocean they practically get licked by the waves at high tide. The surf is strong all along the coast around here, drawing an enthusiastic knot of surfing devotees. At high tide large breakers slam into the pier pilings, turning the frothing water a milky green. The soft, brown-sand beach draws a vibrant young crowd, with surfers congregating around the pier.

Seaside bed-and-breakfasts and outdoor cafés face the beach along Avenida Victoria, which runs beside the ocean for a short distance before looping up, up, and away. On a nice summer day—and all the ones we've

GETTING AROUND THE BIG ORANGE

As a "humor columnist" for a local real-estate publication put it, "Orange County is car culture...You can be sleepless in Seattle, but don't get caught being carless in Orange County. Other cities have mass transit; here it's auto transit en masse."

As his column unfolded, the less amusing reality of this maniacal fume-sucking freeway gridlock reared its ugly head. For example, the dimwitted writer confessed that "some of us spend more time driving than we do with our families. Cell phones keep us connected, but it's a poor substitute for actually being there." Ya think?

He went on to offer these knee-slapping tips about getting around Orange County: "Avoid the El Toro Y at all times." [Ba-da-bump.] "There is never a good time to drive the 22." [Ba-da-bump.] "Avoid the 55 north during daylight hours." [Ba-da-bump.] "And evenings, avoid every road to the beach in the summer." [Ba-da-bump.]

Oh, sorry, apparently he was being serious there.

We know from personal experience that driving in Orange County is no laughing matter. It is a waking nightmare. This reality was brought home to us when we attended an Angels vs. Orioles major-league baseball game in Anaheim one summer evening. It was only 18 miles from our motel in Newport Beach to Anaheim. No problem! Or so we thought. We wound up mired in unmoving traffic jams both before and after the game. At 11 P.M. on a weeknight, traffic was backed up even worse than before the game. We found ourselves stuck on the freeway for what seemed like an eternity. The delay wasn't due to wrecks or a departing game crowd (only 15,000 attended). It was due partly to road construction – the freeway widening and repairing never ends in Southern California – and partly to the traffic that never abates at any hour. As midnight approached, the delay became absurd. An hour and a half to go 18 miles?

Orange County continues subsidizing freeway building and widening projects with revenue from Measure M, a half-cent sales tax approved by voters in 1990 and re-approved by voters in 2006. The proceeds fund countywide transportation improvements, with 43 percent earmarked for freeways. The question is, do more and wider freeways represent real "improvement" or just more problems? Road building has reached such an unutterable state of lunacy in Orange County that the

ever spent in San Clemente have been ideal—the area in the vicinity of San Clemente City Beach has the charmingly upscale aura of a Mediterranean village, with climate to match. You couldn't ask for better weather: average highs of 68 degrees in June, 73 degrees in September (the hottest month), and 66 degrees in December. There are less than 10 inches of rain and 342 days of sunshine per year. In a word, it's perfect.

San Clemente State Beach offers some of the best coastal camping (153 sites, of which 72 have RV hookups) in the state. Whereas the municipal beach is wide and hospitable to swimmers and surfers, the state beach is narrow, prone to rip currents, and almost primevally wild. A campground overlooks the mile-long beach from atop 50-foot bluffs. Trees afford some protection from the summer sun, and the place vaguely recalls national parks of the Southwest—Bryce or Zion Canyon, for instance—in miniature. An asphalt trail leads down a steep, dramatically eroded ravine to the beach. Railroad tracks run extremely close to the water, protected by riprap. Near the water's edge, the sand slopes sharply. Breakers scurry up the beach face, and an occasional tongue of foam licks the dry sand above it. It's great for beach hiking; the solitude and the scenic backdrop are stunning. Diving is popular but swimming is discouraged, and surfers choose to hotfoot

El Toro Y – the infamous bottleneck where the San Diego Freeway (I-405) and Santa Ana Freeway (I-5) meet – has been expanded to 26 lanes at its widest point. Moreover, they're proud of this "modern interchange," which is blithely referred to as "Orange County's Main Street."

Despite the terrible cost in wasted fossil fuel and lost time at home and on the job, Orange County has been slow to implement long-term transportation solutions. They've even nixed mass-transit projects. For instance, plans were drawn up for a light-rail system, the CenterLine, that would have connected some of the most densely populated and highly traveled population centers in O.C. The first phase in this long-overdue project was to be an 18-mile, 22-station line between Santa Ana and Irvine. However, after 12 years of planning and $68 million spent on studies, design, and lobbying, the Orange County Transportation Authority (OCTA) board of directors voted unanimously in April 2005 to indefinitely postpone the CenterLine light-rail project.

According to *Railway Age* magazine, "A primary reason for the board's action was lack of support for the 9.3-mile, $1 billion scheme among the county's mostly Republican congressional delegation, whose help would be vital to obtain $483 million in federal funding." The commentary just writes itself, doesn't it? One thing's for sure: Without decisive action, the Orange crush on the freeways will, if possible, only get worse. Future generations will curse those leaders who have been dragging their feet today.

For now, the most beach-friendly mode of conveyance is the excellent bus system run by the OCTA. Numerous routes operate from inland cities to such coastal locales as Huntington Beach, Seal Beach, Newport Beach, Laguna Beach, Dana Point, and San Clemente. The coast-hugging Bus Route 1 runs along Pacific Coast Highway from San Clemente to Long Beach. Yes, you can travel Orange County's entire coastline for a mere $1.25 fare! Moreover, any and all routes in the county can be ridden for $3 per day or $45 per month. We call that a bargain and a bright note amid all of Orange County's freeway madness.

For information, schedules, and fares, contact the **Orange County Transportation Authority,** 550 South Main Street, P.O. Box 14184, Orange, CA 92868, 714/636-7433, www.octa.net.

---

down to better waves at Cotton's and Trestles, which straddle the San Diego County line from opposite sides of San Mateo Point. If you happen to see a surfer or two studying the distant waves from a freeway off-ramp south of town, they're weighing whether it's worth the long walk to the water. And a long, sandy scramble it is, from the south end of El Camino Real near Carl's Jr. (which is where most people park) down to Trestles, which is part of San Onofre State Beach.

San Clemente is home to the **Surfrider Foundation** (120½ South El Camino Real #207, San Clemente, CA 92672, 949/492-8170, www.surfrider.org), the advocacy group that acts on behalf of coastal environmental matters and other issues of interest to surfers.

❶ SAN CLEMENTE STATE BEACH

Location: Take the Avenida Calafia exit from I-5 in San Clemente and follow it west to park.

Parking/Fees: $10 entrance fee per vehicle; camping fees $29-34 per night with hookups, $20-25 per night without hookups, plus a $7.50 reservation fee

Hours: 6 A.M.-8 P.M. (to 10 P.M. during Daylight Savings Time)

Facilities: lifeguards, restrooms, showers, and picnic areas

Contact: San Clemente State Beach, 949/492-3156

San Clemente

© PARKE PUTERBAUGH

② SAN CLEMENTE CITY BEACH

Location: Avenida del Mar at Avenida Victoria in San Clemente
Parking/Fees: metered street parking
Hours: 4 A.M.–midnight
Facilities: concession, lifeguards, restrooms, showers, and picnic area
Contact: San Clemente Department of Marine Safety, 949/361-8219

RECREATION AND ATTRACTIONS

- **Bike/Skate Rentals:** San Clemente Cyclery and Sport, 2801 South El Camino Real, San Clemente, 949/492-8890

- **Ecotourism:** Orange County Marine Institute, 24200 Dana Point Harbor Drive, Dana Point, 949/496-2274

- **Marina:** Dana Point Marina, 34555 Casitas Place, Dana Point, 949/496-6137

- **Pier:** San Clemente Pier, 611 South Avenida Victoria, San Clemente, 949/492-8335

- **Rainy Day Attraction:** Mission San Juan Capistrano, 31414 Camino Capistrano, San Juan Capistrano, 949/234-1300

- **Shopping/Browsing:** Laguna Village, 577 South Coast Highway, Laguna Beach, 949/494-1956

- **Sportfishing:** Dana Point Sportfishing, 34675 Golden Lantern, Dana Point, 949/496-5794

- **Surf Report:** 949/492-1011

- **Surf Shops:** Rip Curl Surf Center, 3801 South El Camino Real, San Clemente, 949/498-4920; Costa Azul, 689 South Coast Highway, Laguna Beach, 949/4971423

- **Vacation Rentals:** Laguna Beach Oceanfront Rental, 900 Glenneyre Street, Laguna Beach, 949/494-8110

ACCOMMODATIONS

Across the street from San Clemente Municipal Pier is a charming block where a smattering of bed-and-breakfasts offer wonderful beach views at top-end prices. One is **Casa Tropicana** (610 Avenida Victoria, 949/492-1234, www.casatropicana.com, $$$), whose theme rooms (e.g., Out of Africa, Emerald

Forest, and South Pacific) overlook the pier at prices that will quickly bring you down to earth (up to $350 a night). Another is the **Villa del Mar Inn** (612 Avenida Victoria, 949/498-5080, www.seahorsesanclemente.com, $$$), whose condo-style suites offer beach-facing sundecks, big living rooms, and fully equipped kitchens. Rooms run $150–199 in the high season and drop by $70 a night the rest of the year. Since the weather barely changes from month to month, the off-season rates are a real bargain.

The **San Clemente Inn** (2600 Avenida del Presidente, 949/492-6103, www.san clementeinn.com, $$), which abuts San Clemente State Park, operates as a hotel condominium, offering apartment-style suites on grounds that include a pool and spa, shuffleboard courts, and gargantuan pineapple trees. In this largely unfancy town, the **Holiday Inn San Clemente Resort** (111 South Avenida del Estrella, 949/412-6126, $$), a white-stucco wonder convenient to the beach, has the chain-motel competition beat when it comes to amenities: heated pool, spa, fitness center, sundeck with a view, decent on-site restaurant.

COASTAL CUISINE

Look no further than the San Clemente Municipal Pier for dinner. You have two choices: the **Fisherman's Restaurant** (611 Avenida Victoria, 949/498-6390, $$$), on the left side of the pier, and **Fisherman's Bar** (611 Avenida Victoria, 949/498-6390, $$) on the right. They serve good, fresh, Pacific seafood at both places. The restaurant's dinner menu ranges from fish 'n' chips to whole Dungeness crab. If you're toting a huge appetite, ante up for an all-you-can-eat feast of clams, halibut, salmon, swordfish, or crab, served with salad, rice pilaf, sourdough bread, and Fisherman's chowder. The bar tends more toward heavy appetizers.

Across the street, the **Beach Garden Cafe** (685½ Avenida Victoria, 949/498-8145, $) is a cute, modern eatery serving omelets, sandwiches, pizzas, and entrées such as fish 'n' chips. On a more substantial note, the **Rib Trader** (911 South El Camino Real, 949/492-6665, $$$) serves ribs, steaks, and other hearty surf-and-turf fare. It also has a bar area set off from the main dining room that's a favorite place for the surfing cult to congregate and quaff a few after the sun's gone down.

Finally, in deference to the surfing community, we feel obliged to mention **Surfin' Donuts Coffee House** (1822 South El Camino Real, 949/492-1249, and 1110 South El Camino Real, 949/361-2120, $). After all, some of the best surfing spots, surfboard makers, and surfing magazines are headquartered here in unassuming San Clemente. In a town geared to surfers, it stands to reason that you can get some of the best "surfin' donuts" in all creation, too.

NIGHTLIFE

After sunset, best watched from the pier, San Clemente gets quieter than an orange grove. Laguna Beach and San Juan Capistrano are the nearest outposts of serious nightlife. A cocktail waitress at the San Clemente Pier tipped us off to a particularly lively club up the coast where it was reggae night. "Have you ever heard of reggae music?" she asked, as if she were an elementary school teacher introducing a new vowel sound. We didn't feel like letting our dreadlocks down that night and remained happily glued to our perches at **Fisherman's Bar** (611 Avenida Victoria, 949/498-6390), enjoying the pier's relative tranquility.

Capistrano Beach

Enfolding the coastline between Dana Point and San Clemente, the Capistrano Beach area has been rather overoptimistically marketed as "California's Riviera." In actuality, Capistrano Beach is a small and relatively uncrowded seaside sanctuary. That quality, a virtual novelty in overbuilt Southern California, sets Capistrano Beach apart from its neighbors. For instance, San Juan Capistrano—a larger town that has scared away its famous swallows

ORANGE COUNTY

WHERE HAVE ALL THE SWALLOWS GONE?

The story of the swallows of San Juan Capistrano is a major chapter in California's legend and lore. Each year the swallows, ever-reliable in the constancy of their re-appearance, make the 6,000-mile trip from Goya, Argentina, to **Mission San Juan Capistrano.** They arrive on March 19, build nests and hatch their chicks, then depart for the winter on October 23. You can set your calendar by them.

The date of their spring arrival is known as St. Joseph's Day (a.k.a. Swallow Day). Large numbers of tourists turn out to greet the swallows, a ritual highlighted for years by the 8 A.M. ringing of the mission bells. Everybody *oohs* and *ahs* over the return of the little five-inch gliding birds. It's a great day for birds and bird-watchers alike.

In recent decades, however, the truth of the matter has become a little harder to, uh, swallow. On March 19, 1992, a reporter brought an ornithologist to San Juan Capistrano, and not a single swallow was spotted. In 1993, an estimated 25,000 tourists doubled the town's population over the weekend. Thousands turned out in the early morning to witness the flapping of four startled birds who were roused from the mission eaves by the aged bell-ringer. The swallows of Capistrano were outnumbered, according to published accounts, by pigeons. Nonetheless, a celebratory parade of 4,000 people, many on horseback, took place in the afternoon. That's a human-to-bird ratio of 1,000 to 1. Does something seem cuckoo about all this? Driven away by renovations at Mission San Juan Capistrano, among other things, they apparently went elsewhere. In 1997, they set up camp at the Tillman Water Reclamation Plant, in the San Fernando Valley. In 2000, six birds were counted.

In order to entice birds to the mission, it was reported that "mission officials tried to entice swallows by scattering ladybugs on the rose bushes, making mud puddles to be used for nest building, and even building fake ceramic nests to con the birds into thinking there were friends nearby." Do they take the swallows for birdbrains?

The reduction of insects in the area, due to development, has also contributed to the swallows' need to nest elsewhere. And so they no longer darken the skies of San Juan Capistrano, as they once did, though that doesn't stop the community from celebrating their arrival anyway. March 29, 2008, marked the 50th anniversary of the Swallow Day Parade in San Juan Capistrano.

by razing orange groves and constructing shopping malls and boxy stucco homes on every available square inch—offers what more cliché-minded travel writers would refer to as "fabulous shopping opportunities." To us it's just another infernal gash in the landscape drawn to bleed the unconscious consumer. Much of Orange County, particularly its interior sprawl, has come to resemble a Hieronymus Bosch vision of hell, with groaning condominiums and howling land speculators for harpies.

Stick to the beach; it's pleasant out here, and there's plenty to go around. Capistrano Beach has got a nice, unhurried way about it.

Whether you're looking out to sea from the beach or the palisades above, it's a pianissimo passage in the Wagnerian symphony of overdevelopment that characterizes much of the coast from San Diego to Los Angeles.

For more information, contact the Dana Point Chamber of Commerce & Visitor Center, Clocktower Building, La Plaza Center, Dana Point, CA 92524, 949/496-1555, www.danapoint-chamber.com; or the San Juan Capistrano Chamber of Commerce, 31781 Camino Capistrano, San Juan Capistrano, CA 92675, 949/493-4700 or 800/290-DANA, www.sanjuanchamber.com.

BEACHES

Capistrano Beach Park and Doheny State Beach (described later in this chapter) are the main access points in an unbroken stretch that runs along Capistrano Bight up to Dana Point. On a nice day the beaches here look almost too good to be true: a mirage of white sand and emerald water gleaming beneath a bright blue sky. Down on the shoreline, Capistrano Beach boasts a wide, unblemished public beach. A road called the Palisades drops down from steep residential hills to meet Pacific Coast Highway near the entrance to Capistrano Beach. A large parking lot with inexpensive metered parking faces the ocean, and pedestrian overpasses cross the highway at several points. The beach is popular but seldom overrun. At 7 A.M. one drizzly May morning, a group of teenage girls enthusiastically engaged in a little pre-school volleyball practice. Meanwhile, cars idled along the lip of the lot, their drivers lost in meditative contemplation before heading off to a hard day of hammering nails or making deals.

The parking lot runs beside the beach for a good distance, and people aerobicize along it in jogging shoes and in-line skates. By midmorning a furious full-court basketball game was in progress. In the distance surfers congregated off Doheny Point. Just another day in the life of a prime Southern California beach. At the south end of Capistrano Beach, where Camino Capistrano runs out at Pacific Coast Highway, a pedestrian underpass leads to **Poche Beach,** a sandy surfing beach just above the landslide that closed a stretch of PCH in 1993. Incidentally, *Surfer* magazine is published in Capistrano Beach, and surfboards are manufactured here.

⑧ POCHE BEACH

Location: Camino Capistrano at Pacific Coast Highway in Capistrano Beach
Parking/Fees: free street parking
Hours: 6 A.M.-10 P.M.
Facilities: none
Contact: South Beaches Operation Office of Orange County Harbors, Beaches, and Parks, 714/834-2400

④ CAPISTRANO BEACH PARK

Location: El Camino Real at Palisade Drive in Capistrano Beach
Parking/Fees: pay parking lots ($1 per hour)
Hours: 6 A.M.-10 P.M.
Facilities: concession, lifeguards, restrooms, showers, and picnic tables
Contact: South Beaches Operation Office of Orange County Harbors, Beaches, and Parks, 714/834-2400

ACCOMMODATIONS

On the landward side of Pacific Coast Highway is **Capistrano Surfside Inn** (34680 Pacific Coast Highway, 949/240-7681, www.capistranosurfsideinn.com, $$$), a time-share condo complex that also operates like a hotel. Commodious one- and two-bedroom suites come with full kitchens and outdoor balconies stocked with furniture and gas grills. Rooms start at $275. A schedule of optional activities for guests includes day trips to beaches on Mexico's Baja Peninsula. Close by is **Holiday Inn Express** (34744 Pacific Coast Highway, 949/240-0150, $$$). Formerly the Capistrano Edgewater Inn, it offers comparable prices, views, and amenities.

COASTAL CUISINE

A famous Mexican restaurant called **Olamendi's** (34660 Pacific Coast Highway, 949/661-1005, $$) does a big business in burritos across from the beach. Its popularity is easy to gauge from the frequently full parking lot. Inside, moderately priced Mexican food of good quality is served at padded, semicircular booths. Tacos, burritos, and enchiladas are presented every conceivable way (stuffed with shredded beef, steak, chicken, fish, pork, and cheese). The menu carries a one-word endorsement from the late Richard Nixon: "Excellent." Up by the cash register hangs a picture of El Presidente, nervously posed with the kitchen staff. If you're hankering for something more high-end, head to nearby Dana Point or San Juan Capistrano.

NIGHTLIFE

The after-hours options in Capistrano Beach are as weak as the glow from a child's night-light, but you stand a good chance of catching some great music at the **Coach House** (33157 Camino Capistrano, 949/496-8930) in nearby San Juan Capistrano. This 480-seat hall books singer/songwriters, alternative rockers, roots-oriented musicians, reunited New Wave groups, and recherche hair-metal bands. You might see anyone from the Blasters to L.A. Guns, Eve 6, and A Flock of Seagulls on the marquee when you're passing through. Unfortunately, in an age when the live-music scene is struggling, you might also see such god-awful dreck as a Chippendale's male revue. Coach House serves an appetizer-heavy dinner menu.

Incidentally, "San Juan Cap" (as it's known to locals) is a formerly quaint, mission-style community now beset with endless malls whose acreage rivals that of a cattle ranch. The train station is the hub of weekend nightlife. Everyone from wandering minstrels on down performs for the assembled masses, some of whom ride the rails down from Los Angeles just to be part of the crowd.

Dana Point

A nine-foot bronze statue of seaman and writer Richard Henry Dana Jr. looks out over the harbor that's named after him. Dana came here in the 1830s aboard the square rigger *Pilgrim*. He recorded his experiences as a naïf on the high seas in the autobiographical narrative *Two Years Before the Mast,* a California liter-

ary classic. He also described the cliff-backed cove at Dana Point as "the only romantic spot in California." We beg to differ with the estimable writer on this point. Number one, there are plenty of romantic spots in California. Number two, Dana Point is no longer one of them.

Of course Dana himself had nothing to do with the artificial facelift that turned the rugged environment he knew and loved into a sanitized playground for the wealthy, so we won't hold him accountable on this last point. Instead, we'll direct our venom toward those dissemblers of public-relations jive who use his words to promote the arid development that calmed the waves and transformed the landscape. The refashioning of Dana Point (population 35,700) into a 2,500-slip yacht harbor—which began in 1969, when the Orange County Board of Supervisors approved construction of a jetty, harbor, and harborside community—is the sort of tale that would have inspired a salty young sailor like Dana to mutiny. Indeed, were Dana around to see the area today, he would scarcely comprehend the changes that have taken place since his time. The man-made Dana Harbor has stilled the waves for yuppie yachts, while Mariner's Village developers have erected a faux New England fishing village that is a mockery of the real thing.

The brotherhood of surfers is still steamed about what the 1.5-mile jetty did to the surf at Doheny State Beach. "The mellow lines of Doheny are all but gone, replaced by the calm water of Dana Point Harbor," lamented surfing historian and chronicler Allan "Bank" Wright. In an essay entitled "The Boutiquing of the California Coast," lifelong surfer, beach aficionado, and journalist John McKinney writes how he nearly aborted a planned hike on the California coast because he grew so disgusted with the barricading of Dana Point. Stranded outside a gated residential community, McKinney wrote, "As I stand with Dana's memorial…the sun, which I cannot see, drops toward the ocean, which I cannot see, showering golden light on sandstone cliffs, where I cannot legally walk." Of the yacht basin, he wrote, "I walk across the acres of hot asphalt comprising the Dana Harbor parking lot. The sight of the huge antiseptic marina takes the wind out of my sails. A favorite surfing spot of my adolescence has been totally destroyed."

It's not only the squeaky clean fake seaport experience that rankles. Pacific Coast Highway has become clogged with strip malls on both sides through the Dana Point/South Laguna corridor. The buildup along the traffic-choked highway has been torrential since the mid-1980s, with very little unviolated "outdoors" visible anymore. Despite efforts to promote and trade on that very quality, it has all but vanished. Nonetheless, gaily colored ceremonial nylon flags fly from shops and subdevelopments alike. Those flags have lately taken on a patriotic air, being splashed with the red, white, and blue. But this seems as fraudulent as a flag decal on a gas-guzzling SUV. What is so all-American about tampering with what once was one of America's finest chain of beaches? It is, in fact, tantamount to treason.

For more information, contact the Dana Point Chamber of Commerce & Visitor Center, Clocktower Building, La Plaza Center, Dana Point, CA 92524, 949/496-1555, www.danapoint-chamber.com.

BEACHES

Two great Orange County beaches flank Dana Point. **Doheny State Beach** is enfolded by the long arm of the south jetty that protects Dana Harbor. Although the surf has been tamed, it's a great beginner's beach for surfers and still gets some decent peelers on a south swell. Swimmers, meanwhile, enjoy the relative calm of Doheny's wide, white beach, which runs for three-quarters of a mile. An early-morning arrival on summer days is recommended. An interpretive center offers a touch tank and five aquariums. A wooded 120-site campground, grassy picnic area, and bike path make this 62-acre park an exceptional unit in the state-park system.

North of Dana Point, **Salt Creek County Beach** preserves a mile-long stretch of beach, extending from the point up toward South Laguna. It's a historic spot, since it represents one of the earliest volleys fired in the battle for public beach access—especially in Orange County, where Salt Creek became a cause célèbre from the mid-1970s to the mid-1990s. As usual, it pitted public beach advocates against privatization schemers. For the most part, the public won. Situated on the bluffs above and behind the beach is **Bluff Park,** a section of county beach that has everything you could ask for: trails, picnic tables, restrooms, outdoor showers, grills and fire rings, basketball courts, and views of Catalina Island. It is also a good spot for whale-watching during the peak months of February and early March.

Mentioned only for the sake of completeness, there is a small calm-water beach at **Dana Point Harbor** among the shops and boat slips.

5 DOHENY STATE BEACH

 BEST

Location: Dana Point Harbor Drive off Pacific Coast Highway in Dana Point
Parking/Fees: $10 entrance fee per vehicle; camping fees $30-35 per night with hookup, $20-25 per night without hookup, plus a $7.50 reservation fee
Hours: 6 A.M.-8 P.M. (to 10 P.M. during Daylight Savings Time)
Facilities: concession, lifeguards, restrooms, showers, and picnic areas
Contact: Doheny State Beach, 949/496-6172

6 SALT CREEK COUNTY BEACH

Location: Pacific Coast Highway at Ritz-Carlton Drive between Dana Point and South Laguna

ORANGE COUNTY

GOLF COURSE LIVING – OR, SELLING ORANGE COUNTY BY THE HOOK AND SLICE

Orange County is California's cradle of Republican values. Beyond its beautiful beaches, the county has all the lingering warmth and charm of a bank lobby. Every swath of green that doesn't have an ostentatious hacienda plopped onto it, with requisite backyard pool, is devoted to the preternaturally lush contours of a golf course. They even devised a euphemism for their lifestyle: "golf course living."

Orange County's cultural touchstones are Mickey Mouse and John Wayne. The political icon is Richard Nixon, whose library and grave are in Yorba Linda. The irony of all this staunch conservatism is that not so many years ago Orange County was a sleepy rural retreat from Los Angeles. Cities such as Anaheim were where little old ladies dreamed of going to get away from Los Angeles. Most of the land was either grazed by livestock or planted in orange groves.

But the little old ladies passed away. In their place came a determined battalion of mall designers, commercial developers, construction contractors, highway builders and entrepreneurial barracudas of all stripes. All put pressure on pliable government officials, most of whom shared the same party affiliation (read: Republican) to do their bidding. It's the American way, right?

No, it was the will of the Irvine Company, which basically orchestrated the whole scheme. The Irvine Company is the mysterious realty octopus that owns most of the undeveloped land in Orange County. It has built its empire on a real-estate plan whereby it leases land in 99-year increments, thereby ensuring that no one but the company ultimately owns it. Originally, most of Orange County was a land grant called Irvine Ranch. Five times the size of Manhattan, it is the largest private real estate holding in a major U.S. metropolitan area.

Just the name "Irvine Ranch" evokes the "Father Knows Best" patriarchy that governs every square foot of Orange County. Instead of cows, Irvine Ranch is grazed by golfers. Instead of orange trees, palm trees have been geometrically arranged around climate-controlled corporate campuses. To the east, the faceless, interchangeable towns that orbit them have been erected. For example, 134,300 people live in a city

Parking/Fees: pay parking lot ($1 per hour)
Hours: 5 A.M.–midnight
Facilities: concession, lifeguards, restrooms, showers, and picnic tables
Contact: South Beaches Operation Office of Orange County Harbors, Beaches, and Parks, 714/834-2400

ACCOMMODATIONS

Posh and pricey are the bywords in Dana Point. The **Ritz-Carlton Laguna Niguel** (1 Ritz-Carlton Drive, 949/240-2000, $$$$) swaddles guests in five-star luxury. It is probably the premier resort on the Southern California coast. We are hard-pressed to think of one more imposing in its roll call

of amenities: four tennis courts, three restaurants, two heated pools, and an 18-hole golf course—everything but the proverbial partridge in a pear tree. And the view, from a bluff 150 feet above the ocean, is exceptional. As they put it, "We overlook nothing but the Pacific." Well, they also overlook the average wage earner's ability to afford a night at a place like this.

Marriott's Laguna Cliffs Resort (25135 Park Lantern Drive, 949/661-5000, www.lagunacliffs.com, $$$$) is another opulent, sprawling pleasure dome whose 12 acres include biking and jogging trails. All 350 rooms have ocean views. In addition to health clubs, tennis courts, a basketball court (where one of

called Orange. Ever heard of Orange? Does it evoke any tangible associations – natural, historical, cultural? Orange's claim to fame, so far as we could tell, is that it's home to "Southern California's largest entertainment and retail center" (in other words, a mall of monstrous proportions).

Another 202,000 people live in Irvine, a "planned community" that is livable and safe but antiseptic as Listerine. Ditto Costa Mesa, clocking in with 110,000. Another 340,000 live in Santa Ana, 345,000 in Anaheim, and 143,500 in Pasadena. It is a sprawl that never ceases. One morning we saw the following headline in a local newspaper, reported without irony or alarm: "Coto de Caza set to open five new neighborhoods." Coto de Caza is a guard-gated private community with a population of 16,000. In Orange County the old catchphrase "There goes the neighborhood" has been replaced with a new one: "Here comes the neighborhood."

The inevitable toppling of this house of cards came in 2008 with the sub-prime lending crisis, the collapse of venerable financial institutions, and the bottoming out of the Southern California real-estate market. Knowing that fortunes have been lost makes the quiet, upscale neighborhoods of Orange County appear all the more surreal these days. The real-estate crash caused housing prices in Orange County to fall by 20 percent. The housing market is expected to remain soft for a couple of years. Here are some recent headlines in the *Orange County Register* as we were going to press: "How Low Will Mortgage Meltdown Drag O.C.'s Economy?" and "Foreclosures Hit Even High-End Beach Cities." We sure didn't have to look far for bad news.

Okay, enough of all this. To us the beaches are the only parts of Orange County that retain any links to the county's historical, geological, and cultural past. Despite the fact that the moneyed minions have succeeded in snuffing out the Old California feel of Dana Point and Huntington Beach, parts of San Clemente, Laguna Beach, Newport Beach, and Seal Beach retain elements of their original charm.

Huntington Beach and Dana Point lost their battles because they were meccas for surfers – relative non-spenders who are run off the land whenever big money bullies its way into town. Still, some very important lessons about coastal development can be learned from Orange County. As we see it, Orange County represents an endpoint of greed and despoliation against which the rest of America's coastal communities ought to be on guard.

us trounced the other in a game of horse), and spas, it has one of the finest gourmet restaurants in the state, **Watercolors.**

The latest entry in the froufrou market is **St. Regis Monarch Beach Resort and Spa** (One Monarch Beach Drive, 949/234-3400 or 866/716-8116, www.stregismb.com, $$$$). Room rates on summer weekends start at $440. (Yikes!) The 400-room, Tuscan-style resort sits on the east side of Highway 1, peering down at the far Pacific. Yes, it is not ocean side but ocean *view*. It's a beach resort without a beach and a fitting symbol for all that's gone wrong at Dana Point.

For budget accommodations, drive a few miles up the coast to South Laguna, where unfancy beachside motels are strewn along Pacific Coast Highway.

COASTAL CUISINE

We've stated our biases against the exclusivity and landscape-shattering development at Dana Point. That doesn't mean we don't find things to admire about a few properties, particularly the Ritz-Carlton Laguna Niguel and Marriott's Laguna Cliffs. Both are first-class resorts that live up to every expectation. **Watercolors,** the restaurant at **Marriott's Laguna Cliffs Resort** (25135 Park Lantern Drive, 949/661-5000, $$$), went way beyond our expectations. The meal commenced with a pair of appetizers—tuna tartare and spring rolls filled with slices of grilled duck—so artistically rendered that we almost didn't dare disturb them. They proved as delicious to eat as they were to look at. Entrée preparations were similarly sumptuous. The room is light and airy, done in peach tones and brass accents, and the prevailing style is contemporary American cuisine: healthy, creative, and appealing to the eye and palate.

NIGHTLIFE

The lounges at the hotel resorts—particularly the Ritz-Carlton, which has an on-premises nightclub—are your primary options. After a day of tennis, golf, or sailing, and a good meal, you might not feel like much more than a civilized nightcap in any case. If you do, however, there's an old reliable **Hennessey's Tavern** (34111 La Plaza, 949/488-0121) in Dana Point.

Laguna Beach and South Laguna

When people hear the name Laguna Beach these days, they tend to think of Lauren Conrad and her crew from *The Hills* and from its predecessor, *Laguna Beach: The Real Orange County*. Well, these hugely successful MTV reality shows in fact document the *surreal* Orange County, as far as we're concerned. When we think of Laguna Beach, we're reminded of faraway places: the French Riviera, the Greek Isles, the coast of Italy. The town is something of a Southern California anomaly: a cultured seaside village that attracts its share of free spirits. It serves as a kind of Arts and Entertainment channel to the rest of Orange County's *Jackass*-style MTV charades.

Compared to the county's soulless suburban sprawl and fiercely unforgiving arch-conservatism, Laguna Beach is an island, set apart from the rest of Orange County by geography—hills and canyons on three sides, ocean to the west—and the disposition of its inhabitants, which is more creative than mercenary. This

outlook was stated in a local publication by a resident who may have revealed more than she intended when she wrote: "Whatever you do, the waves will take your troubles far out to sea, leaving you mindless."

Above all else, Laguna Beach is an artists' colony. There are more than 90 art galleries in Laguna Beach, the lion's share arrayed along Pacific Coast Highway. Whereas other beach towns in Southern California host surfing competitions, lifeguard races, and volleyball tournaments, Laguna Beach (population 24,000) sponsors three art festivals every summer, among them the nationally renowned event Pageant of the Masters (see the *Laguna Beach's Art Affairs* sidebar). Easels are as abundant as surfboards, especially around sunset, when artists strive to capture the gold fire that illuminates the town's myriad coves and beaches.

South Laguna begins around Salt Creek County Beach and runs north to about Ocean Vista Drive (just below Victoria Beach). The differences between South Laguna and Laguna Beach are strictly jurisdictional and nomenclatural. In the words of a longtime resident, "It's all Laguna Beach to me." Indeed, they blend so thoroughly that only a mapmaker can tell them apart.

People who call Laguna Beach home love everything about it except for one thing: traffic. They revere the intellectual camaraderie that encourages self-expression and tolerates eccentricity; the cool, even climate; the striking beauty of cliffs that plunge to a dramatic shoreline (sometimes taking homes with them); and the quasi-European orientation of the community, with its emphasis on high culture and old money. There's even room for surfers, skateboarders, and all the less intellectual flotsam that washes ashore. Their presence helps keep the community from becoming swamped by its own pretensions.

That's not to say that there's never been trouble in paradise. An October 1993 fire in Laguna Beach destroyed hundreds of millions of dollars' worth of homes, with most of the damage confined to the canyons and

LAGUNA BEACH'S ART AFFAIRS

If you come to Laguna Beach in the summer, chances are you'll spend as much time looking at paintings of the ocean as you will at the actual thing. These three art festivals keep things hopping all summer long in Laguna Beach.

Art-A-Fair (777 Laguna Canyon Road, 949/494-4514) and the **Sawdust Festival** (935 Laguna Canyon Road, 949/494-3030) run from July 1 through August 29. Art-A-Fair is a juried art show that also features demonstrations and workshops. The Sawdust Festival is more of the same, plus food and entertainment, such as a juggler of fiery batons who wouldn't be out of place on Venice Beach.

The venerable **Festival of Arts** (650 Laguna Canyon Road, 949/494-1145) and its highlight, the **Pageant of the Masters,** runs from the first week of July through the end of August; general admission costs $7 for adults and $4 for seniors and students. It has been an annual feature of Laguna Beach life for more than 60 years. The Pageant of the Masters brings to life pieces of classic art using live, human subjects. Actors and locals three-dimensionally re-create paintings by the likes of Matisse, Van Gogh, Magritte, and Seurat for staged, 90-second sittings that take hours (if not months) to prepare. The evening culminates in a grand tableaux vivant setting of Da Vinci's *Last Supper*. The effect is both lifelike and eerily two-dimensional, thanks to creative lighting techniques.

The art scene is strong all year-round, as well. The first Thursday of every month is devoted to the **Artwalk.** Tours are led through the local galleries and the artists leave their studio doors open to all comers and goers.

The quality of the art varies widely. We saw eye-catching expressionist paintings and inventive takes on what would normally be clichéd coastal landscape paintings, as well as exceptional nature photography. But we also saw paintings, in high-end galleries no less, that were little better than paint-by-numbers in quality and others that would not be out of place on a sappy greeting card (e.g., portraits of waifish girls licking ice-cream cones, sailboats resting in harbor at sunset), not to mention cutesy sculptures of frolicking children and frisky dolphins.

Overall, though, the diversity of the galleries and their distribution throughout the nooks and crannies of this rare jewel of a town – a work of art in itself – make them well worth perusing.

houses ill-advisedly built in them. The AIDS epidemic has claimed a lot of local residents in this gay-friendly community.

Laguna Beach has always marched to the beat of a different drummer. Unlike much of California, which was parceled out in the form of land grants by the rulers of Spain and Mexico to friends of the throne, Laguna was homesteaded by tree-planting pioneers following the region's annexation by the United States. It was initially called Lagonas, from the Shoshone word for lakes, because of the freshwater lagoons situated behind the beaches where creeks pour into the ocean. The first arrivals were Mormons, who were followed by Methodists. Laguna's first hostelry opened in 1886 and has been operating ever since as Hotel Laguna.

Artists began forming an enclave here in the early 1900s, around which time the name was changed to Laguna Beach. Gradually, a style known as California impressionism began to evolve after an artist named Lewis Botts painted his famous *Girl of the Golden West* in 1914. Much in the style of Monet's French impressionist school, they painted the natural surroundings with rapid brush strokes and an eye for how sunlight bathed the landscape. The Laguna Beach Art Association was founded in 1918, and thereafter art galleries began popping

ORANGE COUNTY

HANGING OUT WITH THE SURF ADDICTS

The nightlife of Laguna Beach is compacted into the midtown area near Main Beach. One can walk from bar to bar without having to get into a car. That seems a logical enough arrangement, but rarely are clubs laid out so conveniently. Some years ago, we were roaming around Laguna Beach after dinner when we heard live music wafting from this vicinity. Seduced by the siren call of electric guitars, we followed the noise to its source. Imagine our surprise to find three rock bands playing at open-door bars in close proximity.

After sampling all three, we decided to throw our lot in with the Surf Addicts, a local surf-punk trio who were blasting away at Hennessey's Tavern. Their music sounded like the most fun to our ears. The story and sound of this now-defunct band are fairly typical of the Southern California experience. They wrote witty, high-energy songs about the SoCal surfer/party-dude lifestyle.

"I want to live on the edge without falling over," explained the group's singer/guitarist, a live wire named Drew, in a post-show conversation over a table full of beer mugs. For him surfing was an activity as automatic as breathing. He'd found his own slice of wave-filled heaven, a cove beach in South Laguna that few others know about.

His idea of a perfect day in Laguna began with a bout of surfing in the A.M., followed by lunch at Papa's Tacos (a beloved Mexican food joint), and a gig with the Surf Addicts at night. At one time he wanted to join a reggae band. Then one day it occurred to him to write, sing, and play what he knew. In his case he knew about surfing and partying in Laguna Beach.

"We always partied with tourist girls," he told us, "so I wrote a song called 'Tourist Girls.' I grew up partying in Laguna, so I wrote a song called 'Party in Laguna.' I've always imagined what it would be like to surf Hawaii. I thought it would be kind of scary facing waves of that size, so I wrote a song around the line 'Don't hair out' – meaning don't chicken out – 'in Waianea.'"

The Surf Addicts encapsulated the Laguna lifestyle in an entertaining, infectious way that had a damn sight more to do with "reality" than the antics of Lauren and Heidi on *The Hills*. They sounded like the Police, Beach Boys, and Clash all riding the same surfboard. Their tapes were sold in surf shops and local record stores. Having witnessed their bracing, breakneck live show, we still find them hard to forget. They took the fun of riding a wave or chugging a beer and turned it into music that made you want to do both. One thing's for sure: They made two road-weary beach bums glad to be wide awake and rocking at the beach at two in the morning.

up all over. Today, small galleries hang signs in their front windows that read: "We buy Old Laguna and Old European paintings."

The artistic imperative meanders all the way down Laguna Canyon Road to the water. At Main Beach, an art deco chess table fashioned in a colorful mosaic of ceramic tiles sits in the grassy picnic area for all to admire or use. Don't be surprised to see eye-catching professional models posing and preening on the beach. A lot of fashion models and film-industry types live in Laguna Beach. The former estate of Bette Davis is a local landmark. From

its earliest days, the town has been a gathering place for the jet set. Celebrity residents have included Charlie Chaplin, Judy Garland, Rudolph Valentino, and Gregory Peck.

The main artery through Laguna Beach is Pacific Coast Highway, which unfortunately snakes right through the center of town. The steady stream of traffic mars the town's otherwise genteel village atmosphere. There is simply no other way to get from Dana Point to Newport Beach. A proposed freeway bypass a few miles inland was nixed years ago. All the whizzing traffic makes hazardous sport of getting in and out of a parked car. If traffic were rerouted away from town, Laguna Beach would be a far more pleasant place. As it is, the constant thunder of traffic, much of it aggressively hurrying through town on the only coastal artery, seriously blemishes the Laguna Beach experience.

Beyond the vehicular onslaught, Laguna has atmosphere, culture, scenic beauty, and fantastic beaches. The town at one time even had an unofficial greeter, Eiler Larson by name. This friendly, shaggy mountain man from Denmark would stand at the city limits, hollering "How are you?" to those coming and "Leaving so soon?" to those going for eight hours a day. After he died, numerous tributary wood likenesses began appearing on the town's sidewalks.

The community has its own activist beautification council, which successfully battled outside business interests that wanted to refashion Laguna Beach into a convention center during the 1970s. The would-be developers were sent packing and the threatened town center instead became the landscaped, open-air Main Beach Park. Along the coastline such happy endings are all too rare. This one deserves a standing ovation.

Laguna Beach still holds fast to its "walking village atmosphere." Though some grumble about the "mansionization of Laguna" that's taken place on the hillsides—bringing with it the moneyed morons who populate the aforementioned reality shows—the town has by and large maintained its architectural charm. That is largely because Laguna Beach has retained its activist edge. "There is a vocal design and review process in the community," an involved local told us. "People have a say here in what goes on." And what really goes on here is way more interesting than anything you'll ever see on *The Hills*.

For more information, contact the Laguna Beach Visitor Information Center, 252 Broadway, Laguna Beach, CA 92651, 949/497-9229 or 800/877-1115; or the Laguna Beach Chamber of Commerce, 357 Glenneyre Street, Laguna Beach, CA 92651, 949/494-1018, www.lagunabeachinfo.org.

BEACHES

Laguna Beach comes stocked with beaches—more than 20 named ones tucked into coves along a hilly, undulating coastline. To give you an idea of its ruggedness, this small town's elevation ranges from sea level to 1,039 feet. **Main Beach** (a.k.a. Laguna Beach Municipal Park) is just that: the main place to congregate and recreate in Laguna. In a town of tiny coves and pocket beaches, this is the big enchilada. Balls are bounced and batted during daylight hours. With its volleyball and basketball courts, picnicking green, and long, sandy beach bordered by a winding boardwalk, Main Beach is a buzzing hive of activity and a great spot for sitting on a bench and surveying the very eclectic scene.

Beyond Main Beach, smaller beaches can be found in both directions along Pacific Coast Highway. It seems that every side street ends at the cliffs, with a stairway leading to a fan-shaped cove. We'll survey the more noteworthy ones, starting from the south with **1,000 Steps Beach.** It's where Ninth Avenue meets Pacific Coast Highway in South Laguna. You'll have to park a few blocks away on the highway's asphalt shoulder, since all the curbs are red in the immediate vicinity, but the walk from your car to the top of the stairs will warm up your calf muscles for the trek down the lengthy cement staircase to the beach. At the bottom of the stairs is a small beach pinned against steep cliffs. Gibraltar-sized rocks frame the cove, and huge waves run up on the beach with great force. Houses cling precariously to the eroding cliffs, each with its own set of ladder-like stairs. Climbing out of this grotto is the real acid test—and that's an apt choice of words, since Timothy Leary and his LSD-imbibing gang frequented this beach in the 1960s. The ascent actually numbers 219 steps, and you can amuse yourself on the return trip by reading the graffiti scrawled onto the vertical face of each step.

West Street Beach is one of the better bodysurfing spots in a town renowned for its waves. Shoehorned into a small cove at the base of a stairwell at the end of West Street, about 10 blocks north of 1,000 Steps Beach, it has a volleyball court and is seasonally popular with locals.

Aliso Creek County Beach lies along the heart of the motel/taco stand/gas station corridor of South Laguna. Ample metered parking draws the summertime masses, as does the fine board- and bodysurfing. The beach slopes steeply down to the breaking waves, which makes for hazardous swimming. All the same, it's packed with families. You'll also find a playground, fire rings, benches, restrooms, and a short pier with snack bar. When pushed along by the powerful south swell, the waves appear taller than the people playing in them. They break with a mighty crack, sending foam cascading up the brown, sandy beach. We saw happy packs of kids building communal sand castles and getting knocked over by the waves.

The lagoon formed where Aliso Creek empties into the ocean is a popular birdbath, which contributes to its poor water quality. The creek becomes steep-sided on its southern bank as it approaches the ocean. Don't climb into the creek, as its near-constant contamination is an issue that plagues Laguna Beach. Nonpoint source pollution from developments up the canyon fouls the creek, necessitating warning signs. But what to do? Officials haven't figured that out yet, despite much head-scratching, finger-pointing, and public debate. Parents, keep an eye on your young ones here. If the creek is contaminated, it stands to reason that the ocean into which it empties is polluted, too, in the immediate vicinity. The twin threats of water quality and water safety make this a less than ideal family beach, when all is said and done.

The prettiest beach in Laguna, **Victoria Beach** (a.k.a. Vic Beach), is one of the hardest to find. Given the lack of signs, it would appear the locals want to keep it that way. The beach can be entered at several points along Victoria Drive, a street off Pacific Coast Highway that's lined with homes pressed together as close as any block of Victorians in San Francisco. Residents have traded space for easy access to a common, sandy front yard along the ocean. Hiking down from the walkway and stairs at the north end of Victoria Beach, you pass private homes behind a yellow cinder-block wall. A final curve deposits you on one of the nicest beaches in Southern California—one that's especially popular with bodysurfers. It is broad and uncrowded, known mostly by locals, and an inviting spot to drop a beach towel.

Moving north from Vic Beach, **Woods Cove** is a small beach bounded by rocks (there's an especially large one at the north end) popular with locals and largely unknown to others. Diving and tidepooling are the big draws here, but watch out for hazardous surf. Nearby **Pearl Street Beach** (a.k.a. Agate Beach) is another small, locally popular cove beach bounded by rocky reefs. **Bluebird Beach** is right in front of the Surf & Sand Resort, and it's a smooth, sandy beach that's good for bodysurfing, boogie boarding, or just soaking up rays on a beach chair.

As you move more into central Laguna Beach, the distances between the rocky points that bound the cove beaches increase. **Mountain Road Beach** has a wide sand beach, but the surf is strewn with hazards—rip currents, submerged rocks, and offshore reefs—so proceed with caution. At the end of Brooks Street, facing Halfway Rock, is **Brooks Beach,** a rocky beach that surfing authority Bank Wright says serves up "the cleanest, best-shaped big wave in Laguna Beach." Have it your way.... Would you like some southern swell on that wave? Maybe a garland of kelp? A shark-fin appetizer? Brooks Beach is strictly for surfers. Everyone has his or her own favorite hidden cove in Laguna Beach, so there are potentially as many beaches as there are street ends. Don't expect locals to divulge their secrets to a stranger, but feel free to poke around—you might stumble on a deserted cove if you're lucky.

Bring the Frisbee to **Oak Street Beach,** which runs for a block or so on either side of Oak Street. A series of offshore reefs makes this a hot surfing spot, as are adjoining **Thalia Street Beach** and **St. Ann's Beach,** though neither is recommended for swimming because of their rocky reef bottoms. Moreover, St. Ann's has the worst rip current in Laguna Beach. All that changes in the matter of a block or so at **Sleepy Hollow Beach,** whose sandy-bottomed beach makes it fine for swimming and bodysurfing (not so hot for surfing). Sleepy Hollow Beach is popular with guests of Vacation Village Hotel, which overlooks it. At this point you are just south of Main Beach, about which we've already commented.

Jumping north of Main Beach, lovely **Heisler Park** serves as a point of entry to **Rockpile Beach** and **Picnic Beach.** Up at this north end of Laguna Beach, the erodable sandstone coast gives way to sturdier volcanic rocks that form points, with bays cut into the softer shales. The foremost feature at Heisler Park is the walkway that lines the coastal bluffs for about a mile. At dusk it's a magical sight. As fog settles in, the town's twinkling lights come on, rendering a real-life canvas as fanciful as any impressionist's pointillistic study. Rockpile and Picnic Beaches are accessible from Heisler Park via a stairway and ramp, respectively. Rockpile is a rocky, surfers-only spot in front of the Laguna Art Museum, where Jasmine Street meets Cliff Drive. At high tide, the beach disappears altogether. Picnic tables are nestled among the trees of Heisler Park, giving Picnic Beach its name. Down below, the beach is a diver's paradise but no picnic for swimmers.

Along the 600 block of Cliff Drive, at the north end of Heisler Park, is **Diver's Cove,** a family-friendly, football-field-sized beach that draws scuba divers and wading kiddies. Adjoining it to the north is **Boat Canyon Beach,** another rocky-bottomed diver's special that's a no-go for swimmers. A few blocks up, picturesque **Shaw's Cove**—yet another diver's dream (anglers, too)—has the bonus of tidepools at its south end.

The procession of public beaches ends at **Crescent Bay Point Park,** a bluff-top green with views of Seal Rock and Laguna Beach and a beach whose big, tubular waves make for great—and sometimes scary—bodysurfing. Anglers cast from the surf or the rocks, and ocean frolickers brave the somewhat risky (beware rip currents) surf. Because it is one of the longer beaches, running for a quarter mile, it is also one of the more popular in the area, so expect to find weekend crowds.

There are two pieces of good news on Laguna's beachfront. The first is the arrival of a trio of cove beach accesses adjacent to a luxury enclave completed in 2002. To get the permits to build this project, the developers were required to deed a third of the land back to the town of Laguna Beach. As a result, three adjacent coves—**Treasure Island, Goff's Cove,** and **Christmas Cove**—are now accessible to the public. They are the southernmost in a string of 20 city beaches overseen by the indomitable Laguna Beach lifeguards.

The second bit of good news is the **Beach Tram**—a town-run free shuttle bus that services the whole of Laguna Beach, from Aliso Creek to Crescent Bay Point Park. The shuttle also services two parking lots in the canyons. This has not only cut down on traffic and parking woes, but it's a sensible way to curb emissions from vehicles that would normally be stuck in never-ending, nerve-jangling Highway 1 gridlock.

🟨 1,000 STEPS BEACH

Location: Ninth Avenue at Pacific Coast Highway in South Laguna
Parking/Fees: metered street parking
Hours: 6 A.M.–9 P.M.
Facilities: lifeguards
Contact: South Beaches Operation Office of Orange County Harbors, Beaches, and Parks, 714/834-2400

⑧ WEST STREET BEACH

Location: West Street at Pacific Coast Highway in South Laguna
Parking/Fees: metered street parking
Hours: 6 A.M.-10 P.M.
Facilities: none
Contact: South Beaches Operation Office of Orange County Harbors, Beaches, and Parks, 714/834-2400

⑨ ALISO CREEK COUNTY BEACH

Location: 31,000 block of Pacific Coast Highway in South Laguna
Parking/Fees: pay parking lot ($1 per hour)
Hours: 6 A.M.-10 P.M.
Facilities: concessions, lifeguards, restrooms, showers, and picnic tables
Contact: South Beaches Operation Office of Orange County Harbors, Beaches, and Parks, 949/923-2280

⑩ TREASURE ISLAND

Location: just north of Aliso Creek County Beach on Pacific Coast Highway via a ramp at Montage Resort in Laguna Beach
Parking/Fees: metered street parking
Hours: 6 A.M.-10 P.M.
Facilities: none
Contact: Laguna Beach Department of Marine Safety, 949/494-6571

⑪ GOFF'S COVE

Location: just north of Treasure Island on Pacific Coast Highway, accessible via stairs at Montage Resort in Laguna Beach

Parking/Fees: metered street parking
Hours: 6 A.M.-10 P.M.
Facilities: none
Contact: Laguna Beach Department of Marine Safety, 949/494-6571

⑫ CHRISTMAS COVE

Location: just north of Goff Cove on Pacific Coast Highway, accessible via stairs at Montage Resort in Laguna Beach
Parking/Fees: metered street parking
Hours: 6 A.M.-10 P.M.
Facilities: none
Contact: Laguna Beach Department of Marine Safety, 949/494-6571

⑬ VICTORIA BEACH

Location: Victoria Street off Pacific Coast Highway in Laguna Beach, accessed by stairs
Parking/Fees: metered street parking
Hours: 6 A.M.-10 P.M.
Facilities: none
Contact: Laguna Beach Department of Marine Safety, 949/494-6571

⑭ WOODS COVE

Location: Diamond Street off Pacific Coast Highway in Laguna Beach
Parking/Fees: metered street parking
Hours: 6 A.M.-midnight
Facilities: none
Contact: Laguna Beach Department of Marine Safety, 949/494-6571

ORANGE COUNTY

Victoria Beach

15 PEARL STREET BEACH

Location: Pearl Street off Pacific Coast Highway in Laguna Beach
Parking/Fees: metered street parking
Hours: 6 A.M.-midnight
Facilities: none
Contact: Laguna Beach Department of Marine Safety, 949/494-6571

16 BLUEBIRD BEACH

Location: Bluebird Canyon Road off Pacific Coast Highway in Laguna Beach
Parking/Fees: metered street parking
Hours: 6 A.M.-midnight
Facilities: none
Contact: Laguna Beach Department of Marine Safety, 949/494-6571

17 MOUNTAIN ROAD BEACH

Location: Mountain Road off Pacific Coast Highway in Laguna Beach
Parking/Fees: metered street parking

Hours: 6 A.M.-midnight
Facilities: none
Contact: Laguna Beach Department of Marine Safety, 949/494-6571

18 BROOKS BEACH

Location: Brooks Street off Pacific Coast Highway in Laguna Beach
Parking/Fees: metered street parking
Hours: 6 A.M.-midnight
Facilities: none
Contact: Laguna Beach Department of Marine Safety, 949/494-6571

19 OAK STREET BEACH

Location: Oak Street off Pacific Coast Highway in Laguna Beach
Parking/Fees: metered street parking
Hours: 6 A.M.-midnight
Facilities: none
Contact: Laguna Beach Department of Marine Safety, 949/494-6571

20 THALIA STREET BEACH

Location: Thalia Street off Pacific Coast Highway in Laguna Beach
Parking/Fees: metered street parking
Hours: 6 A.M.-midnight
Facilities: none
Contact: Laguna Beach Department of Marine Safety, 949/494-6571

21 ST. ANN'S BEACH

Location: St. Ann's Drive off Pacific Coast Highway in Laguna Beach
Parking/Fees: metered street parking
Hours: 6 A.M.-midnight
Facilities: none
Contact: Laguna Beach Department of Marine Safety, 949/494-6571

22 SLEEPY HOLLOW BEACH

Location: Sleepy Hollow Lane off Pacific Coast Highway in Laguna Beach
Parking/Fees: metered street parking
Hours: 6 A.M.-midnight
Facilities: none
Contact: Laguna Beach Department of Marine Safety, 949/494-6571

23 MAIN BEACH

                 BEST (

Location: between Broadway and Ocean Avenues at Pacific Coast Highway in Laguna Beach
Parking/Fees: metered street parking
Hours: 6 A.M.-midnight
Facilities: lifeguards, restrooms, showers, and picnic tables
Contact: Laguna Beach Department of Marine Safety, 949/494-6571

24 ROCKPILE BEACH

Location: Cliff Drive at Jasmine Street, below Heisler Park, in Laguna Beach
Parking/Fees: metered street parking
Hours: 6 A.M.-midnight
Facilities: none
Contact: Laguna Beach Department of Marine Safety, 949/494-6571

25 PICNIC BEACH

Location: Cliff Drive at Myrtle Street, below Heisler Park, in Laguna Beach
Parking/Fees: metered street parking
Hours: 6 A.M.-midnight
Facilities: lifeguards and picnic tables
Contact: Laguna Beach Department of Marine Safety, 949/494-6571

26 DIVER'S COVE

Location: 600 block of Cliff Drive in Laguna Beach
Parking/Fees: metered street parking
Hours: 6 A.M.-midnight
Facilities: none
Contact: Laguna Beach Department of Marine Safety, 949/494-6571

27 BOAT CANYON BEACH

Location: off Cliff Drive, west of Boat Canyon Park, via stairwell beside Diver's Cove Condominiums in Laguna Beach
Parking/Fees: metered street parking
Hours: 6 A.M.-midnight
Facilities: none
Contact: Laguna Beach Department of Marine Safety, 949/494-6571

28 SHAW'S COVE

Location: Cliff Drive at Fairview Street in Laguna Beach
Parking/Fees: metered street parking
Hours: 6 A.M.-midnight
Facilities: none
Contact: Laguna Beach Department of Marine Safety, 949/494-6571

29 CRESCENT BAY POINT PARK

Location: Crescent Bay Drive at Pacific Coast Highway in Laguna Beach
Parking/Fees: free street parking
Hours: 6 A.M.-midnight
Facilities: lifeguards and restrooms
Contact: Laguna Beach Department of Marine Safety, 949/494-6571

ACCOMMODATIONS

You can expect to pay $300 and up a night for the finer European-inn-type lodgings in Laguna Beach. The **Surf & Sand Resort** (1555 South Pacific Coast Highway, 949/497-4477, www.surfandsandresort.com, $$$$) is the hostelry of first choice. For starters, it is right on Bluebird Beach (named for Bluebird Canyon Road), one of the more pleasant beaches in town. Rooms are pleasantly and airily appointed, and the oceanfront ones are so close to the water that the crashing, splashing symphony of waves lulls visitors into a blissful California state of mind (and a good night's sleep). The rooms are done in light brown earth tones, and the beds are exceptionally comfortable. The pool deck is on the far side of the Surf & Sand's excellent restaurant, Splashes. You literally might wind up making a splash of another sort if you walk through the restaurant in a bathing suit at lunch hour. Seaview rooms at the Surf & Sand run about $395 nightly in summer.

Nearby, **Cap'n Laguna Inn on the Beach** (1441 South Pacific Coast Highway, 949/494-6533, $$$) offers the same paradisiacal setting without the gourmet trimmings and mandatory valet parking.

The **Inn at Laguna Beach** (211 North Pacific Coast Highway, 949/497-9722 or 800/544-9479, www.innatlagunabeach.com, $$$$) also has an unbeatable location—just above Main Beach on a bluff next to our favorite restaurant in town, Las Brisas. Your biggest problem will be deciding how to allocate time: hanging out on Main Beach, sitting on a private ocean-facing balcony, sunbathing on the rooftop sundeck, or strolling Cliff Drive. Moreover, the Inn at Laguna Beach has an amenity worth its weight in gold: an on-site underground garage. Alternatively, if you're feeling sentimental for Old California, you can always stay at the **Hotel Laguna** (425 South Pacific Coast Highway, 949/494-1151, $$$$), a midtown treasure whose beginnings date back to the very founding of Laguna Beach. It's popular with European visitors and is oh-so-civilized.

South Laguna is the site of **Aliso Creek Inn** (31106 South Pacific Coast Highway, 949/499-2271, www.alisocreekinn.com, $$$). Aliso Creek runs through the property, and you can follow it to the beach of the same name, which is only a thousand feet away via a pedestrian underpass. Despite its proximity to the ocean, the inn feels like another world. With views up a canyon and out on mountains, its grounds are woodsy and secluded—a rare find in the midst of a beach town. All rooms are spacious one- and two-bedroom townhouses. The grounds encompass a nine-hole golf course, a large heated pool, and Ben Brown's Restaurant, which serves continental fare. Deer and raccoons, even bobcats and mountain lions, have been spotted on rare occasions.

A string of park-at-your-door motels cut from plainer cloth can be found in South Laguna. The **Laguna Reef Inn** (30806 South Pacific Coast Highway, 949/499-2227, www.lagunareefinn .com, $$) is the nicest of these, offering clean rooms and a heated pool for half the tariff in

Laguna Beach proper. Note: The Laguna Beach Visitor Information Center will assist with hotel and restaurant reservations; call 800/877-1115.

COASTAL CUISINE

The food scene in Laguna Beach is a sensual indulgence bordering on the obscene. After one magnificent meal following another over the years, we've come to understand why the Romans invented vomitoriums.

Stalwart favorites from Laguna Beach's prodigious list of top-flight eateries include **Five Feet** (328 Glenneyre, 949/497-4955, $$$$) and **230 Forest Avenue** (230 Forest Avenue, 949/494-2545, $$$$). At Five Feet, chef Michael Kang oversees the preparation of "contemporary Chinese cuisine," an atypically creative East-meets-West hybrid that results in such signature dishes as catfish with tomato-ginger citrus sauce and wok-fried veal medallions and scallops in Thai basil garlic chili sauce. Kang calls his entrées "whimsical creations"; you'll call them heaven on a plate. With its sleek, urbane atmosphere, 230 Forest Avenue is Laguna's most popular spot for people-watching and martini-downing. Menu choices range from affordable pasta bowls to boldly simple preparations like seared peppercorn ahi, hazelnut-crusted halibut, and macadamia-crusted mahimahi.

Head to **Splashes** (1555 South Coast Highway, 949/376-2779, $$$$) for a refined, cosmopolitan meal in the unparalleled setting of a small, square dining room overlooking the ocean. Located in the Surf & Sand Resort, 25 feet above breaking waves, Splashes occupies a casually elegant setting with an indoor dining room and an outdoor deck a mere wave's splash from the churning Pacific. Chef Christopher Blobaum favors organic ingredients and Mediterranean cuisine. Signature seafood dishes include Pacific swordfish with herb risotto and lemon sauce and sautéed halibut with clams, capers, and black olives. Expect to spend about $80–100 for two, and don't pass up such desserts as chocolate *fondant* with banana ice cream. A postprandial stroll around hilly Laguna Beach will help assuage any guilt pangs.

For fine and fun dining with a view, nothing in Laguna can top **Las Brisas** (361 Cliff Drive, 949/497-5434, $$$). The indoor dining room and outdoor patio overlook Main Beach and the ocean from the bluff-top at the south end of Heisler Park. The house specialty is seafood with a south-of-the-border flair—everything from fresh ceviche to Mexican lobster. The lunch *ensaladas* are too good to be true. Save room for dessert. The restaurant serves a breakfast buffet, lunch, and dinner, with a popular five-course weekend brunch.

The **Beach House Inn** (619 Sleepy Hollow Lane, 949/494-9707, $$$) is another fine-dining option. The glass-walled dining room faces the ocean, so book your reservation at sunset. The menu selections tend toward creative California nouvelle-style preparations of seafood. The broiled filet of sole, for example, is accompanied by bananas sautéed in butter and brown sugar, with chutney and grated coconut. In an old house that used to belong to actor Slim Summerville (one of the original Keystone Cops), the Beach House Inn has retained its original architecture, and a relaxed air pervades the dining room.

The **White House Restaurant** (340 South Pacific Coast Highway, 949/494-8088, $$) is a local institution with a schizophrenic personality. It's a romantic room at the dinner hour that turns into a popular nightspot afterward. The interior of this 1918 vintage restaurant, once patronized by the likes of Bing Crosby, is filled with Tiffany lamps and varnished wood tables. Specialties include fresh pastas and halibut. Later on, the house shakes to everything from reggae bands to local rockers.

After a late arrival in Laguna Beach one Sunday night, we were famished and therefore prepared to take whatever we could find open. Fortunately, we were directed to **Woody's at the Beach** (1305 South Coast Highway, 949/376-8809, $$$), which would be a pleasant surprise at any hour. The tangy Dungeness crab and corn bisque made a soup-erb starter. The miso-crusted mahimahi was masterfully presented, with the filet served atop brown rice with wedges of grilled eggplant arrayed around it and the entire plate swimming in a satay-style peanut sauce. The changeable menu might also include such items as tamarind-glazed rare ahi and roasted striped bass with artichoke ratatouille, saffron cream, and roasted pepper coulis. This is not the sort of inventive fare one would expect from a restaurant whose sign out front is fashioned from a surfboard, or where the background music tends toward softly throbbing disco.

Down in South Laguna, your best bets are Mexican. At least ours were. A surfer/rocker who grew up here turned us on to **Papa's Tacos** (31622 Pacific Coast Highway, 949/499-9822, $), and after feeding on the plate-filling fish tacos and blackened shrimp quesadillas, all we can do is add a hearty "come to Papa's." Another local favorite is the **Coyote Grill** (31621 Pacific Coast Highway, 949/499-4033, $$$), whose motto is "A Taste of Baja at the Beach." A message on the menu says, "When we open our doors, we open our hearts." When we opened their doors, we opened our mouths for things like lobster Puerto Nuevo (whole lobster grilled with all the fixings) and *pescados frescos*. That's "fresh fish" to all of you who don't *habla español*, and it changes daily according to what's available. Coyote Grill is a three-meal-a-day restaurant whose outdoor deck makes a pleasant spot to enjoy a late-afternoon drink.

More and better restaurants arrive with every season in Laguna Beach—certainly more than we can possibly chart. Among the best of the relatively new venues is **Vertical** (234 Forest Avenue, 949/494-0990, $$$). We window-shopped at the latter, a stylish, open-aired, sleekly appointed space. The chef-owner calls his cuisine "casual, bold, exciting, playful, visionary." You are invited to "design" your own meal and pair it with wine by the taste, glass, flight (hence the name *Vertical*), or bottle. Vertical offers "boutique wine" samplings on the second and fourth Thursdays of every month.

Incidentally, a good place to start the day in Laguna Beach is **The Koffee Klatch** (1440 South Coast Highway, 949/376-6867, $), a locals' hangout nestled among the art galleries.

NIGHTLIFE

As the dinner hour wanes, several of Laguna's more popular restaurants morph into nightspots. The **White House Restaurant** (340 South Pacific Coast Highway, 949/494-8088) is popular with locals. Bar bands on weekends and reggae during the week seem to be the rule. **Las Brisas** (361 Cliff Drive, 949/497-5434) also attracts a sizable crowd of folks who hang out at the bar to meet and mingle. The **Marine Room Tavern** (214 Ocean Avenue, 949/494-3027) draws a mixed bag of bands, anything from country-rock to alternative. Across the street, **Hennessey's Tavern** (213 Ocean Avenue, 949/494-2743) is the kind of place that does a good business no matter what. On one of our visits, the band that was playing finished a poor second, in terms of patron interest, to the daredevil boating video on the big-screen TV. It all depends on the band, the night, and the mood as to which club is packing 'em in. Closely quartered down by Main Beach, the Marine Room, Hennessey's, and the White House are the Big Three in Laguna Beach.

Crystal Cove State Park

This state park, between Laguna Beach and Corona del Mar, is a happy surprise on the Orange County coast. Stretching from the ocean into the wooded San Joaquin Hills, its 2,791 acres provide excellent hiking opportunities, three separate coastal accesses (Pelican Point, Los Trancos, and Reef Point), 3.5 miles of beautiful golden-sand beach, an "underwater park" (Irvine Coast Marine Life Refuge), and a 32-site walk-in environmental campground three miles inland. With this bounty, Crystal Cove State Park is known to swimmers, surfers, sunbathers, and divers.

As if that weren't enough, a county-run upland parcel of 2,000 acres known as **Laguna**

BEACH GAMES

The following are some of the most popular games we've witnessed on our beach journeys:

- **Frisbee:** What can we say? The equipment is cheap, and the only rule is not to throw it out to sea. Any game in which a dog can participate is one we feel well qualified to play. Moreover, there's always a chance that the little plastic saucer will get away from you and land near a babe.

- **Hacky-sack:** You generally see circles of shirtless guys (often Deadheads or jam-band fans) kicking the hacky-sack around. Basically, the object is to keep a leather beanbag in the air with the use of your feet. It requires dexterity, concentration, endurance, and a lack of anything better to do.

- **Over the Line (OTL):** This exciting combination of softball, volleyball, and cricket is played on the sand in bare feet. The only equipment needed is a bat, a softball, and gloves (optional for real OTL studs). The OTL field is paced off, 60 feet in width (or 22 paces), with no limit on length. Two teams of three players each compete. As in softball, teams alternate batting and fielding, with three outs per inning, but the game lasts only five innings. Two foul balls or one strike constitutes an out, as does a caught fly ball. Another switch: The pitcher throws to his or her own teammates, kneeling three feet away in the sand and lobbing the ball into an optimum swinging zone (not unlike setting up a spike in volleyball). A "hit" is required to land "over the line" (about 55 feet, or 20 paces, from the batter) and between foul lines. Three hits in an inning scores one run; every subsequent hit in the same inning counts as a run as well. (For more information on rules and tournaments, visit the Old Mission Bay Athletic Club's website at www.ombac.org.)

- **Paddleball:** A combination of tennis, handball, and ping-pong, this game is played

---

Coast Wilderness Park and the 11,500-acre **Irvine Ranch Land Reserve** combine with Crystal Cove State Park to provide a huge mountain-to-ocean tract of natural habitat within otherwise densely populated Orange County. The Irvine reserve is a permanent conservation easement deeded by the Irvine Company to the Nature Conservancy in 2001. On the environmental front, it is not all bad news in Orange County after all.

For more information, contact Crystal Cove State Beach, 8471 Pacific Coast Highway, Laguna Beach, CA, 949/494-3539, www.parks.ca.gov or www.crystalcovestatepark.com.

BEACHES

Reef Point is the southernmost access to Crystal Cove, with a stairway to a beach, hiking trail, bike path, and restrooms. **Los** **Trancos** has the largest parking lot, located on the east side of Pacific Coast Highway, with a tunnel leading under the highway to the beach. **Pelican Point** is the northernmost access, with a bluff-top trail leading to a steep beach access ramp. The beach itself is covered with silvery drift logs, rounded cobbles, and coarse, golden-brown sand. From it you gaze up onto ochre-colored bluffs and grassy, rolling hills beyond. People run, hike, or repose on the beach, whose quietude is a balm from all the automotive mania of the coast cities to the north and south. Modest day-use fees are charged.

One sour note to this pristine coastal glory is the Newport Coast development just north of Pelican Point. Bought by the obsessively acquisitive Disney Corporation, this private community is devoted to luxury time-share

as singles or doubles on a miniature tennis court. The rules are the same as tennis, with the exception of the racket, which is a wobbly-centered thing that looks like an oversized ping-pong paddle. The paddle cuts down on the range of a struck ball and presumably its velocity (although it looked plenty fast to us). When the sport is played well – as it is on the courts in Venice Beach and Santa Monica – it can be as exciting as Centre Court at Wimbledon (well, close). In the limited space of a paddleball court, doubles requires a series of movements as intricate as kabuki dance. Check it out.

- **Volleyball:** If you don't already know the rules of volleyball, move to the back of the bus. What makes this game so "California" are the two-person teams that play on the beach. How, you find yourself wondering in awe, do two people in bare feet cover that much ground? Will that bikini top stay on? And most important, how can anyone ever hope to return one of those spikes, routinely clocked at over 100 miles per hour? (Answer: They rarely do, which is why these games move so swiftly.) On some beaches – Manhattan Beach and Santa Cruz, for instance – volleyball is not just a game but an obsession. It's also a professional sport, one that has been embraced by advertisers, fashion designers, and ESPN. In 2008, Kerri Walsh and Misty May-Treanor beat a Chinese duo to win the gold medal in women's beach volleyball at the Beijing Olympics. They also won the gold medal in 2004, making them the only team to repeat the feat and indisputably the greatest beach-volleyball duo of all time.

- **Whiffleball:** You can make any batter look foolish if you're tossing one of these plastic balls with the wacky waffle holes. The game is played like baseball, though no gloves are needed. The best setup we observed was at Mission Beach, where some guys had placed their beer-laden cooler near home plate and used the ocean as the outfield. If the batted ball went beyond where the waves broke, it was a home run. If it landed in the waves, it was a double. The object was to drink as much as possible from the cooler while at bat.

condominiums for the loophole-loving rich, who will write off the cost of these multimillion-dollar second homes on their taxes. Just across the street from this monolith is the Shake Shack, a 75-year-old smoothie stand that's much more in keeping with the true spirit of the beach life. Buy one of the healthy smoothies—orange-date and raspberry-peach sound good—and thumb your nose at Newport Coast while you're at it.

The long-range plan is to create a Historic District within the state park to preserve and protect a community of 46 small cottages that date from the 1930s. Meanwhile, down at Reef Point, the El Toro mobile home park, which is a bit of an eyesore, is being "converted" to a public campground, picnic area, and lifeguarded beach. Although no one likes to see people displaced, this is ultimately a good

thing for the public and the long-term health of the natural habitat.

30 REEF POINT

Location: Pacific Coast Highway between Laguna Beach and Corona del Mar

Parking/Fees: $10 entrance fee per vehicle; camping fee at hike-in campground three miles inland $11-15 per night

Hours: 6 A.M.-sunset

Facilities: lifeguards, picnic tables, showers, restrooms, and visitors center (at El Moro Canyon)

Contact: Crystal Cove State Park, 949/494-3539

ORANGE COUNTY

31 LOS TRANCOS

BEST (

Location: Pacific Coast Highway between
Laguna Beach and Corona del Mar
Parking/Fees: $10 entrance fee per vehicle
Hours: 6 A.M.-sunset
Facilities: lifeguards, picnic tables, showers,
and restrooms
Contact: Crystal Cove State Park,
949/494-3539

32 PELICAN POINT

Location: Pacific Coast Highway between
Laguna Beach and Corona del Mar
Parking/Fees: $10 entrance fee per vehicle
Hours: 6 A.M.-sunset
Facilities: lifeguards, picnic tables, showers,
and restrooms
Contact: Crystal Cove State Park,
949/494-3539

ACCOMMODATIONS

The big news at Crystal Cove is the renovation of rustic coastal cottages in the Crystal
Cove Historic District. The **Crystal Cove
Beach Cottages** (Crystal Cove State Park,
949/494-3539, $$) opened in June 2006, mak-
ing it possible for beachgoers to rent these
studios and one- and two-bedroom homes,
as well as hostel accommodations. It's a rare
opportunity to stay in some nifty, out-of-the-
way beach bungalows, 13 out of 46 of which
are renovated and rentable. And though they
date back only to the 1930s, this does indeed
qualify as historic in Southern California.
Rates are surprisingly reasonable—two people
can share a room in a dorm-style cottage with
five bedrooms for $63 per night, while $185
per night will net you a two-bedroom cot-
tage all your own. Reservations must be made
through ReserveAmerica (800/444-7275); you

can reserve up to seven months in advance. Do
jump on this one!

COASTAL CUISINE

As if the good news about Crystal Cove Beach
Cottages wasn't enough, they've opened the
Beachcomber Cafe (15 Crystal Cove,
949/376-6900, $$), a restaurant serving three
daily meals, in one of the restored cottages in
the Crystal Cove Historic District.

Corona del Mar

Corona del Mar literally translates as "Crown
of the Sea," but to us it simply means "the good
life." When this book hits the best-seller lists
(hope springs eternal!) or we win the lottery,
Corona del Mar would be high on our list of
places where we'd happily relocate. For one
thing, this small, mostly residential, and fabu-
lously wealthy "neighborhood" in Newport
Beach is blessed with a sweeping vista of the
ocean. The town's financial standing is evident
in the Lamborghini car dealership and chic
boutiques that do a buzzing business along
the main drag. It's a shame there's nowhere
viable to stay in Corona del Mar, because the
beaches and the bluff-top parks overlooking
them are as gorgeous as any in Orange County.
For the most part, people tear through town
on the grievously overburdened Pacific Coast
Highway. It's well worth exploring the beaches
off the beaten path along Ocean Boulevard. In
fact, a whole other world lies off to the side of
the highway clamor.

We took time to get to know Corona del
Mar better on our latest trip; henceforth,
it will become a required annual visit. The
primarily residential oceanfront here is a
visual feast, both seaward and landward. A
fascinating mix of architectural styles gives
the ritzy neighborhood a distinctively civilized air. We came upon a group of plein air
landscape painters, mostly elderly women in

sun bonnets, who gather regularly for sea-side painting sessions. Although they may be deemed amateurs by critics, some of their work is at least as good as the stuff that gets peddled for inflated sums in the galleries of Laguna Beach.

For more information, contact the Corona del Mar Chamber of Commerce, 2855 East Pacific Coast Highway, Suite 101, Corona del Mar, CA 92625, 949/673-4050, www .cdchamber.com.

BEACHES

A linear park runs above Corona del Mar's beaches along Ocean Boulevard. At the south end, a steep road leads down to a wonderfully secluded cove, known as **Little Corona del Mar Beach.** As you're walking, be sure to ogle the estates that line the creekside canyon above the cove. Also notice the rock formations, including a perfect arch, in the water. Little Corona del Mar Beach is a miniature paradise for snorkeling, scuba diving, and tidepooling.

Corona del Mar State Beach (a.k.a. Main Beach)—which is reachable from the other end of Ocean Boulevard via a drive that drops down to it—is gorgeous, as are the people who go there. It is a gigantic triangular drape of sand studded with volleyball nets and beach blankets. More than once, we've been content just to sit and drink for a while in this real-life version of *Baywatch*. It's a state beach that's run by the city of Newport Beach. We don't exactly understand how or why.

Corona del Mar lies on the south side of Newport Harbor. Climbing the rocks at the north end of Corona del Mar Beach, in defiance of the Don't Climb the Rocks sign, will net you a nifty vantage point from which to view the harbor. If you scramble down from Ocean Boulevard to the sandy cove known as **Rocky Point** or Pirates Cove, you can watch boats come and go in relative solitude. Just up from Rocky Point is **China Cove Beach,**

accessible via a stairwell at Ocean Boulevard and Fernleaf Avenue. You can also hike up to Rocky Point and China Cove from Corona del Mar Beach.

Back up on Ocean Boulevard, overlooking China Cove, is **Lookout Point.** It's a wonderful spot from which to gaze out on the harbor jetties, Balboa Peninsula, and the setting sun. Concrete benches provide perches for savoring the magnificent view. The grass is greener here, and we mean that literally. Any of the houses in the vicinity could be featured on the Home and Garden Channel. Especially in the dimming light of day, these contemporary and Spanish-style marvels personify the upscale California lifestyle—an aesthete's dream, with the ocean as heavenly backdrop. By the way, in the unlikely event that anyone who lives along Ocean Boulevard or Poppy Avenue in Corona del Mar wants to invite us to a party, consider this an automatic RSVP. We're there!

33 LITTLE CORONA DEL MAR BEACH

Location: Ocean Boulevard at Poppy Avenue in Corona del Mar
Parking/Fees: free street parking
Hours: 6 A.M.-10 P.M.
Facilities: none
Contact: Newport Beach Marine Department, 949/673-3047

34 CORONA DEL MAR STATE BEACH

Location: Ocean Boulevard at Iris Avenue in Corona del Mar
Parking/Fees: $8 entrance fee per vehicle
Hours: 8 A.M.-10 P.M. PDT (to 8 P.M. PST)

ORANGE COUNTY

Facilities: concession, lifeguards, restrooms, showers, and picnic tables
Contact: Newport Beach Marine Department, 949/644-3151

35 ROCKY POINT

Location: Ocean Boulevard at Harbor Channel in Corona del Mar
Parking/Fees: free street parking
Hours: 6 A.M.-10 P.M.
Facilities: none
Contact: Newport Beach Marine Department, 949/673-3047

36 CHINA COVE BEACH

Location: Ocean Boulevard at Fernleaf Avenue in Corona del Mar
Parking/Fees: free street parking
Hours: 6 A.M.-10 P.M.
Facilities: none
Contact: Newport Beach Marine Department, 949/673-3047

COASTAL CUISINE

While it lacks lodging options, Corona del Mar has some of the glitziest restaurants in Orange County. Among the more notable ones are the posh, contemporary **Trees** (44 Heliotrope Avenue, 949/673-0910, $$$) and the British-themed, jacket-required **Five Crowns** (3801 East Pacific Coast Highway, 949/760-0331, $$$$). The latter is an elegant re-creation of England's oldest inn, Ye Old Bell, that's faithful in every detail, right down to the Elizabethan garb worn by the wait staff.

Our personal favorite is **Oysters** (2515 E. Coast Highway, 949/675-7411, $$$), an informal but elegant (read: no dress code or valet parking) place that has been working magic with Pacific Rim–style seafood preparations since 1989. A recent meal here was one of the finest, from start to finish, we've ever

had in our beach travels. The oyster sampler contained four distinctive types: Fanny Bays, from British Columbia (firm, salted cucumber flavor); Hama Hamas, from Washington State (mild fruity flavor); Hog Islands, from Tomales Bay (plump, smoky flavored, indescribably delicious); and Sunset Beaches, from Puget Sound (crisp and fruity). The kung pao calamari, a popular appetizer, was sheer perfection, a peerless combination of texture and flavors, and the helping was large enough for a meal.

For entrées, the flat-iron seared Hawaiian ahi—a thick, moist slab of crimson as tender as filet mignon—was brilliantly complemented by jasmine-nori rice, spinach, and a soy-chile glaze. The misoyaki northern halibut was another masterpiece of blended flavors and textures, served with fresh soybeans, oyster mushrooms, and a potato-daikon puree. Oysters is commendably participating in a restaurant industry campaign to "Take a Pass on Chilean Sea Bass" by replacing that popular fish with halibut. Without restrictions on the fishing of this species, the Chilean sea bass has been on the verge of commercial extinction for years. Oddly enough, the one thing that may save it is not a positive thing: Chilean sea bass has been found to have extremely high levels of mercury, and consumers are advised that more than two helpings per month is dangerous. Let's all take a pass!

For dessert, the vanilla bean crème brûlée was transformed by a topping of fresh raspberries and a "blowtorch fired" sugar glaze. Our genial waiter, previously a veteran of 10 years in French restaurants, was sold on Oysters, telling us the chef stands so firmly for consistency that restaurant regulars claim to wake up fantasizing about what they will order here, knowing it will be as good as the last time. We will remember Oysters for our next visit. Until then, visions of kung pao squid dance in our heads.

Newport Beach and Balboa

Newport Beach has been mislabeled. The goods are in order, but the writing on the can is all wrong. Before our initial visit way back in the mid-1980s, we'd been led to believe that it was "Nouveau Beach," a land of conspicuous consumption that looked down on anyone in flip-flops and cutoffs. We came expecting manic wheeler-dealer entrepreneurs and bored women dripping with jewelry. After all, Newport Beach was modeled on and named after Newport, Rhode Island, an exclusive community for the old-money yachting set. Indeed, Newport Beach has a few of its eastern kin's amenities, most notably the second largest pleasure-craft harbor in the country (with 10,000 berths). But Newport Beach also has an unpretentious, accommodating side that just doesn't jibe with its designer reputation. After numerous happy visits here, we've come to realize that Newport Beach is, at heart, a fun and funky beach town.

First of all, with a population of 84,200, Newport Beach is not a small town, nor is most of it truly on the beach. Many Newport Beach residents drive expensive imported cars with vanity plates, but they tend to live in gated subdivisions on the mainland or on the exclusive islands in Balboa Bay. The heart and soul of the city is out on Balboa Peninsula, a thin finger of land that reaches into the Pacific, then bends inward to protect the beautiful harbor. Back bays and waterways have been sculpted into the peninsula, and two small inhabited islands, Balboa and Lido, sit close by. Newport Beach is almost always sunny, relaxed, and dominated by watery pastimes. Boats dock right up against the back doors of houses.

The fun begins when you turn off Pacific Coast Highway onto Newport Boulevard or West Balboa Boulevard. The latter runs the length of Newport Beach's peninsula. It's a six-mile stretch ending at the Wedge, by the north jetty at the harbor mouth. To oversimplify, the big money is on the harbor side and all the fun is on the ocean side. Most beachgoers assemble in the general vicinity of the peninsula's ocean piers, Newport Pier and Balboa Pier.

The most boisterous activity can be found at and around Newport Pier. The first pier on this site was built in 1888 by the McFadden brothers, who founded the town and for whom the pier was originally named. Local history lingers here in the form of the beloved Dory Fleet, a fishing contingent that has launched wooden dories from this spot since 1891. Each day, the Dory Fleet leaves before dawn and returns by 7:30 A.M. to sell their fresh catch at Newport Pier. Their motto: Our fish is the freshest fish on earth. A wooden sculpture pays tribute to these stouthearted laborers, and their method of selling fish right on the beach creates an authentic California atmosphere. Nearby, you might see street performers addressing the crowd. We observed a balloon sculptor singing spirituals in an operatic tenor while a long-haired sea dog took Polaroids of passersby posing with his beautifully plumed parrots.

In the 1980s Newport's nouveau-riche elite—exhibiting the shortsightedness that brought them wealth but wound up bankrupting Orange County in 1994—wanted to do away with the Dory Fleet and give the Newport Pier area a sprucing up. They were quickly shot down, offering further proof that Newport Beach's ordinary townsfolk possess the sense and spirit that the more moneyed mullet-brains lack.

Balboa Pier lies two miles farther out along the peninsula. Here, things are a little less crazy. On the harbor side behind Balboa Pier is Balboa Pavilion, a Victorian landmark that dates from 1906. A renowned hot spot during

ORANGE COUNTY

BIKING THE BALBOA PENINSULA

People of all ages flock to the area around the Newport Beach Pier and jam the Balboa Peninsula with traffic. During peak season it's not unusual to find traffic slowed to a standstill on Balboa Boulevard all the way out to the Pacific Coast Highway. Traffic is a thorn in Newport Beach's side. It's partly the result of a decision made many years ago not to have I-5 built closer to the coast here. (Ironically, the decision was made in order to preserve the peace and quiet of the community.) The strategy worked for a while but backfired when Newport Beach exploded with growth in the 1980s.

It goes without saying that driving here can be as gnarly as swimming through a kelp bed. Parking tickets come with stiff fines, and parking at most meters costs $0.25 for 15 minutes, with a six-hour limit. Six hours costs six bucks, and who carries 24 quarters around with them? The city experimented with "smart" meters, which didn't require coins, but went back to the old way of doing business.

The best way to see the beach at Newport Beach is on bicycle, coasting along on the Ocean Front promenade. The peninsula is flat and the city is bicycle-friendly. Local bike-rental outfits carry an excellent map of trails, with detailed tips and rules of the road that are useful anywhere, as well as local points of interest, license information and fees, hazards, and bike lanes along highways. Bike trails run as far east as Irvine, traversing the Upper Newport Bay, a state-managed ecological reserve. So save yourself some hassles – not to mention gas and parking expenses – and have twice the fun with half the wheels.

Here are three places to rent bikes near Newport Pier, right in the heart of the action:

- **Let It Roll Bike Shop,** 3130 West Balboa Boulevard, 949/675-3136
- **Newport Beach Bike and Skate Rental,** 2200 West Oceanfront, 949/675-1065
- **Boardwalk Sports,** 100 McFadden Place, 949/673-1767

the Big Band era, the pavilion still hosts events. You can catch a harbor-cruise boat (see the former homes of John Wayne, King Gillette, and Ron Popeil, inventor of the "Pocket Fisherman"!), take a whale-watching trip, or board a passenger ferry to Catalina Island. A cute quarter-a-ride ferry runs continuously to Balboa Island. It is mostly residential, tightly packed with the homes of wealthy people whose cars chirp like crickets as they approach and exit with electronic keys. The island has a sprinkling of upscale boutiques and tourist shops, but its most appealing feature is the walkway around it, which offers views of the bay and harbor.

Newport Beach is a quintessential California beach town by day and a rock-and-roll party zone at night. Despite the nonstop crunch of

humanity, the peninsula is a friendly place. The most violent blows result from the affectionate pounding of backs, and the loudest shouts are those of approval for some minuscule sashaying bikini. One local restaurant goes so far as to offer "free salad for girls in bikinis." The pedestrian's best friend in Newport Beach is Ocean Front promenade, an asphalt trail that runs along the ocean for nearly the full length of the peninsula. It is the primary route for bicyclists, joggers, and in-line skaters, and the human parade along this walkway is an intoxicating sight in and of itself.

For more information, contact Newport Beach Conference and Visitor Bureau, 1200 Newport Center Drive, Suite 120, Newport Beach, CA 92663, 949/722-1611 or 800/942-6278, www.visitnewportbeach.com.

BEACHES

There are more than six miles of ocean beach and two massive piers on Balboa Peninsula. Starting at the south end, in Balboa, **West Jetty View Park** (a.k.a. The Wedge) is El Dorado for bodysurfers. Extremely rough surf, with waves as high as 20 feet, make the Wedge unsafe for board surfing and suitable only for highly experienced bodysurfers. Just across the harbor from the Wedge is Corona del Mar State Beach. Do not try to swim across. It may look like a short distance, but the water is treacherous. Just watch the boats sailing in and out of the harbor.

The stretch of sand from the Wedge to Balboa Pier is **Balboa Beach.** The dune structure along here is exceptionally healthy. This is what the Orange County coast must've looked like in the predevelopment 1950s, when it was primarily an escape for L.A. day-trippers. Families congregate on Balboa Beach for relaxed sunbathing and swimming.

The main beach on the peninsula is **Newport Beach Municipal Beach,** which runs for two and a quarter miles from Newport Pier to the Santa Ana River Jetty. Along this golden strand surfers prefer the beaches at 52nd Street, North Jetty, and from 61st Street Beach to **Santa Ana River Jetties** (a.k.a. Santa Ana River County Beach), which flanks both sides of the river mouth, just south of Huntington Beach. All beaches on the Newport Beach peninsula are subject to a 10 P.M. curfew.

We're certainly not telling you anything you don't know when we say that traffic on Balboa Peninsula can get hellish on weekends and busy on summer weekdays. The only advice we can give is to bring lots of quarters for the meters—a roll or two if you want to stay all day.

37 WEST JETTY VIEW PARK

Location: end of Channel Road at tip of Balboa Peninsula, in Balboa

Parking/Fees: free parking lot
Hours: 6 A.M.-10 P.M.
Facilities: none
Contact: Newport Beach Marine Department, 949/673-3047

38 BALBOA BEACH

Location: Balboa Boulevard at Balboa Pier in Balboa
Parking/Fees: metered street parking
Hours: 6 A.M.-10 P.M.
Facilities: lifeguards, restrooms, showers, and picnic tables
Contact: Newport Beach Marine Department, 949/673-3047

39 NEWPORT BEACH MUNICIPAL BEACH

  BEST (

Location: Ocean Front at Newport Pier in Newport Beach
Parking/Fees: metered lot and street parking
Hours: 6 A.M.-10 P.M.
Facilities: lifeguards, restrooms, showers, and picnic tables
Contact: Newport Beach Marine Department, 949/673-3047

40 SANTA ANA RIVER JETTIES

Location: Seashore Drive between Summit and 61st Streets in Newport Beach
Parking/Fees: metered street parking
Hours: 6 A.M.-10 P.M.
Facilities: lifeguards
Contact: North Beaches Operation Office of Orange County Harbors, Beaches, and Parks, 949/723-4511

ORANGE COUNTY

© PARKE PUTERBAUGH

Newport Beach

RECREATION AND ATTRACTIONS

- **Bike/Skate Rentals:** Newport Beach Bike Skate Rental, 2200 West Ocean Front, Newport Beach, 949/675-1065
- **Ecotourism:** Upper Newport Bay Ecological Reserve, Newport Beach, 949/640-6746
- **Marina:** Newport Dunes Resort and Marina, 1131 Back Bay Drive, Newport Beach, 949/729-3863
- **Piers:** Newport Pier, McFadden Square, 22nd Street at Newport Boulevard, Newport Beach; Balboa Pier, foot of Main Street, Balboa
- **Rainy Day Attraction:** Newport Harbor Nautical Museum, 151 East Coast Highway, Newport Beach, 949/673-7863
- **Shopping/Browsing:** Fashion Island, Newport Center Drive, Newport Beach, 949/721-2000
- **Sportfishing:** Bongos Sportfishing Charters, 2140 Newport Boulevard, Newport Beach, 949/673-2810; Davey's Locker, 400 Main Street, 949/673-1434
- **Surf Report:** 949/673-3371
- **Surf Shop:** Green Room, 4525 Pacific Coast Highway, Newport Beach, 949/548-3688
- **Vacation Rentals:** Beach 'n Bay Rental Company, 1501 West Balboa Boulevard, Balboa, 949/673-9368

ACCOMMODATIONS

Nightly lodgings directly on the beach are scarcer than gulls' teeth. A particularly nice and fairly pricey one that's only a few bare feet from the surf is the **Newport Beachwalk Hotel** (2306 West Ocean Front, 949/673-7030, www.newportbeachwalkhotel.com, $$$). Formerly a surf shop, its 20 elegant rooms, ranging $175–275, will put you in mind of the Italian Riviera. Only a block from the beach and three blocks from the pier, **Bay Shores Peninsula Hotel** (1800 West Balboa Boulevard, 949/675-3463, $$$) is a salmon-colored, 21-room inn with homey, comfortable rooms.

The inn provides a decent continental breakfast, not to mention everything from beach towels to boogie boards just for the asking. Plus you get a parking space—no small perk in Newport Beach.

Just off Balboa Peninsula, the most reasonably priced ($99 in season) and beach accessible of the motels that line Pacific Coast Highway is the **Newport Channel Inn** (6030 West Pacific Coast Highway, 949/642-3030 or 800/255-8614, www.newportchannelinn .com, $). It isn't fancy but it is clean and serviceable. The motel is across the street—the "street" being Pacific Coast Highway—from the wide, sandy beach at the north end of Newport Beach.

The friendly tone of the town and easy proximity to the sand makes a weekly or monthly apartment rental an appealing prospect here. Two agencies that specialize in beachfront rentals are **Villa Rentals** (427 31st Street, 949/675-4912, www.villarentalsinc.com) and **Balboa Newport Realty** (428 Third Street, 949/723-4494, www.balboanewport.com). The rental units on Balboa Beach are more family oriented, with a casual, kid-friendly ambience. Rates range from $750 for a week to $2,500 for a month. People recline in chaise lounges on back patios, reading newspapers and drinking highballs or coffee, oblivious to the parade passing just feet away on the Ocean Front promenade. The wildest characters you'll run across are adolescents trying to act raunchy. One 12-year-old sported a T-shirt that read "Will Work For Sex." Very funny, junior.

On either side of Newport Pier and continuing to the north end of the peninsula, rentals are snapped up by college kids or groups of party-minded guys whose spartan pads are open to the scrutiny of passersby. Shirtless, tanned, smiling, and perpetually holding beers, they hang loose on every balcony and porch. We peered into one unkempt bungalow where a surfboard lay on a bed and a skateboard hung on the wall. Only in California . . .

COASTAL CUISINE

The **Crab Cooker** (2200 Newport Boulevard, 949/673-0100, $$), one of our favorite eateries in the universe, has been serving its patented smoked and grilled fish for almost 50 years in a building that was once a bank. "We're the only seafood joint that keeps its fish in a vault," jokes owner Bob Roubian, who is an expert on the subject of fish. He is, in fact, obsessed with them. He thinks about fish all day and dreams about fish at night. He sculpts, poeticizes, and writes songs about fish. A recording of a song he penned, "Who Hears the Fishes When They Cry," is sold at the restaurant. (He sounds like Tom Waits.) Music and fish have a lot in common, he says; both have scales. He encourages everyone to "Eat Lots A Fish." This is his motto, and it is emblazoned on the front of the building, along with such nuggets of wisdom as "Slam Some Salmon" and "The main thing is to keep the main thing the main thing."

Near Newport Pier, the Crab Cooker is a local institution for several reasons, not the least of which is that Roubian enforces strict standards on the fish he serves. He buys only fish that have been caught by the hook-and-line method and are eviscerated (bled and cleaned) within five minutes of being pulled from the water, thus assuring their freshness. Fresh fish never smells fishy, he insists; if anything, it smells a little sweet, like watermelon. His fish, shrimp, crab, and scallops are cooked on wooden skewers over a charcoal grill, because that's the way his mother did it. All dinners come with homemade bread, coleslaw, and Romano potatoes. You can actually make a filling meal from the Crab Cooker's incomparably good smoked albacore and smoked salmon appetizers. (Get the large versions, which are $4.25 and $6, respectively.) The food is served on paper plates, like a picnic, and it is beyond compare in quality and price.

This wonderfully ramshackle place is always packed, but don't try to call for reservations or pay with plastic. Just show up and wait your turn in line. To Roubian this is democracy at work, and he'll make no exceptions—not for a U.S. president, not for his grandmother, not even for himself. John Wayne, a longtime regular, always had to wait his turn, as did Richard Nixon. Sometimes the wait can be long, but just settle back on the wooden benches outside, have a cup of the Crab Cooker's famous seafood chowder, and write someone a postcard. (Roubian provides cards and postage, if mailed from the restaurant.) But by all means "eat lots a fish" here as often as possible.

The **Cannery** (3010 Lafayette Avenue, 949/566-0060, $$$) also serves some fine fare. The calamari appetizer is as tender a take on this staple as we've ever had, and the grilled swordfish tomatillo is a winning catch. The restaurant is in a converted cannery, with implements of the trade hung on the wall: wheels, pulleys, conveyer lines, boilers, and processing machines. You can eat inside or on a deck overlooking the water. After dinner, the Cannery morphs into one of the livelier nightspots in Newport Beach.

Even if you're not casting a line you can still land a fish on Newport Pier. At pier's end, **Newport Grill and Sushi Bar** (1 Newport Pier, 949/675-9771, $$$) serves grilled fish, sushi, and steaks from its second-floor dining room. It's easily the best view in town.

For a quick bite with a nice view, hit **Ruby's Diner** (1 Balboa Pier, 949/675-7829, $) at the end of Balboa Pier. The fare is mostly burgers and the atmosphere is faux-1950s diner, rimmed with neon. But the view is the second best in town and the grub is fine, as far as burgers and dogs go. Another local institution is the **Shore House Cafe** (801 East Balboa Boulevard, 949/673-7726, $$), on the main drag.

At the other extreme is **21 Oceanfront** (2100 West Ocean Front, 949/673-2100, $$$$), an elegant fine-dining restaurant that serves fish flown in from all over the world. Abalone is a specialty, and entrées run $25–55. In other words, 21 Oceanfront is high-priced and high-end.

NIGHTLIFE

Most of the action after dark takes place on and around the piers. At **Balboa Pier,** set the wayback machine to the 1950s and step into a world of flirtatious adolescents on parade. Around and around the Balboa Pavilion circles an army of Annettes and Frankies too young to drink but too blitzed out on raging hormones to sit still. Dressed to thrill, they wander about, creating human logjams broken up by friendly beat cops on patrol. They walk around the pavilion again and return to the same logjam—cruising without cars, as it were.

The crowd is older, noisier, and more unpredictable at **Newport Pier.** Motorcycles and muscle T-shirts replace high fashion, and voices get raised a bit louder. The same cops survey the scene, but in a somewhat less amicable manner. Mostly, though, the chaos has a certain California etiquette to it, with lots of backslaps, handshakes, and high fives.

Blackie's by the Sea (21st Street and Ocean Front) is the beer-bar equivalent of the Crab Cooker. It is a timeless, changeless throwback, directly on Ocean Front promenade. On the door is a sign that reads Sorry, We're Open, and on the walls are mounted hammerhead sharks, team pennants, three TVs (each tuned to a different station), pool tables, and a jukebox. It is a classic beer-drinker's oasis at any time of the day or night. We'd give you the phone number, but it's unlisted—part of its homey charm.

Just to the north is **Mutt Lynch's** (23rd Street and Ocean Front, 949/675-1556), a raucous corner joint serving passable pizza, sandwiches, and sports-bar munchies, plus geysers of beer.

Around the corner, off Ocean Front, is the **Stag Bar** (121 McFadden Place, 949/673-4470). It is not, however, a stag bar. That is to say, women are welcome here. Reflecting a cutting-edge collegiate atmosphere, the Stag Bar is a raucous, beer-guzzling, hell-yessing kind of place, with a great jukebox, pool tables, and no pretensions. Draft beer is served in schooners the size of bazookas. On an otherwise slow Monday night in early spring when the rest of Newport Beach was dead, we watched from our bar-side perches as the Stag Bar slowly but surely filled to capacity. By midnight the place was thumping to the beat of pool cues, jukebox jive, and erupting laughter. It occurred to us that, for a so-called stag bar, there were sure a lot of women. In fact, they outnumbered the men, at least on this particular evening. Because you cannot legally smoke in any bar or restaurant in California, the sidewalk outside the Stag Bar gets crowded with barflies taking frequent cigarette breaks. The smoke drifts into the bar, virtually negating the anti-smoking law's directive. We watched three college coeds celebrate the rites of spring by playing pool and drinking beer. The noise level grew and the shots became less accurate with each swig, but no one seemed to notice—ah, the delightful incoherence of youth. Meanwhile, a discombobulated woman who had just panhandled us for a buck wandered outside, where she collapsed in a heap on the sidewalk. We reminisced with the bartender about various punk bands we'd seen over the years, while the jukebox pumped out tunes by Sublime, X, and Social Distortion. We programmed a few selections of our own, including, appropriately, "L.A. Woman," by the Doors. We also played "Whole Lotta Rosie" (the live version) by AC/DC.

Speaking of rosie, you can do a beer-fueled version of ring-around-the-rosie in the Newport Pier area without having to drive a car. Perambulate Ocean Front, McFadden Place, and Balboa Boulevard, angling into the Stag Bar, Mutt Lynch's, Blackie's, **Baja Sharkeez** (114 McFadden Place, 949/673-0292), **Hooters** (2406 Newport Boulevard, 949/723-5800), and **Woody's Wharf** (2318 Newport Boulevard, 949/675-0474). The last of these is another wild hangout with live music (mostly blues and boogie) that gets mobbed on weekends. The clientele seems a bit wanton. It has an outdoor patio and a harborfront dining area, but the main part of the club is configured all wrong and we wound up being wedged against the bar like sardines. Still, it's a hopping place if you want to frolic with the locals, who have been doing so here for 30 years.

Huntington Beach

Huntington Beach is an essentially faceless city whose every move is plotted to best serve the interests of the Orange County business community. Everywhere, it looks and sounds and smells like a city under construction (or reconstruction). This is not necessarily all bad news, but it does mean that Huntington Beach lacks any sort of defining personality. Newport Beach is a funky, low-to-the-ground beach town, and Laguna Beach is cultured and rarefied. By comparison, Huntington Beach feels like a completely sterile asphalt-and-concrete sprawl zone. As if its utter lack of personality weren't bad enough, its beachfront is hemmed between the fuming stacks of a power plant and an active oil field. Inland, the numbing concrete corridor of Beach Boulevard is lined for miles with strip malls and franchises all the way out to I-405.

There's a brief but welcome eruption of bright, squeaky clean commerce by the Huntington Beach Pier along Pacific Coast Highway at Beach Boulevard. The pier and the surfing scene are easily the best things about Huntington Beach. To be sure, the development landward of the beach seems endless (e.g., "4 New Home Neighborhoods Open Soon!"), as Huntington Beach—with a population of 202,500, Orange County's 4th largest and state's 20th largest city—is completely at the mercy of the real-estate industry. It looks like utter madness to us.

Once upon a time Huntington Beach was just another cow town close to Los Angeles with a beautiful beach that was much beloved by the surfing cult. They knew it then as "Surf City," and it still gets called that now,

© PARKE PUTERBAUGH

Huntington Beach

though more by businessmen looking for a marketing handle than by loyal surfers. In Huntington Beach, as Jan and Dean sang in their number-one hit from 1963, the surf was always up and there was the added incentive of "two girls for every boy." During the golden era of surfing in the 1950s and 1960s, the surfers pretty much had the place to themselves. As recently as the mid-1980s, Huntington Beach was a pretty sleepy-looking place along Pacific Coast Highway, lined with unpretentious food shacks (usually Mexican), surf shops, and one-story motor courts. The town would awaken only for the annual Labor Day surfing tournament and the de rigueur riot that often accompanied it.

All that began to change with the arrival of the Waterfront Hilton Beach Resort, a 12-story, 290-room hotel. It has been joined by the Pierside Pavilion and Promenade—clusters of retail stores, restaurants, theaters, and office space that chased a lot of funky old joints off the beach. Hyatt Ocean Grand, a $142 million resort colossus, opened in 2003. This is big news along a coastline where permits for new construction are rarely granted. There's also a gargantuan "mixed use" complex, including a high-end terraced retail mall, that occupies 34 ocean-facing acres. After having remained sleepy for so many years, this flat, foursquare cow town is now an all-too-wide-awake insomniac.

With a bit of imagination, the eye can trace its way across the landscape and imagine what Huntington Beach must have looked like at some remote point in the pre-settlement past: fields of large, fully vegetated dunes extending to the east, backed by lagoons and wetlands. In the early years of this century, the town was actually named "Pacific City" by a developer who wanted to see it become the West Coast's answer to Atlantic City. Pacific City was sold to a group who renamed it Huntington Beach, hoping that by paying nominal tribute to railroad magnate H. E. Huntington he would extend his Pacific Electric Railroad to the young city. (He fell for the ploy.) In 1919 Standard Oil leased 500 acres from the Huntington Beach Company; a year later, a well came in with a roar heard for miles. Nine million gallons a year are pumped out of Huntington Beach. Oil derricks are everywhere (except tourist

LEGEND OF THE DUKE

There's another "Duke" besides John Wayne who left his mark on Orange County. He is **Duke Kahanamoku,** a Waikiki wave-rider who became a California legend. More than anyone else, he spread the word about Huntington Beach, turning a withering, would-be resort into a bustling beach town.

Duke was a Hawaiian native, Olympic swimmer, and a world-class surfer – one of the first, in fact, to make a living at these things. Way back at the turn of the 20th century he publicly promoted the sport, gracefully skiing the sloping surf on his favorite plank. His salary was paid by railroad mogul H. E. Huntington, who wanted to give the public new incentives to travel his freshly laid stretch of track from Los Angeles to Huntington Beach. Duke wowed the locals in the 1920s by surfing under the pier – a dangerous but impressive feat.

Following Duke's lead, a small but growing surfing cult pointed their longboards toward Huntington Beach. In the early 1960s surfing seized the national imagination. When the Beach Boys, Jan and Dean, and the Surfaris took the sport into the Top 40 with a string of catchy surfing anthems, the entire nation suddenly became desirous of coastal access. Surfers trekked the entire West Coast in search of the perfect wave, but it was Huntington Beach that became known as "Surf City," after Jan and Dean's chart-topping hit. The first major surfing competition, the Pacific Coast Surfboard Championships, was held here. Since the early 1970s, the U.S. Surfing Championships have drawn hundreds of thousands to the brown-sugar beach at Huntington.

For many years, a small bust of Duke Kahanamoku gazed seaward from the foot of the Huntington Beach Pier. It has since been moved inside the **Huntington Beach International Surfing Museum** (411 Olive Avenue, 714/960-3483). These days, the late Duke – he died in 1968 at the age of 78 – is recognized as the father of surfing. Remnants and relics of surfing's golden age fill the museum, which is one of the few things worth visiting in Huntington Beach besides the beach itself. Artifacts include wildly designed Hawaiian shirts to a 13-foot, 135-pound wooden longboard. There's also memorabilia from the Huntington Beach Surf Theater, a bygone 1960s-era film house that showed only surf movies.

Ah, yes, those were the days.

brochures): by the highway, in backyards, on the beach, atop offshore platforms. A gigantic active field runs for miles from Goldenwest Street north to Sunset Beach. The pumping drills extend as far as the eye can see, like an aerobics class of metallic black magpies doing toe-touching exercises.

Despite all the changes, Huntington Beach remains a people's beach. Families, surfers, and everyday folks still crowd the city and state beaches that run for a great distance in either direction from the pier. But the retail scenery around these beaches has been drastically altered. At one extreme, there's the Waterfront Hilton, a towering monolith. At the other extreme, fast-food chains now rule the waterfront where once humble but lovable nonfranchised burger and taco huts used to stand. The heart of the action is where Main Street meets Pacific Coast Highway at Huntington Beach Pier. This intersection is home to the Pierside Pavilion and Promenade, a two-story boutique mall aimed at those whose idea of a day at the beach is shopping close to it. Lest we sound too harsh, experience has shown that shops in these glitzy new malls generally have limited life spans, while they displace less trendy stores and restaurants that might have been around for decades. In the process, we've lost—and continue to lose—

many of the beachside stands that stood sentry throughout the years when *American Graffiti* was being lived in reality instead of marketed as nostalgia.

The old Huntington Beach—a motley but likable cluster of surf shops, dive bars, and food stands—has fallen to the wrecking ball. City officials referred to the forced uprooting and relocation of mobile-home-park-dwelling oceanside residents, in *1984*-style double-speak, as a "conversion procedure." We have no delusions: We are not lamenting the passing of great architectural landmarks or businesses that can compete in the latter-day market-place. It's just sad to witness the end of an era. A generation from now, will anyone remember what the beach life was really like?

Consider the squabbling that ensued when Dean Torrance, of Jan and Dean fame, sug-gested to the Huntington Beach City Council in 1991 that they consider copyrighting the name "Surf City" for promotional purposes. "People from Iowa want to come here to the beach," noted Torrance. "All the city has to do is grab onto the coattails of this idea." A great and legitimate hook for reeling in the tour-ists, no? Not in the eyes of one councilman, who whined, "We want people who will spend several hundred dollars a day in our hotels and restaurants. With inland California surfers, we're lucky if they spend $10 or $15 a day." This is how minds in Orange County work: with myopic eyes fixed on the bottom line at all times. And then, ironically, Huntington Beach got in a great big fight with Santa Cruz to brand itself...you guessed it...Surf City.

Whether you're spending $10 or $300 a day, the only part of Huntington Beach that matters is its coastal frontage. The town that sprawls behind it, arrayed along broad, strip-mall-lined arteries that link Pacific Coast Highway with I-405, offers the visitor little that can't be found on or close to the beach. Beach Boulevard is the Big Kahuna of com-merce in the area, offering a lengthy corridor of gas stations, franchise food stands, ATM machines, and strip malls. You can venture down this sun-beaten ribbon of concrete in search of drive-through grub, suntan lotion, film, flip-flops, or a more affordable motel, if you like, but there's not much to distinguish the interior of Huntington Beach from Fresno or Des Moines.

Incidentally, we tried to get a balky laptop PC repaired in Huntington Beach. We hauled it to a computer shop way out Goldenwest Street, farther inland than we care to venture on our beach-research trips. The dude behind the counter informed us of the inflated cost of working on a PC (minimum charge: $75). We lug nearly worthless old laptops on our beach junkets for obvious reasons (i.e., they might get stolen), but they do a perfectly fine job of word processing. When we seemed dis-inclined to leave the malfunctioning PC for servicing, the clerk suggested something we might try to get it to work. Lo and behold, we were able to revive it back in our hotel room. What sticks in our mind about this episode was the youthful clerk's disengage-ment and glassy-eyed expression. He looked like a character out of *Children of the Damned.* It was like communicating with a robot. His detached demeanor is not, we hope, what becomes of people who live in a community where shopping-mall sterility takes over their every remaining brain cell, rendering them numb and dumb.

Here's the best indication we've yet run across of the Orange County mind-set. It was reported that Huntington Beach struck a spon-sorship deal with Coca-Cola, making Coke the city's "official beverage" and forbidding the sale of Pepsi everywhere but private businesses. It's bad enough that fast-food chains, sports arenas, schools, teams, and rock bands sign exclusivity contracts with the corporations that make these sweet, fizzy beverages. But a sponsorship deal with an entire *city*? Is there no bottom they won't plumb for money out here?

This Beaver Cleaver paradise of concrete and stucco has periodically been wracked with divisive issues. From battles over construction of the Waterfront to a debate over what to do with the Bolsa Chica wetlands (develop or preserve was the choice, and of course they developed), Huntington Beach found itself in the hot seat a lot in the 1990s. Even the old reliable surfers, source of the "Surf City" drawing card, have been a scourge on occasion. Back in 1987, the same year in which Huntington Beach was declared the safest city in the United States, a major riot erupted during the Labor Day surfing tournament, making national headlines. They subsequently moved the tournament to August (when crowds would be smaller), beefed up the police presence, and worked to keep alcohol off the beach. We've attended the U.S. Open of Surfing in Huntington Beach and had a blast. The world's best surfers in the water, live rock bands on the beach, a sea of tanned and gorgeous bodies—what was not to like?

This event dates back to 1959 and it's inextricably linked to Huntington Beach. These days it's under sponsorship from Honda. (Yes, it's now the Honda U.S. Open of Surfing.) So who won? It was reported that "Nathaniel Curran overcomes marginal waves and computer glitches to become the 2008 Honda U.S. Open of Surfing men's champion." Yay, Nathan!

Meanwhile, back in the truth-in-packaging department, they still tout Huntington Beach as one of America's safest cities. A little sleuthing on our part, however, turned up the statistic that among U.S. cities with populations between 100,000 and 250,000, Huntington recently placed 167th in terms of number of murders. Just so you know.

For more information, contact the Huntington Beach Conference and Visitor Bureau, 301 Main Street, Suite 208, Huntington Beach, CA 92648, 714/969-3492 or 800/729-6232, www.surfcityusa.com.

BEACHES

Santa Cruz and Huntington Beach have been squabbling for years over which community has earned the right to the title "Surf City," but based on all available evidence, it's not even worth debating. Huntington Beach

rules! Summer surfing championships have been held here since 1928, and it is widely known as the International Surf Capital of the World. In July and August, Huntington Beach hosts the U.S. Open of Surfing, and in June the OP Pro Surfing Championships takes place. There's always something going on here, surf-wise.

People flock to Huntington Beach from the surrounding valley towns, as well as from surf-deprived Long Beach, with boards strapped to the roofs of everything from boat-sized woodies to old VW bugs. The beach is so extensive, sandy, and clean, and the tumbling waves that roll ashore so well formed for surfing, that Huntington was voted the sixth best beach in the world in a poll conducted by (of all things) *Lifestyles of the Rich and Famous*. Surfers tend to get a far-off look in their eyes when they ponder the unobstructed south swells that spill forward in perfect curls of wave and foam (known as "rooster tails"), which can reach up to 12 feet in height.

The beaches of Huntington Beach offer an archetypal Southern California experience. They run for 8.5 miles, encompassing **Huntington State Beach, Huntington City Beach,** and **Bolsa Chica State Beach.** The offshore breezes are refreshing, and the strand is among the widest in Southern California—at least along the adjoining state and city beaches. It costs $10 to park at both Huntington State Beach and Huntington City Beach. There are an incredible 2,400 parking spaces at the city beach, which allows RV camping except during the most popular times of year (late spring through Labor Day).

Bring your running shoes or bicycle, because you can jog or pedal for five ocean-hugging miles (10 miles round-trip) along the **Huntington Beach Path** and **Bolsa Chica Bike Path.** We've taken many rejuvenating morning runs here. Up around Bolsa Chica, the beach starts narrowing. Fences have been put up to keep people back from unstable, crumbling cliffs. In places, the beach has narrowed so severely that it is usable only at low tide. RV camping is available at Bolsa Chica in an "en route" parking lot.

When you've had enough fun on the beach, make your way to the **Huntington Beach International Surfing Museum** (411 Olive Street, 714/960-3483) and the **Surfing Walk of Fame** (Main Street at Pacific Coast Highway). At the museum—opened in 1988, and the largest of a growing number of them—you learn that surfing was first documented in 1778, when Captain James Cook of the British Navy watched Hawaiian natives ride waves on crude longboards. The Walk of Fame starts at Jack's Surfboards and runs up Main Street. Stone monuments salute surfers inducted in such categories as Surf Pioneer, Surf Champion, and Woman of the Year.

41 HUNTINGTON STATE BEACH

Location: Pacific Coast Highway from Santa Ana River to Beach Boulevard in Huntington Beach
Parking/Fees: $10 entrance fee per vehicle
Hours: 6 A.M.-10 P.M.
Facilities: lifeguards, restrooms, showers, and picnic tables
Contact: Huntington State Beach, 714/536-1454

42 HUNTINGTON CITY BEACH

 BEST

Location: Pacific Coast Highway from Beach Boulevard to Goldenwest Street in Huntington Beach
Parking/Fees: $10 entrance fee per vehicle; RV camping fee $60 per night; camping not permitted late spring-summer
Hours: 5 A.M.-10 P.M.
Facilities: lifeguards, restrooms, showers, and picnic tables
Contact: Huntington City Beach, 714/536-5281

43 BOLSA CHICA STATE BEACH

Location: Pacific Coast Highway at Warner Avenue in Huntington Beach
Parking/Fees: $10 entrance fee per vehicle; RV camping fee $39-44 per night oceanfront, $29-34 per night inland, plus $7.50 reservation fee
Hours: 6 A.M.-10 P.M.
Facilities: lifeguards, restrooms, showers, and picnic tables
Contact: Bolsa Chica State Beach, 714/846-3460

RECREATION AND ATTRACTIONS

- **Bike/Skate Rentals:** Dwight's Beach Concession, 201 Pacific Coast Highway, 714/536-8083

- **Ecotourism:** Bolsa Chica Ecological Reserve, Amigos de Bolsa Chica, 714/897-7003

- **Marina:** Huntington Harbor Marina, 4281 Warner Avenue, 714/840-5545

- **Pier:** Huntington Beach Pier, Main Street and Pacific Coast Highway, Huntington Beach, 714/536-5281

- **Rainy Day Attraction:** International Surfing Museum, 411 Olive Avenue, 714/960-3483

- **Shopping/Browsing:** Ocean Promenade, 101 Main Street

- **Surf Report:** 714/536-9303

- **Surf Shop:** Huntington Surf & Sport, 300 Pacific Coast Highway, 714/841-4000; 5th Street Surf Shop, 217 Fifth Street, 714/969-8930

- **Vacation Rentals:** Western Resorts Vacations, 8907 Warner Avenue, Suite 260, Huntington Beach, CA 92657, 714/596-2015

ACCOMMODATIONS

The posh, 12-story **Waterfront Hilton Beach Resort** (21100 Pacific Coast Highway, 714/960-7873, $$$$) claims to be the only oceanfront hotel between Laguna Beach and Redondo Beach. On Pacific Coast Highway between Main Street and Beach Boulevard, it's an attractive tower with rooms whose balconies look out onto Huntington Pier. No creature comfort is unmet. A large, shallow pool and hot tub occupy a landscaped courtyard teeming with greenery. The marble-filled lobby, with its enormous, arching walkways, is unusually opulent for a seaside hotel. The comforters are thick and heavy, making for blissful, mummified sleep. Every aspect of the Waterfront's design and landscaping envelops the visitor in an illusion of tropical delight.

The only sour note is the "Legend of the Surf Hero," a promotional motif. In this "legend," Huntington Beach's legitimate past as a surfer's mecca is turned into cheesy fiction. We quote: "The Surf Hero lived more than 200 years ago in a Native American village on what is now called Huntington Beach. His name was Mankota, and he was the greatest surfer of all time, in a region where surfing was a way of life. During one summer, the spirits became angry and threatened to make the ocean's waves cease forever unless the people offered a human sacrifice. To the surprise of the people, it was Mankota who volunteered. Later that night, Mankota paddled out to the waves for the last time. He caught a massive, churning wave, dropped into the curl and was never seen again...Today, on the beach where the Surf Hero took his final ride, the legend has been carefully preserved by the Waterfront Hilton Beach Resort."

C'mon now, give the surfers a break, not to mention some respect. The real legend of the local surfing scene is far more intriguing than this corporate tall tale. Duke Kahanamoku is no doubt rolling over in his grave. Moreover, the Waterfront can stand on its own without it.

The **Hyatt Regency Huntington Beach Resort & Spa** (21500 Pacific Coast Highway, 714/698-1234, $$$$) is next door to the Hilton. It is the latest dramatic surgery done on Huntington Beach's oceanfront since we began visiting in the early 1980s. On the other side of the Hilton is yet another gigantic, fenced-off lot. Behind it, earth movers have erected a new commercial/real estate complex. It never ends in Huntington Beach.

If you're after something a little more down to earth, try the modestly likable, single-story **Huntington Shores Motel** (21002 Pacific Coast Highway, 714/536-8861, $$). Likewise, the **Quality Inn** (800 Pacific Coast Highway, 714/536-7500, $$) has location (three blocks north of the Huntington Beach Pier, across from the beach), price (significantly less than the Waterfront), and condition (contemporary, clean) going for it. There's a string of small motels close to the beach between Beach Boulevard and Goldenwest Street on Pacific Coast Highway.

COASTAL CUISINE

The Huntington Beach dining scene is, like the town itself, rather undistinguished. One piece of good news is that down by the Huntington Beach Pier you have two upscale franchise options: **Duke's** (317 Pacific Coast Highway, 714/374-6446, $$$) and **Savannah Supper Club** (315 Pacific Coast Highway, 714/374-7273, $$$). "Duke's" refers to Duke Kahanamoku, the Hawaiian legend considered the father of surfing. The restaurant specializes in Hawaiian-style cuisine, such as *huli huli* chicken (grilled with soy, garlic, and ginger) and hibachi-style teriyaki ahi (grilled with lime salsa, papaya, ginger, and soy). Savannah Supper Club served contemporary American cuisine and has an extensive wine list.

Main Street, from the beach up to Olive Avenue, has some shops and restaurants that are fun to duck into. Not all of them are yuppiefied and/or nationally franchised, either. We hit **Wahoo's Fish Tacos** (120 Main Avenue, 714/536-2050, $) for a quick bite. We were first attracted by all the decals on the door and then by the casual, let-it-all-hang-out ambience of the place. You can get a combo plate with a tasty grilled fish taco (plain or Cajun-spiced) accompanied by black or white beans and rice. You could spend an entire afternoon watching surf videos or browsing the bric-a-brac on the walls at Wahoo's, which has a few other franchises in Southern California.

You can grab a decent breakfast or lunch at the **Sugar Shack** (213 Main Street, 714/536-0355, $). Surfers and local characters hang here, too, probably because it's one of the few old haunts that hasn't been given the bum's rush by developers with a myopic "vision" of Huntington Beach's future.

Out on PCH, **Tsunami Sushi Bar** (17218 Pacific Coast Highway, 562/592-5806, $$) draws twenty-something locals who jam the small place for drinks and raw fish. If there's a line, hang in there—it's worth the wait.

At the other extreme, you can always "run for the border." The local **Taco Bell** (818 Pacific Coast Highway, 714/536-1951, $) is crawling with surfers. They stand on the tiled floor, topless, shoeless, shirtless, and dripping wet, waiting for their orders to be called. This particular one, while outwardly no different than the 4,151 other Taco Bell franchises in the United States, is something of a landmark with the surfer crowd, and it was the first in the chain to serve Baja fish tacos. However, this fast-food rendition of the venerable fish taco is a pale imitation of more substantial fare to be found at countless authentic Mexican restaurants between Mission Beach and Malibu.

NIGHTLIFE

Surfers and party dudes with long memories still lament the passing of the Golden Bear, a great hangout that got nuked by the redevelopment prerogative. Most of the old bars in the vicinity of the beach, which we remember as being a little rough, have met a similar fate. In many cases, it was no great loss, but it doesn't appear that much of worth has come along to replace it beyond studied plastic re-creations of the 1950s surf-diner motif. And

so party-minded people in Huntington Beach head to **Hurricane Bar and Grill** (200 Main Street, 714/374-0500), which has live music seven days a week. Across the street is the **Huntington Beach Beer Co.** (201 Main Street, 714/960-5343), an excellent brew pub with live music on Saturdays.

Huntington Harbor, Sunset Beach, and Surfside

Huntington Harbor is a ritzy marina and residential development that split a significant wetland in two. Some of the remains of that wetland have been preserved as **Bolsa Chica Ecological Reserve,** southeast of Huntington Harbor, and as the **Seal Beach National Wildlife Refuge,** just inland from Sunset Beach and Seal Beach.

The saga of the Bolsa Chica wetlands reads like some sort of environmental soap opera. The story dates back to 1970—nearly 40 years ago—when Signal Landmark Inc. purchased 1,600 acres of coastal wetlands from the Bolsa Chica Gun Club, with the intention of building homes on them. This was just about the time that the environmental movement began gaining steam and people came to appreciate the ecological significance of wetlands. Thus began a three-decade tug of war over the Bolsa Chica wetlands. Part of the fun of tracking this story has been keeping up with all the name changes on the real estate side: Signal Landmark became Koll Real Estate Group, which became California Coastal Communities, which is now attempting to do business at Bolsa Chica as, rather absurdly, Hearthside Homes.

Seemingly every month, there's some new twist, lawsuit, filing, proposal, or decision, and yet everything and nothing changes. The initial plan, approved by the California Coastal Commission in 1985, was to build 5,700 homes and a 1,300-slip marina with

A SURFER LOOKS AT 50

One afternoon during lunch we overheard a fellow named Brian talking to a waitress at Woody's Diner, right on the Pacific Coast Highway in Sunset Beach. She was having a bad day, and he urged her to "fluff up her aura" and "receive some of our positive vibes, 'cause we're full of happiness." He was sitting with his 15-year-old son, plotting his future (surfing adventures on the Baja Peninsula) while leisurely downing a plateful of Super Spuds: hash browns fried in a skillet with mushrooms, onions, green peppers, and cheese. This stick-to-your-ribs concoction has been warming surfers' tummies at this location since the 1950s.

We engaged him in conversation, and he openly shared his life story and opinions on what's been happening along the California coast in recent decades. Of Huntington Beach, on whose sands he learned to surf, he said: "We're disgusted with it. We don't go to Main Street anymore."

As thick as the development of Huntington Beach's shoreline has grown since the arrival of the colossus known as The Waterfront, Brian revealed that plans were in the works to make it worse – plans that he, as an active member of the Surfrider Foundation and a concerned resident, has been diligently battling at the grassroots level. He is quick to point out that rules can be bent when influential Orange County businessmen want their bidding done. He rhetorically asks, "How did the Hilton Waterfront resort get around Proposition 13, which clearly forbids the further construction of high-rise fortresses along the ocean?"

Brian has been leading the good life while fighting the good fight, but for him the "Old California" of the 1950s and 1960s has become a fond, fading memory. He told of nights spent sleeping sitting up in a Jeep at Bolsa Chica (then known to locals as Tin Can Beach) in order to surf with the rising sun. A wearying day on the waves would be followed by a hearty plate of Super Spuds at a bait and donut shop on the site of what is now Woody's Diner. Today, here he is, decades later, still surfing waves and scarfing spuds on the same spot, but disenchanted with the takeover and makeover of his beloved California coast. He mourned the loss of Dana Point as a surfers' mecca since the man-made harbor eliminated one of the most challenging point breaks on the West Coast.

He's got his eyes pointed south, beyond California, where he'll stake his claim and surf out his days. Already, he shares a year-round lease on a shack at a beach on the Baja, well south of anything that could be described as Americanized. A paltry $900 gets it for the whole year. Divide that by six tenants, and you're talking next to nothing in living expenses. It's a sweet life. The locals like the gringos, and vice versa.

His smile was genuine and constant, the sense of pleasure he derives from his largely non-materialistic life an inspiration as he approaches his fiftieth birthday. Unlike those who fret over adjustable rate mortgages on their Huntington Beach condos, Brian is living free and easy, able to pull up anchor and move on at a whim.

"I've still got places to go and things to see and waves to ride," he concluded with a gleam in his eye.

ORANGE COUNTY

luxury hotels on a 2,000-acre wetland tract. It was met with opposition from grassroots environmental groups like Bolsa Chica Land Trust and Amigos de Bolsa Chica. In August 1994, the Orange County Planning Commission readied a proposal to rezone the Bolsa Chica wetlands from agricultural to residential use. However, the county's environmental impact statement was challenged by the city of Huntington Beach, which threatened to sue. By November the California State Coastal Conservancy, the cities of Huntington Beach and Seal Beach, the Sierra Club, and the League of Women Voters had all weighed in with preservation opinions. In addition to its inherent value as a wetland, it was pointed out that Bolsa Chica is a valuable archeological site. More "cogged stones"—used in Native American rituals between 6,000 and 3,500 B.C.—have been found here than anywhere else. "It is the mother of cogged-stone sites," said Pat Ware, president of the Pacific Coast Archeological Society.

Gradually, it dawned on people that, having destroyed 95 percent of its coastal wetlands, the state of California could ill afford to lose another acre. As regards Bolsa Chica, the state acquired 300 acres of its wetlands from what was then Signal in 1978. But the tide really turned in 1997 with the purchase by the state's Lands Commission of 880 acres of Bolsa Chica wetlands. Meanwhile, both before and after that sale, plans to develop Bolsa Chica kept shrinking in size. The dimensions of the proposals have gone down from 5,700 homes (1985) to 4,884 homes (1989) to 3,300 homes (1994) to 2,400 homes (1997) to 1,235 homes (1997) to 388 homes (2001). As it stands, Hearthside homes is building 356 homes on 105 acres of the upper mesa. The development is called Brightwater. The good news is, after all the wrangling, the Bolsa Chica wetlands are mostly preserved.

Shoreward of Bolsa Chica are the small communities of Sunset Beach and Surfside. The latter is a private beach colony accessible only to pedestrians and bicyclists through a gate. Sunset Beach is more in line with the old ways of Huntington Beach back when surfers had the run of this stretch of the coast. Remnants of that time are still evident in some of the funky restaurants and bars lining Pacific Coast Highway. Still, Sunset Beach is a confusing hodgepodge of upscale and downscale, old and new, fancy and decrepit. There seems to be no rhyme or reason to the retail landscape along Pacific Coast Highway, which grows more incoherent with each passing year.

BEACHES

Sunset Beach is the principal beach in this area of wetlands, man-made harbors, and private residential communities. While the developers make their move on Bolsa Chica, life goes on at Huntington Harbor and Sunset Beach. The first of these is a private marina that has some public docks and overnight slips for rental. The community of Sunset Beach, arrayed like a centipede along Pacific Coast Highway, has a linear park with restrooms, playground, and volleyball nets that runs between Warner Avenue and Anderson Street. This county park was acquired and constructed in the early 1970s to provide a public beach for those who couldn't gain access through the privatized beachfront of the Sunset Beach colony.

Surfside Beach is a small beach accessible at Anderson Avenue through the gates of the private Surfside community, just north of Sunset Beach. The beach at Surfside, though, is not worth the trouble it takes to get to it, as parking is virtually nonexistent. Most visitors to the area would do better to head down to the massive city and state beaches of Huntington Beach.

44 SUNSET BEACH

Location: Warner Street off Pacific Coast Highway in Sunset Beach
Parking/Fees: free parking lot
Hours: 6 A.M.–10 P.M.

Facilities: lifeguards, picnic tables, restrooms, and showers
Contact: North Beaches Operation Office of Orange County Harbors, Beaches, and Parks, 714/723-4511

45 SURFSIDE BEACH

Location: Anderson Avenue at Pacific Coast Highway in Surfside
Parking/Fees: no parking; accessible only via pedestrian gate
Hours: 6 A.M.-10 P.M.
Facilities: none
Contact: North Beaches Operation Office of Orange County Harbors, Beaches, and Parks, 714/723-4511

COASTAL CUISINE

Vestiges of the area's comfortably unglamorous past can be seen in places like **Harbor House Cafe** (16341 Pacific Coast Highway, 714/592-5404, $) and **Woody's Diner** (16731 Pacific Coast Highway, 714/592-2134, $). Harbor House has been around since 1939, and the site occupied by Woody's has a long and storied history as well. Both have menus heavy on omelets, seafood, and burger variations, offering something for everyone in pleasant surroundings.

Seal Beach

Seal Beach was named for the flappy sea mammal that was once so popular with the garment trade. By Orange County standards it's a modest town in the best sense of the word. It could just as easily have been named for its good fortune at having been "sealed" off from its neighbors. At the north end of Orange County and just across the San Gabriel River from Los Angeles County, Seal Beach is a seal among sprawling sea monsters.

Pacific Coast Highway swings wide of Seal Beach, sparing the town center the nonstop wall of traffic between Long Beach and Huntington Beach. One must vigilantly search for the turn-off at Seal Beach Boulevard or miss the town completely. Seal Beach (population 24,000) is a world unto itself, existing primarily for those who live here. It has a Main Street that looks like a Main Street should—shaded with trees, cobbled with bricks, and as civilized as one of Grandma's bedtime stories. It has a grassy park named for an American president, Dwight D. Eisenhower, whose memory is synonymous with a more reassuring past. There's a tiny historical museum housed in an antique railroad car, an art deco movie house with a Wurlitzer organ, an Irish pub, a couple of seafood restaurants, a municipal pier, and a city beach.

The main drag along the beach impresses with its lack of gratuitous commerce and its gosh-darn normalcy. The hottest ticket in town when we last visited was a Lion's Club fish fry. The community bulletin board was filled with solicitations for recipe-swapping and pen pals. Of course, we quickly signed up for the latter.

For more information, contact the Seal Beach Chamber of Commerce, 201 8th Street, Suite 120, Seal Beach, CA 90740, 562/799-0179, www.sealbeachchamber.com.

BEACHES

For all its small-town charm, **Seal Beach** is not completely undiscovered, as the surf here is middling popular. Many of the surfers who make the trek are too young to drive, so they ride the bus from Long Beach, boards tucked under their arms like briefcases. At 9:30 on a Monday morning, we counted 78 surfers on the north side of Seal Beach Pier. Looking like tropical fish in their fluorescent wet suits, they sat passively on their boards and stared west, bobbing up and down, not speaking to one another, just waiting for the perfect wave.

The wait can be a long one. The surf here approaches the beaches that run for half a mile on each side of the pier at a southerly angle. Sometimes this produces ideal waves, sometimes not. The surf's erratic quality

SWINDLIN' USA

(sung to the tune of "Surfin' USA")

If every realtor had an ocean
Across the USA
There'd be a selling off the coastline
Like California
You see 'em building marinas
Time-sharing condos, too
Goofy goofy golf courses
Swindlin' USA
You'll catch 'em boutiquing Del Mar
Up to Orange County Line
Installing spas and Jacuzzis
And pouring vintage wine
All over the Southland
Like down Doheny way
Developmental frenzy
Swindlin' USA

They'll all be planning out a ruse
They'll pay some bribes real soon
They're shaking down their bankers
To fund a building boom
They'll be bulldozing all summer
Phase One by fall, hooray!
Tell the surfers they're comin'
Swindlin' USA
At Huntington and Newport
They always get their way
They're draining Bolsa Chica
Big homes and green fairways
All over the coastline
They're wrecking beach and bay
Developers gone crazy
Swindlin' USA

keeps the town from becoming another Huntington Beach. Even when the waves aren't cooperating, though, the currents and crosswinds are swift and potentially treacherous. Signs warn: Beware of Beach Hazards, Long Shore Currents, Rip Currents, Inshore Holes, Sand Bars, Underwater Objects, Pier Seawall, and Rock Structures.

The El Niño winter of 1997–1998 devastated Seal Beach. It's taken a lot of work to get the beach in working order. Nearby jetties and the cement base of the Seal Beach Pier, which acts as a kind of groin, conspire to impact natural sand-transporting mechanisms, to Seal Beach's detriment. The beach is narrower on the north side than on the south. Planners who constructed the jetty did not intend this to happen—instead, the jetty was meant to hold the sand equally on both sides.

Surfing is allowed on the shorter stretch of beach north of the pier and on Surfside Beach, below the south jetty (and belonging, in fact, to the small community of Surfside). The longest and widest stretch of beach, between the pier and the south jetty, is reserved for swimmers and sunbathers. The 1,885-foot pier was destroyed in January 1983 by the same storm that leveled Huntington Pier. The Seal Beach Pier was rebuilt the next year, with a placard to commemorate the town's industriousness and a cute bronze sculpture of a seal.

Oh, so you noticed the oil platforms offshore? Well, that's part of the scenery over which the town has no control. Occasionally, in fact, Seal Beach is the unwilling recipient of an oil spill that closes the beach until it's cleaned up. During one of our visits, Seal Beach was hit by a small but nasty spill from a leaky pipe on an offshore platform. While the oil-company execs ducked culpability, the town mobilized with bulldozers and volunteers to clean up the mess. As we were leaving, the beach had been reopened. Meanwhile, angry letters to the editor began to appear.

"The rigs not only besmirch the coastline," wrote one citizen, "they pose a constant threat to our beaches and sea life." Let's guess: Next came the press release from the oil company publicists reassuring the townsfolk how environmentally conscious they are. Then local officials reminded the citizens about the money and jobs the oil companies bring the local economy. Everyone forgets for a while, then another small but nasty spill occurs, and the cycle beings anew.

Anyway, here's to the good folks of Seal Beach. May your sand remain clean and may your beach stay in place for another year.

46 SEAL BEACH

Location: Main Street at Seal Beach Pier in Seal Beach
Parking/Fees: metered street parking
Hours: 4:30 A.M.-10 P.M.
Facilities: lifeguards, restrooms, and showers
Contact: Seal Beach Lifeguard Station, 562/430-2613

ACCOMMODATIONS

In this homey town, there's really only one large motel, the **Pacific Inn of Seal Beach** (600 Marina Drive, 562/493-7501, www.pacific inn-sb.com, $$). This former Radisson Inn is an easy walk from the beach, pier, and Main Street. Two small pools are on the premises.

You may opt for the 24-room **Seal Beach Inn and Gardens** (212 Fifth Street, 562/493-2416, $$$), a restored 60-year-old inn with splendid gardens. It combines the best of bed-and-breakfast and hotel amenities under one roof.

COASTAL CUISINE

Walt's Wharf (201 Main Street, 562/598-4433, $$$) attracts the most devoted following. It's more upscale than most other restaurants in town, drawing a gregarious crowd in the late afternoon. There are nearly as many fish to choose from as there are imported beers on tap, and the seafood is as fresh as it comes.

NIGHTLIFE

Don't leave **Walt's Wharf** (201 Main Street, 562/598-4433) if you're looking for something to do after dinner. It's got a great bar with a kick-back-and-relax ambience and excellent appetizers to go with the brew. There's also a **Hennessey's Tavern** (140 Main Street, 562/598-4419) across the street. Hennessey's, a Southern California chain mining an Irish-pub theme, is an old reliable watering hole no matter the location.

MOON LOS ANGELES & ORANGE COUNTY BEACHES

Avalon Travel
a member of the Perseus Books Group
1700 Fourth Street
Berkeley, CA 94710, USA
www.moon.com

Editor: Naomi Adler Dancis
Copy Editor: Kay Elliott
Graphics Coordinator: Kathryn Osgood
Production Coordinators: Amber Pirker,
   Elizabeth Jang
Cover Designer: Kathryn Osgood
Map Editor: Albert Angulo
Cartographers: Jon Twena, Kat Bennett

ISBN-13: 978-1-59880-332-7

Text © 2009 by Alan Bisbort and
Parke Puterbaugh.
Maps © 2009 by Avalon Travel.
All rights reserved.

ABOUT THE AUTHORS

© TOM HEARN

Alan Bisbort

Alan Bisbort is a writer, editor, and researcher who has authored or coauthored nearly 20 books of history, biography, travel, and poetry, and contributed to numerous other books. He has worked for the Library of Congress, on staff or on contract, since 1977. As a freelance journalist, he is a regular contributor to *The New York Times*, the *Hartford*, *Valley Advocates*, *Yale Environment Journal*, *Yale Medicine*, *Connecticut*, *American Politics Journal*, *AMP*, and *Ugly Things*. His work has also appeared in *The Washington Post*, *Rolling Stone*, *American Way*, *Los Angeles Times*, *City Paper*, *Creem*, *Biblio*, and *Washingtonian*.

Though Alan lives on the East Coast, he has spent a great deal of time in California over the past ten years, researching four editions of *Moon California Beaches* with Parke Puterbaugh. Since high school he has been guilty of unrepentant California dreaming. Alan lives near New Haven, Connecticut with his wife, award-winning journalist Tracey O'Shaughnessy, their son, Paul James, and their ageless dog, Sam.

© ALAN BISBORT

Parke Puterbaugh

Parke Puterbaugh is a writer, editor, and educator who mainly works in the music and travel fields. A rock-music enthusiast and scholar, he is a former senior editor for *Rolling Stone* magazine. After nearly a decade in New York City, he longed to work in more natural surroundings, and the idea of writing beach guidebooks – inspired by a lifelong love of coastal environments – came to him. The publication of *Moon California Beaches* coincides with the 25th anniversary of his and Alan's decision to ditch their respective jobs to embark on lives of itinerant beachcombing and full-time freelancing. They have written several celebrated beach guidebooks, and have visited every public beach in the continental U.S. that can be reached by car, foot, or ferry.

Parke further pursued his interest in beaches and barrier islands in the classroom. He earned a master's degree in environmental science, with emphases in coastal geology and coastal-zone management, from the University of North Carolina at Chapel Hill. He has written a guide to Southeastern wetlands for the U.S. Environmental Protection Agency, as well as several music-related titles, including a forthcoming biography of the rock group Phish. Parke's work has also been published in more than 30 magazines and newspapers. He has served as a freelance writer, historian, and curatorial consultant for the Rock and Roll Hall of Fame and Museum since its inception. Presently, he teaches in the music department at Guilford College in Greensboro, North Carolina, where he lives with his wife, Carol, and daughter, Hayley.